THE
OPTIMIZATION
EDGE

THE
OPTIMIZATION
EDGE

Reinventing Decision Making
to Maximize All Your
Company's Assets

STEVE SASHIHARA

New York Chicago San Francisco Lisbon London Madrid Mexico City
Milan New Delhi San Juan Seoul Singapore Sydney Toronto

The **McGraw·Hill** *Companies*

1 2 3 4 5 6 7 8 9 10 11 12 13 14 15   QFR/QFR   1 9 8 7 6 5 4 3 2 1

ISBN   978-0-07-174657-1
MHID   0-07-174657-9

This publication is designed to provide accurate and authoritative information in regard to the subject matter covered. It is sold with the understanding that neither the author nor the publisher is engaged in rendering legal, accounting, securities trading, or other professional services. If legal advice or other expert assistance is required, the services of a competent professional person should be sought.
> —*From a Declaration of Principles Jointly Adopted by a Committee of the American Bar Association and a Committee of Publishers and Associations*

McGraw-Hill books are available at special quantity discounts to use as premiums and sales promotions or for use in corporate training programs. To contact a representative, please e-mail us at bulksales@mcgraw-hill.com.

This book is printed on acid-free paper.

CONTENTS

PART 1

OPTIMIZATION AS A COMPETITIVE ADVANTAGE

PART 2

PUTTING OPTIMIZATION TO WORK

PART 3

THE OPTIMIZED WORLD OF TOMORROW

PREFACE

In today's turbulent, competitive business environment, the old axioms for creating an enduring competitive advantage can no longer be relied on. Long-term strategy. Low-cost provider. Customer loyalty. Competitors as enemies. "Golden goose" products that keep on giving. All are dated notions that need reexamination. Survival and sustained growth depend on rethinking the management fundamentals.

Certainly, one fundamental that needs rethinking is how executives make decisions related to asset management. Fierce global competition for resources; gyrating prices of raw materials; Web-based start-ups with global reach being built on a fraction of the fixed-asset investment of many established companies; and the new skinnied-down organization, with vastly diminished head count: all of these require executives to rethink how human, capital, and financial assets are deployed and how they can be made to yield maximum value.

Make no mistake about it: downsizing, which has become the management weapon of choice, is not a long-term strategy for asset management—never mind one designed for future growth and success. But *Optimization* is another matter, which is why this book is written for executives on the firing line: those who are intent on moving beyond cutback management to achieve breakaway competitiveness by changing the fundamental approach to how their organizations are led, decisions are made, and assets are managed.

Optimization can be an intimidating word. I define it simply as harnessing the new breed of software that not only presents data, but also makes explicit recommendations to help you achieve your goals. Optimization applications, which couple fast computers and sophisticated algorithms, often juggle and evaluate millions or tens of millions of choices before presenting what they recommend as the optimal, or best, choices. This is particularly useful in cases where the data are voluminous and change rapidly, which when you think about it, are those facing just about every manager every day.

Optimization spans multiple technical fields and often travels under names such as Operations Research, expert systems, decision support, artificial intelligence, and advanced analytics, to name a few. Not surprisingly, many books on these topics are well above average on the academic-abstraction scale. Over the past several years, as interest in Optimization has grown outside academia, a new genre of literature has appeared that attempts to bring the optimization discussion to a broader audience. Books such as *Super Crunchers*, *The Numerati*, *Competing on Analytics*, *Fooled by Randomness*, and *The Black Swan* have made a significant contribution to promoting the importance of the new "smart": being smart about numbers.

The Optimization Edge: Reinventing Decision Making to Maximize All Your Company's Assets has a different focus than any of these. It is the first business book to deal exclusively with Optimization: what it is and what makes it a unique way of looking at—and operating in—business reality. The central question it asks is, How can executives improve their game using Optimization to make decisions? Since I write for an executive audience, my focus is on relating the experiences of a forward-thinking breed of executives who have begun to distance their companies from competitors by deploying a widely underutilized weapon—*Optimization*—to make complex judgments and recommendations about the best way to deploy assets. They are doing this faster, better, and more consistently than those who are making decisions the old-fashioned way, that is, without the support of Optimization.

In the chapters that follow, I define what Optimization is; examine how successful companies are using it to drive up value; and explore the unique technical, organizational, and cultural requirements for the successful application of Optimization to managerial decision making. Along the way, I provide a variety of examples drawn from our experience at Princeton Consultants, working with clients across industries, as well as from nonclient companies that are at the forefront of this new type of decision making. This book is not a tutorial on software, hardware, or algorithms. I have avoided Greek letters, sophisticated mathematical discussions, arcane explanations of software programming, and all the other accoutrements of complexity. Optimization is presented not simply as a technology, but as a set of principles and a way of thinking that are achieving superior business results as they reshape businesses, industries, and the competitive landscape.

Leaders who apply Optimization effectively build an "optimization culture" that goes beyond the traditional management imperatives of improving quality, reducing cost, speeding up product-development cycles, and decreasing customer-response time. Such a culture puts highest value on staking out the best solutions to strategic and operational challenges. While the book is decidedly pro-Optimization, it does not ignore the many practical challenges associated with implementing optimization projects. It takes the reader to the front lines, where the battle is being waged to change the way organizations make decisions. In doing so, it pays close attention to the social dynamics of organizational decision making and presents a general change framework—together with a detailed five-step process—for successfully conducting an optimization project in any organization. Each step in the process is illustrated by multiple case examples of real executives and their companies.

After reading *The Optimization Edge*, you should:

- Have a grasp of the power of Optimization
- Know what to look for when considering acquiring it as a capability
- Understand the preconditions that ensure its success
- Know how to harness the power of Optimization in order to keep your organization ahead of competitors

I have included in the book a guide and evaluation test to assess the Optimization-readiness of your organization. I also discuss a key metric that can help determine the likelihood of success of any optimization project.

My goal is to provide a framework for executives in companies of all sizes, across industries and geographies, to think about Optimization, explore the implications for decision making, and provide a road map for using it to drive up the value of key assets. In the concluding section of the book, I venture out on a limb to paint a picture of the shape of things to come. Our digitized world is still in its infancy. The result: not just gigabytes, terabytes, or even petabytes of data, but rather 1.8 zettabytes of digitized information—129 million times more information than is contained in the Library of Congress—and growing every minute. I believe that the accessibility of this data, combined with high-powered miniature computers, will create a world in which Optimization takes center stage in helping not just companies, but also individuals make increasingly well-informed decisions about asset utilization on a minute-by-minute basis. As organizations attempt to thread their way through the many challenges ahead, Optimization will provide a powerful way for them to create value and build competitive muscle.

If you are unfamiliar with Optimization and the ways in which it is reshaping both organizational and personal decision making, this book should serve as a starting point for your journey. If you are already aware of Optimization or are considering introducing it into your organization, then *The Optimization Edge* will provide the how-to guidance that will enable you to avoid the booby traps and proceed wisely as you move ahead.

ACKNOWLEDGMENTS

I owe a great debt to the clients of Princeton Consultants and to my colleagues at the firm for the opportunities to work together and explore how Optimization can be used to create greater competitive advantage in the real world. My business partner of the last 30 years, Jon Crumiller, deserves special credit for having pioneered much of our Rapid Action Delivery (RAD) project methodology. He was one of the first who showed me that successful optimization projects are as much about the "people factors" as the math or the technology.

I am deeply grateful to the individuals that we interviewed for allowing me to share their stories with our readers. Barry List, director of communications, INFORMS, has been an invaluable source of information and ideas. My fellow members of the INFORMS Roundtable have been tremendous sources of wisdom and encouragement. Thank you!

Peter Tobia, my literary agent, and his Market Access team provided terrific support throughout every phase of *The Optimization Edge*.

OPTIMIZATION AS A COMPETITIVE ADVANTAGE

CHAPTER 1

THE WINNERS AND
THE ALSO-RANS

W hy do some companies become industry leaders, while others never rise to the top? For example:

- McDonald's versus Roy Rogers
- Walmart versus Kmart
- Marriott versus Howard Johnson's
- Google versus Yahoo!
- UPS versus Airborne Express
- Amazon versus Borders

What has McDonald's discovered about cooking burgers and fries that has eluded Roy Rogers? Why are Walmart's aisles bustling with customers, while at Kmart even Blue Light Specials can't fill the stores? Why, after more than 50 years as close competitors, did HoJo become history and Marriott a megachain? Why does Google appear on the verge of putting Yahoo! into the dustbin of history? When you must get a package delivered on time, why do you dial up the "tightest ship in the shipping business" instead of Airborne Express? And why has Amazon managed to leave a host of venerable, already established booksellers at the starting gate?

Theories abound about the drivers of industry dominance: strategy, leadership, sticking to the knitting, customer centricity—the list goes on and on. While these theories may go far in explaining why some companies rise to the top, they just do not go far enough.

Take McDonald's. Underlying the Big Macs, Egg McMuffins, french fries, and now first-rate coffee, there is a hidden advantage: McDonald's remarkable consistency. Visit just about any McDonald's restaurant: from burgers to bathrooms, from coffee to counter service, you know what to expect and you get it. Or look at Walmart. Not too long ago, the pundits were predicting the demise of the general merchandise stores that had become part of the post-World War II business landscape. Indeed, Montgomery Ward, Sears, J.C. Penney, Kmart, and others have either fallen off the charts or appear to be hemorrhaging uncontrollably. Walmart, on the other hand, weathered the most recent economic downturn quite handily, remaining profitable while so many others in its industry were gasping for air.

In yet another industry, consider Google. It certainly did not invent the Internet search engine. In fact, Google was a relatively late bloomer that suddenly burst on the scene in 1998, two or three years after a host of other search engines—Lycos, AltaVista, InfoSeek, and Yahoo!—were already up and running. And then there is Amazon. It has left every other online mall in its wake, with revenues more than double that of its closest rival.

How do you account for the difference between these stars and the also-rans? Is there a common denominator that differentiates them from other companies? There are undoubtedly a number of reasons for their stellar performance, but one that has largely gone unnoticed is this: these companies possess an uncanny *ability to make complex decisions faster, more accurately, and more consistently than their competition.*

Optimizing Decision Making: The Competitive Edge

In today's fiercely competitive world, the notions of long-term strategy and enduring competitive advantage seem like quaint anachronisms, part of the detritus of the 1980s and 1990s. Now, "strategy on the run" and tactical advantage rule the day. McDonald's, Walmart, Marriott, Google, UPS, Amazon, and many others have demonstrated that competitive advantage comes from tight focus and riveting attention on making optimal decisions that squeeze every ounce of value from the assets under management. As we will see, *Optimization is a decision-making process and a set of related tools that employ mathematics, algorithms, and computer software not only to sort and organize data, but to use that data to make recommendations faster and better than humans can.*

The McDominator

McDonald's vaunted mastery of consistent, cost-conscious quality is a tribute to its laserlike focus on hundreds of microdecisions made by employees every day, all over the world: when to turn hamburgers and dump old coffee; how often to fry a new batch of chicken McNuggets and how many to fry; how many times a day to clean bathrooms. These decisions have been translated into rules that govern the behavior of McDonald's employees. The rules are deceptively easy to follow, but many factors have to be considered in order to make the right decisions for each individual restaurant: location, season, weather, day of week, time of day, customer preferences, projected volume, and on and on. Then just the right balance must be struck between turning hamburgers and turning a profit. Mickey D's learned early on that the best way to ensure the quality of its decisions was to introduce Optimization and build a strong culture to support it. It obviously worked: in 2008, when the U.S. stock market lost two-thirds of its value, McDonald's was one of only two companies among the Dow Industrials whose stock actually *gained value*. Which was the other? You guessed it: Walmart—another big user of Optimization.[1]

Everyday High Profits at Walmart

Walmart supplies a wide array of decent goods, all at reasonable prices. How does the megachain do it? Volume buying helps, but it is not the real differentiator. What makes Walmart unique is its command of logistics. It continually deconstructs its entire supply chain, from supplier to distribution centers to customers, and treats each link as a decision point, asking a battery of microquestions: Where and how much to buy and at what price? Where to route goods? How to resupply and reorder? It optimizes assets all along the supply chain, decision by decision. Its obsession with squeezing value from every link in the chain has enabled it to develop *smart rules* for making decisions and managing its business.

Take air conditioners, a relatively mundane product in today's high-tech world. Many of Walmart's competitors, like Kmart, tend to use simple rules to regulate their stock: "In the summer, make sure that every store has lots of air conditioners" or "Stockpile air conditioners for our mid-August sale." Not Walmart, where the management of air conditioners and every other asset is guided by optimization decisions, which employ *smart rules*, such as: "In the summer, track the weather; find out where heat waves are predicted; and be prepared at a moment's notice to redirect air conditioner shipments to the areas with highest demand."

As a result of its optimization prowess, Walmart—which was originally created by Sam Walton to serve rural areas too small for Kmart to bother about—has driven Kmart to the brink of extinction.

The Price Is Right at Marriott

For decades, Howard Deering Johnson and J. Williard "Bill" Marriott appeared to be moving in parallel universes. In 1925, Johnson borrowed $2,000 to buy a small drugstore in Wollaston, Massachusetts; two years later, Marriott borrowed $6,000 to open a nine-stool A&W root beer stand in Washington, D.C. By 1937, Johnson had established, through franchising, 56 Howard Johnson's restaurants that graced the nation's expanding highway system with their distinctive orange cupolas and 28 flavors of ice cream.[2] Marriott's small root beer stand initially grew into eight Hot Shoppes restaurants along the Washington-Baltimore corridor,[3] and by 1938 the company was supplying box lunches to passengers on Eastern Air Transport's 22 daily flights from Washington to New York. Each company opened its first travel lodge in the mid-1950s and for a decade competed in serving travelers on the country's new interstate highway system. The 1960s and early 1970s were boom years for both Howard Johnson's and Hot Shoppes, which changed its name to Marriott in 1967.

The companies' paths, however, soon diverged. As changing public taste, tougher economic times, and soaring fuel costs caused Americans to cut back on vacations and long drives, Howard Johnson's profits sagged. Like many executives before and since, Johnson and his executive team chose to respond by downsizing, but their efforts to cut costs, reduce the number of employees, and serve cheaper food only accelerated the public's flight from HoJo's doors. Finally, in 1979, the chain accepted an acquisition bid from the Imperial Group PLC of Britain for all of its 1,040 restaurants and 520 motor lodges.

Meanwhile, Marriott was meeting the same challenges in a different way: optimizing rather than downsizing. It moved aggressively first into international property management—opening the company's first European hotel in Amsterdam, Holland, in 1975—and in 1982 into the then-lucrative time-share market. As its properties and assets grew, Marriott took one additional important step to strengthen its competitiveness. As a longtime partner of the airlines, Marriott had a front-row seat as the industry turned to mathematical algorithms and optimization software to make minute-by-minute price adjustments to maximize plane loads. It soon became the first company in the hospitality industry to adopt the airlines' "revenue management" pricing techniques.

The end of the story? In 1985, Marriott purchased Howard Johnson's assets from the Imperial Group, subsequently selling them to Prime Motor Inns.

Google: Master of the Search

Then there's Google. In 1992 there were only 26 websites; eight years later that number had soared to one billion; another eight years later Google's new content links registered one trillion unique page links.[4] A prodigious rate of "inventory" expansion, indeed! Recent estimates of the number of Google customers are difficult to find, but a study conducted in late 2008 reported that Google had registered 7.23 billion search requests that year, or approximately 10 million search requests per hour.[5] Google's challenge involves nothing less than deciding in seconds, for each request, which of the trillion pages are most relevant. What is Google's secret, and how has it come to dominate Internet search so completely? Quite simply, Google outoptimized its competitors. It found a way for its computers to make decisions more quickly and accurately than everyone else. In 1998, when two Stanford graduate students founded Google, Yahoo! had a four-year head start. Yahoo!'s approach to optimizing searches involved hiring experts to grade websites for relevance. The approach worked well for 26 websites—and maybe even for a million. But for a trillion? There just weren't enough experts!

Google, in contrast, thought like an optimizer and in the process invented a new model. Rather than use experts, Google discovered that it could leverage its customers themselves! Google could track how often a given Web page was referenced, or linked to, by other Web pages. This allowed Google to build its now-famous PageRank algorithm. The pages most frequently referenced for a particular topic became the most relevant sites. No paid experts need apply to Google. The decision algorithm that Google developed not only surpassed Yahoo!'s panel of experts in providing relevant content, it proved capable of searching through a trillion pages as many as 10 million times an hour. For a period of time, Yahoo! actually retained Google to do its index searches, before realizing that the decision-making optimized search engine was the core competency that would propel the winner across the finish line. Google stands as the quintessential decision optimizer. Its competitors have simply not been able to keep up.

UPS Takes the Right Turn

Although not quite as old as UPS, Airborne Express's history stretched back to 1946. The company had developed a U.S. air-and-ground express-delivery service, as well as business logistics services much like those of UPS. However, in August 2003, Airborne's shareholders approved the sale of the company to Belgium-based package-delivery service DHL. Five years later—in the face of stiff competition and a declining economy—DHL shuttered Airborne Express's U.S. delivery operation.

While the ink was drying on Airborne's sale to DHL, UPS was pondering how it could increase the fuel efficiency of its delivery trucks. With a fleet of 88,000 trucks, even small savings could be leveraged across the fleet, adding up to major economies company wide. One area of waste that UPS identified was the time its trucks spent idling while waiting to make left-hand turns. UPS's response: optimization routing software that favored right-hand turns. By developing routes that balanced directness with the fewest possible left-hand turns, in 2005 the software helped UPS eliminate 464,000 driving miles in Washington, D.C., alone, saving 51,000 gallons of fuel.[6] The competition and economic downturn proved no match for the "tightest ship in the shipping business."

Rewriting the Book at Amazon

Amazon is to the Internet what Walmart is to bricks and mortar. Not only were its revenues more than double that of its closest Internet rival in 2009, but the gap is widening. During 2009, Amazon's North American Web sales grew by 25 percent, while U.S. online retail as a whole grew by just 6 percent. How does this Web behemoth do it? It wasn't the first Internet retailer; it wasn't even the first cyberspace bookseller. But Amazon optimized better than its competitors—at both its front and its back doors.

At the front of its electronic store, Amazon's Web servers send out millions of personalized recommendations to customers each day, informing them of new and used items that closely match their personal interest. Over the years, Amazon has become so adept at managing its Web portal that competitors like Borders have outsourced the management of their websites to Amazon. In May 2008, in an effort to regain control of its Web sales, Borders launched its own e-commerce engine. The result? While at the height of a recession Amazon reported its "best Christmas ever" in 2008—with spending per customer growing by 18 percent—Borders reported an 11.7 percent decline in 2008 holiday sales on its new, non-Amazon website.[7]

Now consider Amazon's back door. When it opened for business 14 years ago, Amazon shipped just *a few items a day* out its back door—so few, in fact, that employees rang a small bell to celebrate each sale. By December 2008, at the height of the global recession, Amazon was selling *72.9 items a second*. If you stacked the copies of the bestseller *Breaking Dawn* that Amazon sold during the 2008 holiday season, they would reach the peak of Mount Everest eight times over! When you stop to consider that orders are typically filled and shipped one book at a time, the magnitude of the accomplishment is astounding and undoubtedly keeps competitors awake at night.[8]

Reinventing Decision Making

The importance of effective decision making in business has not gone unnoticed. A quick search—using Google, of course—of "methods for making complex decisions in business" returns a well-prioritized list of 26,200,000 Web pages. A number of consulting firms have made a good living offering structured decision-making approaches to companies around the world. Nobel laureate Daniel Kahneman—after a long and illustrious career studying the foibles of human judgment and decision making—has argued that decisions are an organization's most important product and that companies should begin applying quality-control processes to decision making.[9]

While interest in business decision making is not new, there is a powerful new decision-making capability available: one that has largely gone unnoticed despite its success in vaulting a number of companies from bit players to industry powerhouses in relatively short order. That capability is Optimization, and it is increasingly playing a pivotal role in separating winners from the rest of the pack.

Optimization has been around, in various forms, for some time. Originally growing out of a discipline labeled "Operations Research," or OR, it began as an academic discipline and then—as we will see in Chapter 2—became a key factor in the Allied victory in World War II. After the war, Optimization was deployed to help manage large-scale, asset-intensive operations such as oil refineries, power plants, and the U.S. space program. As the availability, speed, and capacity of computers increased in the last decades of the 20th century, optimized decision making moved from the public to the private sector and was soon adopted by both larger and smaller enterprises in a variety of industries.

Optimization is known by different names in different communities: to the computer scientist it is artificial intelligence; to economists it is modeling; mathematicians know it as game theory or applied mathematics; engineers, with a nod toward tradition, have stuck with Operations Research. Most recently, it has been referred to in some business circles as advanced analytics. What is common to all of these groups when they speak of Optimization is that each is typically referring to large *data sets*, *decision algorithms*, and an *empirical approach* to deciding what works best. Computers and sophisticated software are being used to make increasingly complex decisions more quickly and accurately. When effectively applied, Optimization can become a competitive game changer, as it has for many companies, including computer-chip maker Intel, which is featured in the accompanying sidebar. If your organization is not using Optimization, it may be strategically vulnerable. Chances are that one of your competitors has already tapped the power of Optimization.

OPTIMIZING FOR INNOVATION AT INTEL

Continuous innovation is what keeps Intel at the top of the semiconductor industry, and that innovation comes from the company's most important asset: its people. To maximize their contributions, Intel must carefully assemble product-design teams with just the right mix of circuit engineering, software development, and system validation skills, to mention just a few.

The teams in any product-design group may be working on dozens of major development projects at any one time, each employing hundreds of highly skilled individuals spread across multiple geographies. The status and priorities of these projects are in constant flux. The result is a recurring cycle of assignments and reassignments guaranteed to keep project managers awake long into the night.

For many years, team assignments and reassignments were made using large, group-specific spreadsheets. Juggling the personnel could take a full day or more. Worse still, the resulting solution often involved moving more people among teams than necessary, costing time, money, morale, and—a game stopper for Intel—creativity.

When one product-design group asked Karl Kempf and his team of optimizers from the Decision Engineering (DE) group to improve its personnel-assignment process, the team set about developing a

continued

decision-support software program. Inputs included everything from skill requirements to projected completion dates to individual location preferences. The program even took into account hiring projections. The output: an optimal personnel-assignment plan matching personnel and projects over an extended time period. A user-friendly graphical interface clearly identified trouble spots such as under-resourced projects or underutilized talent. It also allowed planners to test alternative assignments in what-if scenarios.

When the Resource Planning Tool, as it was dubbed, was introduced, it reduced the time needed to make assignments and reassignments from more than a day to less than an hour. Equally important, the computer-generated solutions invariably moved fewer people, thereby creating tremendous cost savings while helping to sustain creativity. The decision tool was so successful that other product-design groups immediately began asking for it.

Within 18 months, all product-design groups at Intel were using the tool, drastically cutting workforce planning time and saving multiple person-years of effort per year. When fully deployed, the Resource Planning Tool made it possible to roll individual team plans up to top managers, allowing them to make superior product-design resourcing decisions across the organization.[10]

The Institute for Operations Research and the Management Sciences (INFORMS) is the largest professional society in the world for professionals in the field of Operations Research, or Optimization. Its annual Edelman Award recognizes outstanding, money-earning examples of the application of these techniques. A glance at the award finalists since 2005 illustrates the increased emphasis being placed on Optimization by industry leaders. Among others, the finalists have included HP, IBM, Marriott International, Coca Cola, P&G, Swift & Co., Eli Lilly & Co., Zara, and the Memorial Sloan-Kettering Cancer Center. The INFORMS Roundtable, an optimization interest group, counts among its members AT&T, Bank of America, Boeing, Cisco, FedEx, GE, HP, IBM, Intel, McDonald's, P&G, Verizon, and Walt Disney: all companies working on improving their competitive position by optimizing decisions.

Every Executive a Quant?

The physicists, mathematicians, psychologists, engineers, and computer programmers who crunch numbers, develop decision algorithms, and write optimization software are commonly known as "quants" (short for *quantitative analysts*). If you are an executive exploring whether or not Optimization will help your company raise its level of competitive play, I don't advise running out to sign up for a crash course in advanced mathematics. There's no need for you to become a quant, but it would help to think a bit like one.

Begin by asking a few optimization questions, such as:

• **What are my company's underutilized assets?** For example, for a newspaper, it might be ad space; for a pharmaceutical company, it might be the "face time" that sales reps spend with doctors; for an agricultural company, arable land or available seeds might be the undervalued asset; for a railroad, train capacity might qualify. Which of your assets, if tapped for optimal value, have the potential to take your organization to a significant new level?

• **Where and how are repetitive decisions about key assets being made in my company?** Assume you could improve the accuracy of these decisions by 10 percent—or perhaps make them twice as fast. What would be the potential impact on profitability, customer service, or sales?

• **When and how are we forecasting? How accurate are our forecasts?** What would be the impact on your competitive position if the accuracy of these forecasts could be improved by 10 percent—or if they could be derived one month earlier?

• **Where are we repeatedly having lengthy debates over strategic decisions or operational issues?** Can you collect better data upon which to base these decisions? Could you make these decisions more empirically, rather than relying so heavily on the "three Hs": history—"It's the way we've always done it," hunches—"It feels right," and hierarchy—"Because I say so, and I'm the boss."

• **What does "best" mean?** The next time you hear someone in your organization say, "This is the 'best' decision," ask what factors constitute *best*: cost savings, service, profitability, speed of resolution, capacity utilization? Are these factors the right ones, and are they carrying the right amount of weight in the decision process?

Final Note

The Optimization Edge examines optimized decision making from multiple perspectives:

1. Part 1 continues with Chapters 2 and 3.
   - Chapter 2 will take you on a brief historical tour of Optimization to help you better understand what it involves, where it came from, and a bit about where it seems to be heading.
   - Chapter 3 will put you inside a variety of companies and industries to learn how decision optimization is being used for competitive advantage in applications as far-ranging as getting greater yield from print ads to scheduling airplanes to predicting hit songs.
2. Part 2 will take you, step-by-step, through a proven process for successfully implementing Optimization in any organization.
   - First, Chapter 4 will compare Optimization to other decision-making approaches and to other popular organizational-improvement initiatives. It will explore some of the reasons that people resist adopting Optimization and why it is often underutilized. Finally, Chapter 4 will provide you with a set of questions that you can use to evaluate your company's preparedness to undertake an optimization project.
   - Also in Part 2, Chapter 5 will discuss the differences between *good* and *great* optimization projects and will introduce Princeton Consultants' five-step process for successfully executing an optimization project. Chapter 5 will take you through the first two steps of the process—the charter and the vision—using examples from real-life companies as illustrations.
   - Chapter 6, the final chapter in Part 2, will explore the remaining three steps of our company's process: the early win, the scale-up, and the harvest.
3. In Part 3, we will look over the horizon to trace the future of Optimization. Chapter 7 will include a discussion of the vast potential of Optimization as well as some of the challenges that could possibly slow its implementation.

CHAPTER 2

OPTIMIZATION: FROM CAVE TO CUBICLE

"If you would understand anything, observe its beginning and its development," advised Aristotle in the fourth century B.C.E. A while later, Machiavelli pointed out another way in which examining the past can be of value: "Whoever wishes to foresee the future must consult the past." In the spirit of Aristotle and Machiavelli, this chapter overviews the history of Optimization and aims to give you a better idea of where Optimization came from and where it is going.

The cave people who had to decide who should go on the hunt and who should stay behind to guard the camp faced an optimization problem. Alas, there were no computers back then; without sophisticated ways of framing the problem or of calculating and testing alternative solutions, our cave-dwelling ancestors functioned at a distinct disadvantage.

Our forbears were not analytical slouches, however. There is evidence that they did attempt to improve their decision-making techniques. The use of "models" to represent real-life situations can be traced back 20,000 to 35,000 years. Artifacts found in Africa and France suggest that women—or perhaps men—made early attempts to quantify time by using notched sticks to track menstrual cycles.[1]

Now fast-forward to the 21st century.

Modern-day Optimization employs mathematical models and algorithms to make complex decisions in an empirical fashion, often using high-end, sophisticated computer software. The word *empirical* refers to testing solutions in a measurable fashion to achieve a desired outcome. For example, in determining whom to take into battle—and whom to leave behind to guard the camp—today's military officers are apt to employ sophisticated optimization software, enabling them to pinpoint the precise combination of men, women, and equipment that will turn the battle in their favor.

Humankind's journey from modeling the passage of time with notched sticks to employing decision-making algorithms and computers capable of "outthinking" their makers represents a rich tapestry in which theory and application, necessity and invention, brilliant minds and pragmatic doers are all woven together to form the story of Optimization. As we briefly review this story, we will find that the most brilliant strands of theory include applied mathematics, computer science, and what today is called decision theory. One of the most powerful accelerators of Optimization has been that ultimate competitive endeavor: warfare. Here, as in many other applications, Optimization provided a powerful competitive advantage.

To keep the story of Optimization manageable, I have divided its history into four periods:

1. **Prior to 1900:** when many of the foundational ideas first emerged
2. **1900–1950:** the birth of modern-day Optimization
3. **1950–1980:** postwar proliferation of optimization practices in the public and private sectors
4. **1980 to the present:** when personal computers and the Internet brought Optimization to the masses

During each of these historical periods, including the time prior to the 1900s, important advances in our three foundational areas—applied mathematics, computer science, and decision theory—occurred. At times, one area seemed to outpace the others, but not for long, as each discipline fed off—and fed—the others.

1. Prior to 1900: Early Foundations

Some refer to the years from 1600 to 1900 as the golden age of math and science. Certainly, many of the foundational ideas behind modern-day Optimization first emerged during this period—including their application to decision making. Some of the most important ideas involved finding ways to mathematically represent probability, as well as additional inferential statistical techniques, to better anticipate future outcomes of decisions. Some foundational ideas of modern computing even emerged. We will start our journey through this early period with an application of optimization thinking to war and conclude it with an important business application. In between, we will touch on some important advances in applied mathematics, as well as in decision theory.

Warfare has been not only the creature of technology, but also its creator. Way back in 214 B.C.E., the Romans began laying siege to the Sicilian city of Syracuse. It was then that Hieron II, king of Syracuse, tapped the considerable computational smarts of Archimedes, one of the greatest mathematicians of antiquity, to devise ingenious weapons to repulse the Roman invaders. Among these were Archimedes' claw, designed to lift and sink attacking ships, and Archimedes' heat ray (see Figure 2.1), which involved positioning a series of reflecting mirrors or polished shields to focus the sun's rays on attacking ships and set them on fire.

FIGURE 2.1   Archimedes' Heat Ray[2]

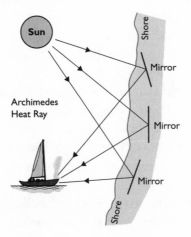

Archimedes didn't label himself an optimizer, but he certainly was one at heart. We can imagine him carefully looking over the situation and asking, "How can we maximize the assets under our control to beat the enemy?" While Archimedes' heat ray may not have succeeded in incinerating any attacking ship, he has been cited by some as the "patron saint"[3] of Operations Research, a discipline crucial to contemporary Optimization, for his use of mathematics to devise improved methods of attack and defense. We will encounter an eerie similarity between Archimedes' efforts and the work of British operations research scientists in World War II—more than two millennia later.

Wresting the Future from the Gods

For the greatest part of human history, the future has been viewed as unpredictable: little more than the whim of capricious gods. A monumental step toward optimal thinking was the wresting of prediction and forecasting from the hands of seers, shamans, and fortune-tellers. Peter Bernstein argues that, "The revolutionary idea that defines the boundary between modern times and the past is the mastery of risk. . . . The ability to define what may happen in the future and to choose among alternatives lies at the heart of contemporary societies."[4] The ability to project forward to anticipate the future, with all its attendant probabilities and risks, and then construct optimal alternatives to shape it to your advantage lies at the very foundation of decision Optimization. Much wresting of the future from the whims of the gods occurred during a 300-year period between 1600 and 1900, as advances in mathematics, calculating machines, and decision theory provided humankind with a new, more predictable perspective on the world.

Here are two key questions related to chance and risk: Can they be represented mathematically? And if so, can this mathematical representation help us make decisions about the future? It took a 17th-century compulsive gambler, who went by the name of Chevalier de Méré, to get an answer to these questions from his good friend, noted mathematician Blaise Pascal. Chevalier asked his friend to solve the following problem involving a ball game from the period, "balla":

A and B are playing a fair game of balla. They agree to continue until one has won six (by scoring six goals). The game actually stops when A has won five and B three. How should the stakes be divided?[5]

This puzzle, known as the "problem of the points," had been the cause of animated debate for 200 years. The crux of an optimal solution is the answer to the question: How confident are you about what will happen in the future? It seems clear that the leading player has a greater chance of winning, so the odds should be set in his or her favor. But what are the odds, and what should these be worth?

Centuries of dice playing had generated ideas about the frequency with which different combinations turn up. But no formal representation of the laws of probability existed to resolve such questions. Once this was accomplished, probability could—and would—be applied well beyond the gaming table, to encompass the great human issues of war and peace, commerce, finance and investments, technology, and personal success.

Pierre de Fermat, a 17th-century French lawyer credited with the early developments that led to modern calculus, not only solved the puzzle but developed a systematic way to represent outcomes. His technique was based on the ratio between all the ways in which something can occur compared to the possible occurrences. Today, when we are able to determine that an event has, say, a 50 percent, or 0.5, chance of occurring, we have Pascal and Fermat to thank for our ability to express probability in these terms.

Pascal was involved in constructing two additional foundational blocks of Optimization. Late in life, he entered a monastery where, in 1662, the monks published *Logic, or the Art of Thinking*, which was still being used as a textbook in the 19th century. The book contains four concluding chapters on probability, along with the statement, "Fear of harm ought to be proportional not merely to the gravity of the harm, but also to the probability of the event."[6]

This idea of assigning degrees of probability and seriousness of consequence to each possible outcome is what we today refer to as an "expected return." In the realm of finance, for example, if you can determine or accurately estimate both the magnitude of an outcome and the likelihood of its occurrence, then you can go about evaluating expected outcomes and rationally decide where best to invest your money. Suppose, for example, that with investment A you have a 5 percent chance of losing $1,000, while with investment B you have the chance to earn the same amount, but there is also a 70 percent chance of losing $100. Other things being equal, which investment is worse? Until probability could be represented mathematically, there was no clear way to decide. Today, we know that the first investment has an expected loss of $50, while the second has an expected loss of $70. It is easy for us to see that we are likely to lose less with choice A than choice B. One could point to expected return as a very early foundational concept for optimizing choices. Again, thank you, Pascal.

Computers: In the Beginning

Pascal's third important contribution to Optimization came about from daily watching his father, a tax collector, calculate long lists of taxes paid and owed. When he was not quite 19 years old, Pascal constructed a mechanical calculator—the Pascaline—capable of adding and subtracting numbers.[7] Although Pascal eventually produced 50 calculators of increasing sophistication, none were widely used, given their high cost of construction. The idea that machines could calculate numbers better than people, however, had long legs and subsequently great power for optimizing decisions.

Any discussion of early calculating machines also needs to include mention of Gottfried Wilhelm Leibniz (1646–1716) and Charles Babbage (1791–1871). In fact, Leibniz[8] could well be labeled the first "computer scientist." Early in life, he documented the binary number system and in 1671 began work on his own calculating machine, the Stepped Reckoner, which could execute all four arithmetical operations: addition, subtraction, multiplication, and division. In addition, while developing his ideas about binary arithmetic, Leibniz conceptualized a machine in which binary numbers were represented by marbles governed by what could be viewed as rudimentary punch cards. Leibniz was also the first to recognize that the coefficients of a system of linear equations could be arranged into a matrix and manipulated to find a solution. As we will see, the ability to solve a series of equations is a core capability for optimizers. Without it, today's optimizers would surely be back in the Dark Ages.

Accolades for the design of the first "mechanical computer," however, are generally reserved for the Englishman Charles Babbage.[9] The new focus on mathematics led to the need for a variety of mathematical tables. The people who developed such tables were called "computers," or those who compute. Not surprisingly, their efforts were often replete with errors. Distressed by this, Babbage set out to devise a means of doing the work mechanically. In 1822, he began the development of the steam-powered Difference Engine, thus labeled because of its use of differences, or subtraction, to multiply and divide. Not satisfied with simply calculating numbers, Babbage went on to design a machine to print the tables produced by his Difference Engine.

Babbage never completed construction of the Difference Engine. Budget overruns and a business partnership that went bad when his mechanic left with all the construction tools killed the project. The London Science Museum, however, subsequently built a working engine from Babbage's designs that went on display in 2008 and appears in the photograph in Figure 2.2. As a point of comparison to your handheld calculator and laptop computer, the constructed Difference Engine contained 25,000 parts and weighed 15 tons.

FIGURE 2.2   London Science Museum's Working Difference Machine[10]

Babbage soldiered on in spite of his construction problems. His next project was based on an even bigger and better idea: the Analytical Engine. Also never built in Babbage's time, the Analytical Engine was a succession of designs that Babbage worked on until his death in 1871. The main difference between the two calculating machines was that the Analytical Engine could be programmed, using punch cards, to undertake a specific set of calculations. As conceptualized, the Analytical Engine had other features of modern-day computers, including sequential control, branching, and looping.

Ada Lovelace, a contemporary of Babbage, became the world's first "computer programmer" when she wrote a program for the Analytical Engine. In 1890, Herman Hollerith and James Powers, working for the U.S. Census Bureau, developed devices that could read information automatically from punch cards.[11] In the next century, IBM, Remington, and Burroughs all adapted this system to feed data and programs into their calculators and computers.

We tend to think of calculators and computers as modern-day inventions. But key ideas, together with some early working models, go back a long time.

Optimization: Laying the Foundation

Let us leave the vaporous field of steam computing to examine some additional important early developments in probability, applied mathematics, and decision theory, all of which contributed to 20th-century Optimization.

The 300-year period from 1600 to 1900 also saw the ascendance of one of history's most remarkable families: that of Nicolaus Bernoulli (1623–1708). During this period, no fewer than eight Bernoullis were recognized as celebrated mathematicians.[12] Two Bernoullis of particular interest to decision making were Nicolaus's son, Jacob (1654–1705), and Jacob's nephew, Nicolaus II (1695–1726). Jacob collaborated with "computer scientist" Leibniz to develop techniques for estimating a population value from a sample. In addition, he proposed the idea of placing a confidence interval around the estimated value. So when you hear that a Nielsen poll found that 46 percent of Americans support health care reform, 95 percent confidence level plus or minus (±)

3 percent, think Bernoulli and Leibniz. What the pollsters are saying is that based on their drawn sample, they are 95 percent certain that the percent of Americans supporting health care reform lies between the interval of 43 and 49 percent.

Why should optimizers care? Because when you make decisions, you are often called upon to estimate values from a sample of information, using probability to determine accuracy. If you are in manufacturing, this is precisely the mechanism that your quality-control team is most likely using to set quality-control limits, get samples of output, and decide if everything is running as it should.

Let's consider a slightly different problem. Often, we have an initial idea of the likelihood that an event will occur, but then we receive additional information with its own associated probability. How do we combine the new information with the old? Or, asked slightly differently, How should we adjust the first probability based on what we have just learned? The ability to combine probabilities is key to optimizing.

Unfortunately, the average human brain tends not to be very good at this task.

Consider, for example, the following contemporary medical challenge, outlined in an explanation of Bayes' theorem:

> One percent of women at age 40 who participate in routine screening have breast cancer. 80 percent of women with breast cancer will get positive mammographies. 9.6 percent of women without breast cancer will also get positive mammographies. A woman in this age group had a positive mammography in a routine screening. What is the probability that she actually has breast cancer?[13]

The problem begins with a pretty simple piece of information: the chance that a woman 40 or younger undergoing routine screening has breast cancer is 1 percent. But now we suddenly have a good deal of new information, with associated probabilities. Unless you are a mathematics whiz, you probably have no idea how to compute the probability. You are not alone. When a group of contemporary physicians were asked what they would tell the young lady, 85 percent of them, as we shall see, gave not just a wrong answer, but a *really wrong* answer!

Nicolaus II, Jacob Bernoulli's nephew, was one of the first to work on this problem of combining probabilities, together with French mathematician Abraham de Moivre (1667–1754) and subsequently, British theologian Thomas Bayes (1702–1761). Prior to their joint contributions, probability had been represented by a frequency with a clear reference such as, "The chance of rolling an even number with a toss of a fair six-sided die is 3 in 6 or 0.5." The Bayesian, or stochastic, perspective framed probability as a belief with a level of certainty that can, and should, be adjusted as new information becomes available.

With this perspective in mind, let's return to our doctors' problem and ask: What should our doctors think about the young patient? Most of the doctors surveyed thought that the probability of the patient having breast cancer was between 70 and 80 percent. If they had known and used the Bayesian probability formula for adjusting initial probabilities, they would have been able to calculate and plan their next step based on the correct likelihood: 7.8 percent. With greater awareness of how to apply probability thinking to patient care, doctors would be better able to assess risk, communicate with patients, and make better decisions tailored to a patient's situation. It's a way to optimize the doctor-patient experience!

The fertile period of discovery between 1600 and 1900 also saw advances in general decision theory. Once again, a member of the Bernoulli family provided an important early insight. Daniel Bernoulli (1700–1782) was initially encouraged by his father, Jacob Bernoulli's brother Johan (1667–1748), to study business because of the low salaries being paid mathematicians. Being a Bernoulli, however, Daniel's real love was mathematics, and he later convinced his father to tutor him.[14]

In 1738, Daniel Bernoulli published an article in the *Papers of the Imperial Academy of Sciences in St. Petersburg*, questioning the proposition that "expected value" should be computed simply by multiplying each possible gain by the probability that it will occur. He argued that this was unrealistic, given the way people make real-life decisions. In real life, similar outcomes mean different things to different individuals. Bernoulli went on to propose that the perceived value or desirability of an outcome—destined to be called *utility* in modern decision theory—varied inversely to the quantity of goods that one possesses. In other words, the value or utility of $100 to a millionaire is less than the value of $100 to a pauper.

Thus at an early date, Bernoulli proposed a method for measuring something that could not be seen and counted directly. Likewise, modern-day optimizers focus great attention on measurement and often find ways to measure things that many of us think can never be measured. Bernoulli was an early member of this club. We will return to his idea of utility when we review the 20th century.

If you are wondering how early the ability to measure probability began to affect business decisions, you need not look further than the evolution of the insurance industry.[15] This industry was a *very early* adopter of the concept. Way back in 600 B.C.E., the Greeks and Romans introduced the idea of health and life insurance by organizing guilds, or "benevolent societies," in which a regular small payment provided funeral and family-care expenses after death. A similar system operated throughout Europe during the Middle Ages. In addition, the British government raised money through the sale of "life annuities." Pricing decisions, however, were based on intuition or trial and error. As late as 1540, a person could buy an annuity from the British government that repaid the purchaser in seven years, regardless of his or her age!

This one-size-fits-all approach began to change with the development of probability theory and the groundbreaking work of British astronomer and mathematician Edmond Halley (1656–1742). Inspired by an earlier study of London's population by John Graunt (1620–1674), Halley analyzed birth and death statistics from the German town of Breslau for an article that he had promised to write for a new Royal Society journal. Halley created a "life table" and used probability theory to compute the probability that a person of a particular age would not die within a year. He then used this table to calculate the life expectancy of different age groups.

Surprisingly, after the publication of Halley's paper in 1693, a century would pass before the British government and insurance companies such as Lloyd's of London would begin to price annuities based on age and life expectancy. Once this happened, underwriting left the gambling halls for the world of actuarial science, where applied mathematicians provided an insurance company with a clear competitive advantage.

ON THE SHOULDERS OF GIANTS

Looking back, it is astounding to see how many foundational ideas of modern-day decision making and Optimization had been articulated prior to the 20th century. Some of the most important were:

- The use of mathematics and probability theory to help predict and make decisions about the future
- Calculating machines more accurate than humans, together with designs for future "computers" that included binary arithmetic, programs, punch cards, and control programs
- Ways of estimating population parameters and confidence intervals from drawn samples
- The foundational mathematics underlying inferential statistical techniques such as regression and correlation analyses
- Methods for solving a series of linear equations, as well as first-order optimization procedures for minimizing or maximizing functions
- Recognition of the importance of utility, or perceived value, in human decision making
- Ways to measure things that cannot be directly counted
- The value to be gained from applying mathematics and probability theory to business problems such as the pricing of insurance

The long sweep of years prior to 1900 effectively set the stage for the arrival of Operations Research and Optimization.

2. 1900–1950: The Birth of Modern-Day Optimization

The first 50 years of the 20th century proved to be a defining period for modern-day Operations Research and Optimization. It was during this era that mathematics began to be rigorously applied to warfare and industry, making decision making more of a discipline and less a matter of gut feel and intuition. It was also a period that witnessed the birth of modern-day computing and the development of the most widely used mathematical model and algorithm for optimizing decisions: linear programming and the simplex algorithm.

Scientists and Soldiers: Light Meets Might

Until late in the 19th century, during a war it was possible for a supreme commander to personally plan and take charge of operations. However, as the complexity of weaponry, ammunition, fuel, and training increased, and the theater of war expanded worldwide, it became impossible for a single individual to master all of the details and make timely decisions. The result was an increased reliance on an ever-expanding "general staff," which subdivided the planning process and came to rely increasingly on subject matter experts.[16] Unlike King Hieron's reliance on Archimedes, 20th-century commanders in chief would come to rely not just on one individual, but on large groups of scientists and mathematicians.

The early 20th century saw continued expansion of applied mathematics into industry and wartime planning. A notable example was the work of Frederick Lanchester (1868–1946), builder of the first British motor car and power boat. Lanchester was also fascinated by air power and its ability to extend the reach of an armed force over the horizon. In 1916, he published *Aircraft in Warfare: The Dawn of the Fourth Arm*, which included a series of differential equations that dealt with the relationship between the concentration of opposing forces and their effective fighting strengths. The equations and mathematical formulas that Lanchester developed during World War I were able to predict quite accurately the outcome of engagements, adding impetus to the use of mathematics to make strategic decisions.[17]

The early 1900s also saw the expanded application of mathematics to decision making in business, including application of the mathematical formula for Brownian motion—the random movement of particles suspended in liquids—to model movements in the stock market (Louis Bachelier, 1900), use of probability theory to manage incoming telephone traffic (Agner Erlang, 1909; E. C. Molina, 1927), development of scheduling models (economic order quantity) to minimize inventory (F. W. Harris, 1913), and design and application of quality-control charts at Western Electric Company's Bell Telephone Laboratories (W. A. Shewhart, 1920s).[18]

World War II, however, was the game changer. Given the magnitude of the Axis threat, the Allies had to reach deeply into their moral, ideological, economic, military, technological, and scientific reserves to overcome the most powerful military force ever assembled. If, as Arnold Toynbee argued, history is nothing more—and nothing less—than a series of challenges and responses, then World War II was the perfect crucible for extracting the optimal potential from "the greatest generation." The unique stress and demands of World War II brought forth modern-day Operations Research, a forerunner of Optimization.

Late in 1934, H. E. Wimperis, director of scientific research for the British Air Ministry, was a desperate man. By then, the Versailles Treaty was no longer being taken seriously, especially by the Nazis. Germany had quietly begun to rearm in 1933. The prospect of a Nazi invasion of Europe and England was in the air, and Wimperis and others could envision squadrons of German bombers raining destruction on British cities. In the spring of 1935, Adolph Hitler punctuated the threat by boasting that the *Luftwaffe* had achieved parity with the Royal Air Force (RAF). The new German bombers were only 20 minutes from their British targets, leaving British fighters insufficient time to launch and intercept them in the event of an attack.[19]

Wimperis recommended that a Committee for the Scientific Study of Air Defense be established under Henry Tizard, a distinguished chemist and rector of the Imperial College of Science and Technology. The Tizard committee's charge was to consider "how far recent advances in scientific and technical knowledge can be used to strengthen the present methods of defense against hostile aircraft."[20] Members of the committee represented the crème de la crème of Britain's scientific, military, and political elite. Reminiscent of Archimedes' heat ray, one of the committee members suggested that the superintendent of the radio department of the National Physical Laboratory, Robert Watson-Watt, be consulted about the feasibility of developing a "death ray" to kill German bomber crews at the controls of their planes.

Watson-Watt didn't buy into the plan. After immersing himself in the situation, he concluded that the death-ray idea was impractical. But he did not give up. He thought more deeply about the challenge and then inspiration struck. Why not use radio waves as an early-aircraft-detection device? By July 1935, he and a small group of scientists had demonstrated that radar was capable of detecting aircraft from a range of 33 miles and could guide planes and antiaircraft fire to the target.

Radar was a revolutionary idea, no doubt about it. But the challenge moved quickly from discovering a breakthrough idea to putting a battle-ready system in place. The specific challenge: using radar as a defense against German bombers required a series of complex decisions about how to integrate the radar installations with the existing national networks of ground observers, antiaircraft guns, and interceptor aircraft.

Two separate groups set about tackling these issues. The first was the Bawdsey Research Station, comprising a small group of scientists whose focus was radar experimentation and development. The station also served as the headquarters for Britain's coastal chain of radar stations. The second was a small group of Royal Air Force officers at Biggin Hill in Kent, which was formed to study how the radar chain might best be used for aircraft interception. Between 1936 and 1938, the Biggin Hill group, working closely with the scientists at Bawdsey Research Station, conducted a series of experiments to determine the best way to integrate radar with other early-warning systems and with control command centers for the fighters and antiaircraft guns.

Contemporary Optimization is built on the use of rigorous scientific and mathematical concepts as the basis for practical problem solving and decision making. It is also built on a close working partnership between technical experts and their pragmatic counterparts in industry, the military, and government. In this, World War II played a pivotal role.

The close collaboration between British scientists and RAF officers has been cited by historians as the first example of modern-day Operations Research. P. M. S. Blackett, a physicist and member of the Tizard committee established to study air defense, wrote: ". . . the Biggin Hill experiments were the first step towards the fully fledged operational research[21] sections (ORS) eventually attached to all the major commands of all three services."[22] By 1941, Blackett had developed the rationale and general principles for assigning civilian scientific analysts to operational military units. One such principle: "OR units should be formed at the request of the unit commander."[23]

There is little doubt that the operations research teams of soldiers and scientists were instrumental in Britain's winning the air war in the summer and autumn of 1940, as Germany fought to gain air supremacy in preparation for an invasion. At times, the British achieved 80 percent interception rates through the coordinated use of radar and Observer Corps spotters. In the end, the RAF achieved a decisive victory over an air force twice its size, handing the Germans their first major defeat of the war.[24]

Apart from helping configure the defense networks, Operations Research played a key role in a strategic decision that likely saved Britain. In May 1940, France pleaded with Prime Minister Winston Churchill for British fighters to help repulse the German advance. Initially, Churchill seemed inclined to acquiesce. However, a group of analysts in the Stanmore Operations Research Group undertook a mathematical analysis of expected British aircraft attrition in France and the effect it would have on the RAF's ability to defend British skies. They concluded that the expected losses would so weaken the RAF that it would be unable to counter a German air attack. A summary of the report was presented to the War Cabinet, leading Churchill to deny the French request. The involvement of the Stanmore Group in a matter of higher policy was a significant departure from the mostly tactical studies it had been undertaking and set a precedent for operations research involvement in predicting the outcome of operations, with the objective of helping determine higher-level policy.[25] Optimization had arrived in the boardroom!

In their search for allies, the British communicated frequently with the United States, including sharing the success of their operations research efforts. The United States itself had engaged in a few early attempts to incorporate scientists and mathematicians into military operational decisions. Following the sinking of the *Lusitania* in 1915, the U.S. secretary of the Navy established a naval consulting board and asked Thomas Edison to serve as an advisor. Edison used empirical research and statistics to analyze the operations of German submarines and the vulnerability of British and U.S. shipping routes. He proposed to the British Admiralty a number of measures to reduce ship sinkings, upon which, unfortunately, it never acted. One important lesson in Operations Research that was learned early on by Edison—and is still relevant today—is that studies are likely to be ignored or actively discredited in the absence of direct contact with field commanders (or line management).[26]

By 1942, following the British example, operations research units had been established in the U.S. Navy as well as the U.S. Army–Air Force. Like their British counterparts, the U.S. operations research groups were involved in helping solve a wide variety of problems, including:

- Performance evaluations of weapons and equipment
- Analysis of operations, particularly those related to issues of weapon selection and use
- Outcome predictions of both tactical and strategic future operations
- Efficiency studies of groups wielding various weapons in battle

As for the competition, none of the Axis powers developed an effective operations research component during World War II. This contrasted sharply with the British and American operations research units in the field, who were credited with an impressive array of accomplishments. A short list of examples illustrates the extent of Operations Research's contribution to victory[27]:

- It markedly increased the percent of bombs striking their targets. One analyst concluded that by 1944, 250 bombers were doing the work that would have required 1,000 bombers in 1942.
- It reduced the number of rounds of antiaircraft fire needed to down one German aircraft from 20,000 in the summer of 1941 to 4,000 in 1942.
- It increased flight hours by 61 percent, through improved management of component parts and maintenance schedules.
- It raised the probability that an attack on a German submarine would sink it, from 2 to 3 percent at the beginning of the war to over 40 percent by 1945.
- It reduced Allied shipping losses in the Atlantic by more than a third, through modifications in the convoy system.

The Magic of Linear Programming

During and shortly following the war, a number of significant advances in mathematics, computer science, and decision theory accelerated the advancement of Optimization. The most significant of these was the development by George Dantzig of linear programming and the simplex solution algorithm in the summer of 1947, in response to a specific need of the military. To help coordinate the incredibly complex planning of a worldwide air conflict, in 1943 the Air Staff had created a program-monitoring function, under the direction of Harvard professor E. P. Learned. The "program," or planning activity, was started with a high-level war plan containing key objectives. In successive stages, the plan specified individual-unit deployment to combat theaters, training requirements of flying and technical personnel, supply and maintenance, and so on. The complexity involved was so great that the scheduling process could take as long as seven months to complete.[28]

It became clear to the Air Force that efficient coordination of the energies of a nation would require scientific "programming"[29] techniques. Intensive work began in June 1947 by a group that subsequently was given the official title of Scientific Computation of Optimum Programs, known informally as "Project SCOOP." George Dantzig was a member and took on the planning challenge. The result was the development of linear programming[30] and the simplex solution algorithm. These techniques play such a central role in modern-day Optimization that it is worth taking a few moments to examine how they work and why they represented such a breakthrough.

Informally, linear programming is a method for mathematically determining the best outcome—such as maximum revenue or lowest cost—using a series of linear equations. As stated in Chapter 1, Optimization involves squeezing value from assets under management; this can now be done in a disciplined way, thanks to Dantzig's breakthrough.

Let's take a very simple example to illustrate the concept.[31] Farmer Jones has a tract of land and has to decide which combination of wheat and barley he should plant. Each crop requires different amounts of expensive fertilizer and pesticide, and each commands a different market price per acre. Unfortunately, due to financial constraints, Farmer Jones has a limited amount of fertilizer and pesticide available to him for the planting season. "How can I maximize my revenue?" Farmer Jones asks. Not familiar with linear programming, Farmer Jones must guess about different combinations and rely on trial and error to maximize his revenue.

Enter Farmer Jones's daughter, Mary, a college graduate with a degree in mathematics and the mind of an optimizer. She puts intuition aside, at least temporarily, and begins by representing both the goal and the constraints—such as cost and amount of available fertilizer—in a set of mathematical equations. Mary then calculates how many acres of wheat and barley would maximize the revenue from her father's farmland. The series of equations looks something like this:

First, Mary represents the goal she wants to maximize by the statement $S_W x_W + S_B x_B$. This is simply the price of an acre of wheat (S_W) times the acres of wheat planted (x_W), added to the price of an acre of barley (S_B) times the acres of barley planted (x_B). In optimization parlance, $S_W x_W + S_B x_B$ is the "objective function," or what we want to maximize or minimize: in this case, revenue.

Once Mary has mathematically represented the goal, she then represents each constraint. A constraint is simply something that limits the possible solutions. For example, one limit is how many acres of land the farmer has available. Mary represents this limit as $x_W + x_B \leq A$, where A represents the acres available and $x_W + x_B$ is the sum of acres planted with wheat and those planted with barley. The formula simply says that the acres planted in wheat plus the acres planted in barley must equal or be less than the total acres. In other words, Farmer Jones cannot plant on his neighbor's land.

The complete mathematical model for Mary's problem, with an explanation for each formula, can be represented this way:

Maximize the value of:

$S_W x_W + S_B x_B$ (S_W and S_B are the selling price per acre of wheat and barley, respectively, and x_W and x_B are the acres planted with wheat and barley.)

Subject to the constraints:

$x_W + x_B \leq A$ (The sum of acres planted in wheat and barley must equal or be less than the total acres available, A.)

$F_W x_W + F_B x_B \leq F$ (The fertilizer put on an acre of wheat (F_W) times the acres of wheat planted (x_W), plus the fertilizer put on an acre of barley (F_B) times the acres of barley planted (x_B) must be equal or less than the total fertilizer available, F.)

$P_W x_W + P_B x_B \leq P$ (This is the same formula as the previous, except that it is the constraint for pesticide, P, rather than fertilizer.)

$x_W \geq 0$ (Simply said, the acres planted in wheat must be equal to or greater than zero.)

$x_B \geq 0$ (Same as the previous for the acres of barley planted.)

Solving for x_W and x_B in this series of equations allows Farmer Jones to set aside the precise number of acres for barley and wheat needed to maximize his revenue. This should make Farmer Jones a very happy man. He not only knows how to optimize his investment, but he also realizes that he has spent wisely on his daughter's education!

Representing a problem with a series of equations is one thing; solving for x_W and x_B is quite another, especially when faced with a more complex problem. For example, in 1951 the Air Force developed the first computer-based linear program solution dealing with deployment and support of aircraft between combat sorties and training, with an objective function of optimizing sortie success. Its representation of the problem involved 48 equations with 71 unique variables.[32] Hardly a homework assignment for a beginning algebra student!

To meet the solution challenge, Dantzig developed what he called the simplex algorithm. The mathematics are beyond this book, but conceptually the simplex method involves representing the set of equations as a geometrical shape in an x-dimension space. A 3-simplex, for example, is a tetrahedron, or what we would call a three-sided pyramid. The simplex algorithm moves along the edges of the shape until it reaches an optimal solution for the objective function.

The impact and power of Dantzig's discovery for arriving at optimal solutions are hard to overstate. In an early illustration of the technique, Dantzig discusses assigning 10 people to 70 jobs. Incredibly, the number of possible assignments exceeds the number of particles in the universe! By representing the problem as a linear-program problem and using the simplex algorithm, Dantzig was able to arrive at a solution in a few minutes.[33] It was a technique that would come to be used by optimizers more often than any other.

Realizing the full potential of linear programming and the simplex algorithm would require additional computing power. Before we discuss computers in the first half of the 1900s, however, there were several additional important developments in applied mathematics and decision theory that contributed significantly to the evolution of modern-day Optimization.

Games, Computers, and the Genius of John von Neumann

Following the chaos and destruction of World War II, many European intellectuals fled the continent and came to America. An impressive number of them—including Albert Einstein, George Dantzig, and John von Neumann—found their way to Princeton University and the nearby Institute for Advanced Study. Some believe that Hungarian immigrant John von Neumann (1903–1957) possessed the greatest intellect of the three. Whether or not that was the case, his contributions to Optimization were substantial and spanned all three disciplines: applied mathematics, decision theory, and computer science.

While in his early 20s, von Neumann became fascinated by "games." Not games like chess—which he believed were computational exercises with a correct answer for every move—but rather games more akin to real-life situations, in which the best response depends on trying to anticipate the future moves of an opponent. As he is reported to have said, "Real life [games] consist of bluffing, of little tactics of deception, of asking yourself what is the other man going to think I mean to do?"[34] His work in this area culminated in 1944 with the publication of the *Theory of Games and Economic Behavior*, coauthored with the Austrian-born economist Oskar Morgenstern.

Game theory involves using mathematics to model behavior in strategic and tactical situations, where an individual's success in making choices depends on the individual's wins at the expense of another. The theory was subsequently expanded to encompass a diverse set of decision-making situations, including both symmetrical and asymmetrical interactions, interactions involving simultaneous versus sequential moves, interactions involving perfect versus imperfect information, and as mentioned, zero-sum games versus possible win-win interactions.

Few theoretical frameworks have had as broad an impact on decision making in so many different disciplines, including economics, biology, engineering, political science, international relationships, philosophy, and of course, computer science. Von Neumann's study of games impacted the evolving science of Optimization in several ways:

- First, game theory gave additional impetus to the application of mathematical rigor for understanding and deriving solutions to a wide range of practical problems: problems that had previously been viewed as ill defined or intractable. These range from international relations among countries to business negotiations to predicting patterns of consumer behavior.

- Second, it provided a framework for solving problems that lent themselves to discovering equilibrium, or end points to which an interaction is likely to evolve, suggesting strategies for maximizing or minimizing outcomes for the players. The mathematics of game theory lent themselves directly to questions of Optimization.

- Third, it advanced the theory of utility by identifying a means of measuring more precise than Bernoulli's general notion of proportionality. Bernoulli's suggestion for measuring utility produced only an ordinal scale of measurement. That is, the most that this type of measurement permits is a gross ranking, such as stating that the prize is worth more to individual A than to individual B. But Bernoulli was unable to answer the question, How much more? Von Neumann and Morgenstern used probability theory, in conjunction with asking people about different imaginary lotteries that they would or would not be willing to play, to determine more precisely how much more one person values an object than another person does or how much more a person values object x over object y. As we have noted, an important element of successful Optimization is being able to measure things accurately, including some things that may initially appear hard to measure.

As mentioned, von Neumann's contributions to Optimization extended beyond applied mathematics and decision theory to computing. New developments in mathematics, large-scale planning, linear programming, and now game theory have all created a strong impetus to search for better ways to compute all the numbers, formulas, and game iterations. Computing became von Neumann's passion during the second half of his life.

The Dawn of the Modern Computer

In 1936, while still a student at King's College in Cambridge, Alan Turing had devised a theoretical device to simulate the logic of any computer algorithm. Subsequently, in 1937, while working on his Ph.D., Turing built a digital multiplier, using Boolean logic with electromechanical relays.[35] This quickly led to the construction of the first general-purpose electronic computer.[36]

The project began in 1943 and took three years to complete. It was led by John Eckert and John Mauchly at the Moore School of Electrical Engineering at the University of Pennsylvania. The building of this machine, the Electrical Numerical Integrator and Calculator (ENIAC), was funded by the U.S. Army to calculate artillery firing tables. It used 17,468 vacuum tubes; took up 1,800 square feet of floor space; weighed 27 tons; and consumed 160,000 watts of electrical power. Although the machine could receive data from punch cards, it had to be hardwired for each set of calculations. The rewiring task was so complex that it could take weeks to complete. Computer programs on punch cards would have to wait until the second generation of machines.[37]

Although the U.S. Army's Ballistic Research Laboratory sponsored ENIAC, one year into the three-year project John von Neumann became aware of its existence. At the time, von Neumann was working on the hydrogen bomb at Los Alamos. He and the Los Alamos engineers became so involved with ENIAC that the first test run was a series of computations for the hydrogen bomb that used one million punch cards of data.

Von Neumann was subsequently heavily involved in discussions at the Moore School concerning a successor to ENIAC. These included groundbreaking concepts such as storing programs as data, and conditional control transfer to allow the use of subroutine calls in a program. Von Neumann prepared a lengthy memo discussing these and other concepts, which was widely circulated outside the University of Pennsylvania. It became the basis for the following generations of computers, which, incidentally, wound up spending more time solving linear programming problems than carrying out any other mathematical problem.[38]

The first mass-produced commercial computer, the Universal Automatic Computer (UNIVAC I), was built by Remington Rand and delivered to the U.S. Census Bureau in 1951 at a price of $1 million. (The equivalent cost today would be $8.2 million.) To illustrate the advancements made since the 1946 ENIAC, this machine used

5,200 vacuum tubes; weighed 13 tons; and could run approximately 1,905 operations per second. Eventually, 46 of the computers were produced. Besides the U.S. government and Armed Forces, early clients taking delivery of a UNIVAC I prior to 1955 included General Electric's Appliance Division, Metropolitan Life, U.S. Steel, Franklin Life Insurance, Pacific Mutual Life Insurance, and Westinghouse's Early Adapter Group.

The first linear program and simplex algorithm were coded on the National Bureau of Standards computer under the auspices of the U.S. Air Force to deal with the deployment and support of aircraft. This was the problem we mentioned earlier, which required 48 equations and 71 variables. The computer needed 73 simplex iterations and 18 hours to arrive at the optimal solution. It was an astounding accomplishment for the period. Today, it could be solved in seconds on your laptop or desktop computer!

By the mid-1950s, computers were winding their way into industry as well as government. Operations Research and Optimization had clearly demonstrated their value in business as well as in war. Advances in computational power, together with advances in applied mathematics and development of new algorithms such as the simplex method, were creating new capabilities for finding optimal solutions to increasingly complex problems.

The foundation for Optimization was firmly in place. It was becoming increasingly possible not only to analyze complex problems and vast amounts of data but to prescribe what the optimal solution should be. The next 30 years would witness rapid expansion of optimization techniques into new industries and increasingly complex decisions.

3. 1950–1980: Postwar Proliferation at the Speed of Business

Theory never rests. The years between 1950 and 1980 continued to see new mathematical models being applied to decision making. For example, nonlinear programming techniques and queuing theory were being used to optimize an ever-increasing array of modern-day challenges, from shortening customer-service lines to abating highway congestion to dealing with the growing complexity of computer networks. But what most clearly defines this 30-year period in the history of Optimization is the rapid development of computing power and the proliferation of computers—together with optimization applications—throughout the world of business.

Computers: From Number Crunchers to Problem Solvers

IBM quickly followed Remington Rand, bringing its own computer to market in 1952. By 1957, IBM was shipping the 608-transistor calculator, the world's first completely transistorized computer. Replacing vacuum tubes with transistors proved to be an astonishing accomplishment. The size of the computer shrank by 50 percent, its speed more than doubled, and its power consumption decreased by 90 percent. The 608 machine could perform 4,500 additions a second: 2.5 times faster than IBM's 607 model, which had been introduced a mere two years earlier.

Even more impressive, customers could purchase the 608 for only $83,210, compared to the million-dollar price tag the Remington computer had carried six years earlier. Moore's law, which predicted the doubling of the price-performance ratio of computers every 18 months, had already been passed a decade before Moore would write it down!

In 1964, IBM introduced the 360 series that became the business workhorse of that and the succeeding decade. The engine of Optimization—calculations—became faster, cheaper, more powerful, and more readily available.

With this new availability, programs emerged that were specifically designed for problem solving and decision making. In 1955, Allen Newell, Herbert Simon, and J. C. Shaw developed the Logic Theorist (LT), an artificial intelligence (AI) program invented to mimic the problem-solving skills of human beings. The program used heuristic rules to prove mathematical theorems. Building on this early effort, in 1965 Edward Feigenbaum and his Stanford University students developed two AI programs: DENDRAL and MYCIN. In addition to using a rule-based language, these programs introduced an important language feature that simplified future development of AI programs: They separated the knowledge base (rules) from what was labeled the inference engine, or how the rules were to be evaluated.[39]

MYCIN was designed to help physicians identify which bacterium was most likely causing a severe patient infection and then recommend an antibiotic regiment. This program included many features of current-day optimization software. The program would first pose to the physician a series of contextual questions about the patient and his symptoms. After completing the analysis, MYCIN presented a list of possible infectious agents, together with the probability of each diagnosis and a recommended drug and dosage. MYCIN would also list the questions and rules that it used in its diagnosis. This enabled the physician to understand the logic behind the program's decisions.

Researchers at Stanford Medical School tested the effectiveness of MYCIN and found that it proposed an acceptable therapy in 65 percent of the cases. While this might seem low—particularly if you are the person infected—MYCIN's accuracy exceeded the performance of a group of infectious disease experts.[40] For a number of ethical and practical reasons,[41] MYCIN was never used in a clinical setting. However, the concepts derived in its development would be extended in the future to a wide range of optimization software problems.

The development of computer languages such as LISP and AI programs like MYCIN not only advanced optimization software techniques; they radically altered how computers began to be viewed. Initially, computers were seen primarily as number-crunching "calculating" machines. These new developments led people to see computers as "thinking machines" that could analyze situations, solve problems, and make better recommendations than their creators.

Early Adopters

Beginning in the early 1950s, optimization techniques such as linear programming and AI began to be used by business organizations at an ever-accelerating pace. Several members of Arthur D. Little, Inc. (ADL) had taken leave during World War II to work with the government. This exposed them to the military's Operations Research. In 1949, after returning to the private sector, Harry Wissman established a group within ADL to explore the use of Operations Research in industry. Early clients included Sears, Roebuck & Co.; the baby products division of Johnson & Johnson; and Republic Steel. This was only the beginning. A small sample of the businesses adopting operations research and optimization practices over the following 30 years provides a snapshot of the speed and breadth with which Optimization caught on and augmented human decision making:[42]

- 1950: The "Transportation Problem" is first programmed on a computer, using linear programming and the simplex algorithm. The solution is applicable to a wide range of industry situations that require moving goods from multiple sites to multiple locations as efficiently as possible.

- 1954: *Operations Research for Management* by Joseph F. McCloskey and Florence Trefethen (editors) is published. This is the first publication describing the relationship between management and Operations Research. It covers, among other things, statistics, linear programming, queuing theory, computers, and game theory.

- 1955: The first international congress concerning the application of probability theory to telephone engineering and administration problems is held in Copenhagen.

- 1955: *Linear Programming: The Solution of Refinery Problems* by Gifford Symonds is published, presenting a formal account of the use of linear programming to solve refinery problems at Esso Standard Oil Company. These problems include blending of aviation gasoline, selection of crude oils to meet production demands in ways that maximize profit, and selection of production runs and inventory levels to meet seasonal fluctuations in demand.

- 1956: *Linear Programming: A Key to Optimum Newsprint Production* is published, describing the application for cutting standard-width rolls of paper into smaller-width rolls of different sizes in ways that minimize waste.[43]

- 1960: Ronald Howard of Arthur D. Little develops the Markov decision process (MDP), using stochastic probability to help Sears, Roebuck & Company determine which customers it should send catalogues to, based on the likelihood of their making a purchase.

- 1964: Publication of the *Vehicle Routing Savings Algorithm* by G. Clarke and J. W. Wright. This algorithm provided a near-optimal solution for minimizing costs when routing a fleet of delivery vehicles of varying capacity to make deliveries to diverse locations.

- 1969: The Media Evaluation Using Dynamic and Interactive Applications of Computers (MEDIAC) model is developed by John Little and Leonard Lodish. The first marketing-decision-support system had arrived! It used mathematical models to maximize total marketing sales potential, subject to constraints on exposure, media usage, and budgets.

- 1971: Michael Morton of MIT proposes the concept of the Management Decision System (MDS), later relabeled Decision Support System, or DDS. He described the system as ". . . an approach involving the analysis of key decisions and the design of support for these decisions . . . [involving] the use of interactive graphics, terminals, a multiple-access computer, and a data bank and model bank relevant to the problem."

- 1973: Fisher Black and Myron Scholes publish their formula for determining the fair value for pricing options, paving the way for the subsequent massive market in financial derivatives.

- 1974: Shortly after its founding in 1973, FedEx establishes an operations research department, reporting directly to its chairman and CEO, Frederick Smith. Smith subsequently notes, ". . . All major system changes, such as number and location of hubs and fleet-composition analysis, were first modeled by the OR [operations research] analysts several years in advance of the actual system changes."[44]

- 1978: New York City's Department of Sanitation uses Optimization to manage collection and disposal of 22,000 tons of refuse collected each day from 6,000 miles of city streets. Areas to which Optimization is applied include manpower forecasting, truck sizing, and load assignments. Mayor Ed Koch reports that the initiative results in productivity increases of 17 percent over a two-year period.

- 1982: American Airlines (AA) hires its first director of Operations Research, who subsequently establishes SABRE Decision Technologies, the AA subsidiary credited with the development of "yield management," the ticket-pricing system designed to maximize revenue through continuous ticket-price adjustments. It was a pricing approach tailor-made for computers—and CFOs.

Human Decision Making: Facts and Foibles

Optimization's ability to solve complex problems quickly and accurately was clearly the driving force behind its initial acceptance by some businesses, government, and the military. A supporting contributing factor, however, was the increased study and documentation by economists and cognitive psychologists of the foibles of human judgment. An important early work was the 1957 publication *Models of Man* by Herbert Simon in which Simon introduced the concept of "bounded rationality." Simon argued that the rationality of individuals is limited by the information they have, their own cognitive limitations, and the finite amount of time available to them in which to make a decision. He goes on to suggest that because decision makers lack the ability and resources to arrive at an optimal solution, they apply their rationality only after greatly simplifying the available choices. They do this by applying heuristics, or simple rules of thumb, to guide them. Simon concludes that in most situations people are "satisficers," not optimal decision makers.[45]

In the 1970s, Daniel Kahneman and Amos Tversky elaborated further on the limits of human decision making in their articulation of prospect theory, which dealt with how people make decisions about risk.[46, 47] In a series of ingenious experiments, Kahneman and Tversky demonstrated that human decision makers (1) place too much importance on small probabilities, (2) weigh losses disproportionally more heavily than gains, and (3) are susceptible to judgment errors resulting from framing or anchoring effects—judgment distortions caused by the way information is presented. As a simple demonstration of the last phenomenon, Kahneman shows that if you ask a group of people to write down their Social Security number and then ask them how many physicians they believe reside in New York City, the group with high Social Security numbers will estimate more physicians by as much as 30 percent, compared to people with low Social Security numbers. Obviously, Social Security numbers have nothing to do with one's ability to make estimates. What creates the bias is the action of having in mind a large versus a small number just prior to making an estimate.

Daniel Kahneman would subsequently receive a Nobel Prize for his work in uncovering judgment biases. His and others' demonstrations of the ephemeral nature of human perceptions and judgments provided additional impetus for finding better ways of making good decisions using operations research and optimization software.

Although Optimization made impressive inroads into business between 1950 and 1980, for the most part its spread was limited to large, well-financed organizations with the capital to invest in computing power, consultants, and large IT departments. But change was coming—and fast. Moore's law was slicing the cost of computing in half every 18 months. The laptop computer, digitization, and the Internet were about to bring Optimization to the people.

4. 1980 to the Present: Optimization to the People

The more recent the history, the greater the interpretive challenge. However, there have clearly been several revolutionary trends and events in the past 30 years that are having a profound impact on Optimization. One of these, of course, is the incredible shrinking—and rapidly proliferating—computer. A second is the omnipresent Internet, with its vast digitized databases, instant global communication, and aggregated computing power. These advances are accelerating the adoption of Optimization, moving it from government and Fortune 500 companies into smaller companies and even into the hands of individuals.

Computing Power: From Floor Model to Handheld

In the 1970s, VLSI—the placing of thousands of transistor-based circuits onto a single chip—generated striking increases in computer power in ever-shrinking packages. By the late 1970s, three separate companies had brought to market out-of-the-box, ready-to-run desktop computers: the Apple II, the Commodore Pet, and Radio Shack's TRS-80. Businesses were initially hesitant to let these "toys" into their halls of capitalism. However, in 1981 IBM introduced its first desktop computer, complete with an inventory of business software. With IBM's stamp of approval, the desktop, or personal computer (PC) quickly became a business essential.

Throughout the 1980s, computers were not merely becoming smaller and less expensive; they were growing in power and connectivity. By the end of the decade, desktop computers had become more powerful than their minicomputer predecessors and were typically networked together into a local area network (LAN). In another 10 years, even more computing power was available on a laptop computer that fit easily into a briefcase and had modem access to a corporate data center. Today, with 85 percent of American adults owning cell phones, the smartphone is on its way to becoming the computing device of choice, and a cloud of interconnected computers—from a vast number of companies—all interconnect to provide user-friendly applications, or apps.

As important to the growth of Optimization as readily available computing power was the arrival of powerful new software that followed in its wake. In 1979, Dan Bricklin introduced the VisiCalc spreadsheet for desktop computers, giving nonprogrammers the ability to build computer models, run what-if scenarios, and conduct statistical analyses to help them make decisions.[48] Then in 1984 Sam Savage of LINDO Systems, Inc., introduced spreadsheet add-in software that could solve both linear and nonlinear sets of equations. Linear programming and the simplex algorithm arrived on the desktop![49]

In addition to spreadsheets, AI shells began to proliferate, designed to assist in the development of knowledge bases, decision rules, and expert systems. A 1995 analysis of business AI applications found that by 1987, 40 percent of the AI systems described in the literature had been built using a shell rather than a computer language.[50] This represented another advance for Optimization: you no longer had to be a computer programmer to create decision-making software models.

Optimizing with Global Resources

As it has for almost all aspects of life, the emergence of the Internet changed Optimization forever. First, the Web has made it possible to link computers together into powerful, distributed-computer networks. One of the most famous was the SETI project. This effort asked participants to download the data gathered by telescopes to their home computers and analyze it for signs of intelligent life. More than 5.3 million personal computers eventually become part of the search for extraterrestrials.[51]

Optimizers are data hounds. Consequently, the second important way in which the Web enhanced computing power and optimization efforts was to make available very large digitized databases, many of which could be accessed in real time. As we will see in a moment, such data sets have brought individuals into the optimization arena. The recent Mobile Century experiment provides one example of just how powerful real-time data points and a network of distributed computing devices can be for real-time problem analysis. Most cell phones now have GPS positioning capabilities accurate enough to identify the device's position as well as track its movement. The Mobile Century experiment used the phones of 100 students to track traffic flow along I-880 in California. The result? Traffic congestion could be tracked accurately simply by monitoring the average speed with which the 100 cell phones were moving along the highway—no satellites or cameras needed, thank you.[52] The day appears to be quickly approaching when many of us will use our handheld computing devices to monitor our immediate surroundings and recommend optimized walking and driving routes that take into consideration distance, traffic, and even potential chores we wish to accomplish along the way.

Empowering Small Companies

Over the past 30 years, government, the military, and large companies have continued to expand their use of Optimization to make decisions. For example, in the late 1980s, Yellow Freight commissioned Princeton University professor Warren Powell to create optimization software that would enable it to plan and run its vast less-than-truckload (LTL) freight network.[53] Other trucking companies soon followed.

In another application, Hewlett-Packard's Strategic Modeling and Planning Group, working with Hau Lee and associates of Stanford University, developed a series of new computerized models for supply chain management. The U.S. military took advances in computerized supply chain management to new levels in Desert Storm, when it successfully moved 155,000 tons of equipment and 164,000 personnel to Saudi Arabia in 75 days.[54]

As impressive as these applications were, a bigger story over the past 30 years has been the increased use by smaller companies—and private individuals—of optimization software to more effectively manage an increasing array of assets. Consider the following examples:[55]

- 1997: Visteon Automotive Systems, a Ford parts supplier, began using simulation-based decision-support software to improve scheduling of training, production operations, and production planning at its Sterling Heights, Michigan plant. The result? Over a two-year period, the plant improved productivity by

30 percent and saved $10,000,000 from the cost of expanding its production line.

- 1999–2000: The Jan de Wit Company, a Brazil-based international grower and seller of ornamental lily plants, began using linear programming to optimize its profit margin, after factoring in a lengthy list of constraints, including country-defined sales limits, import requirements, bulb origination, germination cycles, bulb inventory, and greenhouse limitations. During a two-year period, the company's income from operations increased by 60 percent, while return on owner's equity grew from 15.1 percent to 22 percent.

- 2002: Texas Children's Hospital was faced with the daunting task of managing—and continuously renegotiating—150 contracts with insurance companies and managed care providers. Overwhelmed with the complexity, the hospital developed optimization software to assist in managing contract revenues. One year later, the hospital had increased contract revenue by $6 million.

- 2003: Rhenania, a German mail-order company, developed a multilevel modeling system to dynamically evaluate key customer segments according to purchasing history. The system helped executives decide when, how often, and to whom catalogs and marketing material should be sent. The system was so successful that Rhenania outperformed the market and in a short period of time rose from fifth to second in its industry.

- 2003–2005: Travelocity reinvented its business. As a result of market changes, Travelocity's revenue and market share began to take a nose dive. To solve the problem, Travelocity teamed up with American Airlines' Sabre Research Group to model customer behavior, product pricing, and supplier agreements. The exercise prompted Travelocity to overhaul its business model. The result: between 2002 and 2006, Travelocity more than doubled its annual revenues and drove millions of dollars per year to its bottom line.

- 2005: Google introduced Google Analytics, a set of enterprise-strength analytics programs designed to evaluate and make recommendations about Web-page changes and marketing campaigns. The core set of tools was offered free of charge, putting Optimization into the hands of small companies around the world.[56]

- 2008: Barack Obama's Web team used Google's Website Optimizer to conduct conversion-rate tests on the candidate's Web pages to far outpace other candidates in fund-raising through the Web.[57]
- 2010: Apple Computer bought Siri, the maker of a mobile personal-assistant app for iPhones that searches out information on the Web to book reservations and make recommendations based on personal preferences, location, and past activities. Optimization found its way into the consumer's pocket.[58]

Individual Optimizers

Certainly, one of the biggest steps in the development of Optimization is its sudden, widespread availability: not just to armed forces, governments, and companies, but to individuals. While "yield management" is Optimization that advises businesses what to charge, the same science can be used in reverse—to tell customers what to pay. In his book *Super Crunchers*, Ian Ayres introduces us to his friend, Princeton economist and wine aficionado Orley Ashenfelter.[59] Ashenfelter earned the ire and disdain of wine critics around the world, including the world-famous Robert Parker, by using weather statistics combined with an Internet database of wine prices to predict the quality of Bordeaux wine vintages without actually tasting them. Ashenfelter's mathematical model takes into consideration factors such as summer temperatures and the amount of rain that falls during harvest time.

Ashenfelter's big advantage over the wine tasters who traditionally make such pronouncements is not only his accuracy, but his timeliness. Bordeaux wines spend 18 to 24 months in oak casks before being set aside in bottles for final tasting. While the average wine buyer waits, Ashenfelter calculates! When the 1989 Bordeaux wines had lain in their casks for barely three months, Ashenfelter proclaimed them to be far superior to the then-highly praised 1986 vintage, before even the earlier "barrel tastings" had begun. Later, his model ranked the 1990 vintage even higher. While this bucked the conventional wisdom, today, as Ayres notes, first-growth '89s are selling at auction for more than twice the price of the '86s, and the 1990 bottles are going for even more.

As noted, Google's Analytics services are available to individuals free of charge. The series of optimization programs use multivariate statistical techniques to "isolate and analyze subsets of your Web traffic with a fast interactive segment builder." Google Analytics also "monitors your Web traffic reports and alerts you to significant changes in data patterns."[60] Furthermore, you can create alternative Web pages, with varying messages or text placement, and continuously measure their relative effectiveness in increasing the browsing time of visitors to your site. Google Analytics even lets users set optimization goals and track progress toward reaching them. If you have a website, why not begin to optimize right away? Just click on google.com/analytics.

Final Note

The quotations from Aristotle and Machiavelli that introduced this chapter point to the power of history to help us both look back to understand how things evolved and look ahead to envision future possibilities. As I reflect on the history of Optimization with both men's points in mind, here are the lessons that I draw:

- Humans are optimizing animals. They always have searched—and always will search—for better ways to model their environment to make better, faster, and more accurate decisions.
- From war to gambling to business, Optimization affords early adopters a competitive advantage. Being the best and fastest decision maker separates you from the crowd.
- Success in the application of Optimization requires more than just quants. It depends on taking a practical, experienced-based approach, in which applied theorists work closely with practitioners and frontline personnel. Each member of the interdisciplinary team needs to understand at a conceptual level what the others are doing to achieve maximum success. And each needs to bring his or her unique perspective to the discussion to ensure that the human-computer relationship leads to truly optimal solutions.
- Optimization's penetration of our world is accelerating. For many years, the high cost of Optimization limited its application to large, financially wealthy institutions. These barriers are disappearing. Small companies and individuals are depending

increasingly on optimization techniques to outperform, or at least keep pace with, their competitors.

The rate of improvement in optimization software's ability to make decisions is accelerating much more rapidly than our brain's ability to make complex decisions. Make no mistake, there is no substitute for human brainpower, experience, and judgment. But decision making is becoming more complex, the need for speed is ever greater, and the value placed on "the right decision" is increasing. Optimization is destined to occupy a central seat at the decision-making table.

This chapter examined where Optimization has been—its historical roots—and included some initial speculation on where it might be headed. We will speculate more about the future in the book's concluding chapter. The following chapter will take us inside real-life organizations to examine, up close, how Optimization is being deployed and how it is playing an increasingly important role in the quest for competitive advantage.

CHAPTER 3

OPTIMIZATION IN ACTION

We live in an Optimization-ripe era. For much of human history, competition for goods and services was primarily regionalized, and resources seemed almost boundless. Expanding global empires, the Age of Exploration, and Manifest Destiny all reflected the drive of a few powerful nations to dominate a resource-rich world. Following World War II, the United States was left the uncontested master of the industrial universe, driven to satisfy the pent-up demand for goods and services at home and abroad. Given the situation, who needed to worry about competition and resource conservation? Certainly not the United States.

But what a difference a few decades make! Today, the world is marked by ferocious global competition for every imaginable product and service. Each year, the World Economic Forum publishes a report evaluating the global competitiveness of countries around the world. Its 2010 ratings range from 2.58 to 5.60, based on a composite rating for each country, which include such factors as infrastructure, macroeconomic stability, education levels, market efficiency, financial sophistication, technology readiness, business sophistication, and innovation. For many years, the United States, together with a handful of highly industrialized nations, dominated the ratings. In the 2009–2010 report, however, 19 countries had ratings of 5 or higher, and for the first time the United States fell from the vaunted first position to number two.[1] No doubt about it: businesswise, the world has become a very competitive place.

As for unbounded resources, the stress imposed on the world's environment and its resources by seven billion inhabitants shows itself every time we read the news, listen to or watch a news broadcast, or travel. Some optimists argue that the world could support nearly twice as many inhabitants. However, as Jared Diamond points out in his book *Collapse*, such arguments fail to persuasively show how so many inhabitants could be supported. Today, citizens in the United States, Western Europe, and Japan consume 32 times more fossil fuel—and extrudes 32 times more waste—than do inhabitants of the Third World. If all the members of the Third World were to adopt the living standard of the industrialized nations, the impact on resources would increase by a factor of 12.[2] It takes blind faith—never mind optimism—to believe that this could be feasible without vastly improving the efficiencies of our resource use.

Given the hyper-competitive, resource-drained world in which we live, Optimization holds great promise. Two resources that the world is not short of are data and computing power, the very stuff of Optimization. Today, companies such as Amazon Web Services and Elastic Compute Cloud are leading the way in providing customers with vast amounts of low-cost computation and storage on demand, much as utility companies supply water and electricity. With computing power and data increasingly being commoditized, let's take a look at how a variety of organizations are using Optimization to manage their assets and extract greater value from scarcity.

What Is the Real Value of Your Assets?

Accountants have a fairly narrow definition of *assets*. To optimizers, assets include *any resource that an organization owns or controls that can potentially add value to the business*. Some are traditional accounting assets, such as buildings, equipment, and inventory. Others are human assets, such as your employees, vendors, and customers. Still others are intangible assets, such as your reputation, brand, customer loyalty, intellectual property, and access to capital. Whatever the asset, optimizers are driven to maximize its yield.

Identifying assets can be tricky. What you see may not immediately reveal the true value of what you have. Take a national long-haul trucking company. Its highest-cost assets are its fleet of trucks, but the real value of these assets comes from how well they are loaded and deployed: Where should you position them to get the most freight? Which loads should you accept? Which should you turn down? Are they loaded coming and going, or do they have to deadhead one way?

If you are a printer, your presses are clearly large and expensive assets. But their real value is driven by how you decide to load and run them: Are you able to keep them running at full capacity a high percentage of the time? Are you able to provide printing capacity to the most profitable customers on a reliable basis? Can you organize the printing queue in ways that minimize packing and shipping costs?

For a grocer, shelf space is a key asset, but not all shelf space is equal. No matter what you place at eye level, at the front of the store, it sells much more; put the same product near the floor, in the furthest corner, and you will spend more time dusting than restocking. For airlines, planes are clearly assets. But what determines the planes' true value—and competitively makes or breaks the airline—are the thousand and one decisions that an airline makes about pricing, plane positioning, flight crew assignments, and maintenance schedules.

At Ann Taylor Stores Corporation, time and people are key assets, so maximizing value from them becomes everything. To improve the value per hour from its sales force, the company installed an optimization program that stipulates which employees should work, when, and for how long, with the best sales performers scheduled for the busiest hours.[3] Optimizing workforce management—it makes great sense, given the criticality of human assets to most organizations' success.

No matter which of your assets you focus on, the goal of an optimizer is not simply to utilize the asset. After all, what is the value of running a machine 100 percent of the time if it works on low-value activities, creates bottlenecks, or produces a product that fails to meet specifications or customer requirements? The goal of an optimizer is not simply to keep an asset busy, but to *utilize the asset in a way that adds the greatest value to an organization's long-term profitability.*

How well you accomplish this goal typically depends on a series of complex and often repetitive decisions that juggle constraints and balance multiple interdependent objectives. For example:

- Which prospects should your sales force focus on?
- Should you expand your office space at headquarters or invest in a regional office?
- How much raw material should you order to balance customer demands and inventory expenses?
- What products should you discount this week, where, and what will be the likely cross-impact on other offerings?
- If you add a "plus" feature to a "regular" product or service, do you drive up high-margin volume?
- Should your employees be stocking shelves or waiting on customers?
- Which employees should you pull away from their current assignments to serve on the committee preparing a new proposal?

These and hundreds of other repetitive decisions continuously add or subtract value from your enterprise. Optimization can improve the quality of each of those decisions, each time they are made, adding millions and even billions to the bottom line, as McDonald's, UPS, Marriott, Walmart, Amazon, Google, and other early adopters have discovered.

Decisions: Man—or Woman—Versus Machine

Optimization is about making decisions and choices. What sets today's optimizers apart is their ability to use voluminous data, computers, and software to make decisions about assets better, faster, and more consistently than others can. And therein lies their power: optimizers give us computer programs that are capable of making *accurate and lightning-fast recommendations.*

Computers have become the paper, pencils, and filing cabinets of the modern enterprise. They are used in the workplace to gather, store, and manage data. But when it comes to the moment of truth, when a choice must be made among competing alternatives, the old-fashioned "computer" that sits atop our shoulders is all too often the decider. Most software programs juggle data and supply us with volumes of well-organized information at the push of a button. They tell us what is happening, but not what we should do about it. They do not make recommendations. But optimization software is different. Beyond analyzing data, it takes the next step: *deciding on and making a specific recommendation.* This is what distinguishes it from the vast majority of software used by businesses today.

Before we look at some concrete examples of how companies are strengthening their competitive position through decision-making software, let's examine how people and computers stack up against one another as decision makers.

Where Computers Shine

A person can juggle a few dozen permutations, or combinations, of data. Optimization software can juggle millions or even billions.

To understand why this is such an important capability, assume that you are managing an emergency room and have to decide the order in which three patients, all of whom arrived around the same time, will be examined. The total number of combinations is six, or three factorial (written as "3!"). Not too tough a problem to sort out. But now let's make it a little more complex. By increasing the number of patients to 10, you increase the number of possible orders in which to attend to them over 3 million (10! or 3,628,800). Add just three more patients, and the number of possible combinations rises to over 87 billion (13! = 87,178,291,200).

To put 13! into perspective, suppose you tried each combination in your head and could do so at the rate of 10 per second. If you did that 24/7 and never slept, you could get through 13! combinations in about three centuries. Not too bad. But 13 isn't that large a number of patients to consider. Suppose we upped the ante to 20 patients, such as might occur following a natural disaster. At the same speed, 20! would take you over *11 billion centuries.*

So how do emergency room (ER) personnel cope? They use simple rules of thumb to help set priorities, such as "first come, first served" or "move forward anyone who has lost consciousness." Even if there are more efficient and better combinations, no unaided human being has time to consider even a tiny fraction of the possible arrangements.

By being able to search many thousands or millions of times more possibilities than humans, computers can make better recommendations. But examining or testing permutations is just one significant advantage in the decision-making process that computers and optimization software possess. There are others.

One is the ability to access extremely large and complex databases at lightning speed. When I am considering buying a book on Amazon, its optimization software can instantly combine my current selection with a search of millions of past purchases to create a profile of my interests and then suggest other books I might like, based on what other recent shoppers "like me" have purchased. Imagine a salesperson in a bookstore trying to compete with Amazon's software just using his own memory and reading experience. When making an optimal decision depends on accessing, reviewing, and sorting large amounts of pertinent information, the computer wins hands down.

The power of a computer to make decisions extends beyond simply accessing and sorting information. Computers typically are also better than humans at combining information. One important area mentioned in Chapter 2 is combining probabilities. People are fairly capable of estimating simple probabilities in areas in which they have experience. For example, if I were to ask you what the chances are that this year your hometown will have a white Christmas—defined by at least one inch of snow on the ground—your guess would probably be fairly accurate. If you live in the United States, you can test this by first making an estimate and then checking your accuracy on the map in Figure 3.1.

However, if I asked what the chances are of a white Christmas *and* the day being sunny, you would likely have a much harder time making an estimate. The answer would require not only knowing two likelihoods, but knowing how to combine them correctly.

Here is another example of just how difficult it is for us to juggle multiple probabilities. Suppose I were to estimate the probability that a person randomly sitting next to you has the same birthday as you. Most people would come up with an answer of 1 chance out of 365, which would be fairly accurate (although not perfect, since birthdays are not distributed evenly throughout the entire year). But now suppose you are sitting in a room with 22 of your closest friends. What are the chances that 2 people in this relatively small group have the same birthday, assuming that none of them are twins? Surprisingly,

FIGURE 3.1   Probability of a White Christmas Based on 1961–1990 Climate Normals[4]

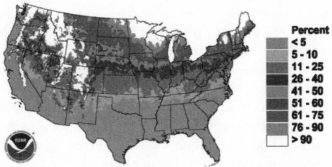

the answer is 50-50. If you should be so lucky as to be together with 56 friends, there is a 99 percent probability that two of them were born on the same day.[5] Most people are surprised by such a high probability. Our intuitions are simply not wired to accurately estimate probability problems of this nature. A computer, however, can easily compute the answer with a relatively simple program. Optimal solutions often require estimating and combining probabilities.

Computers Lack Biases

Another advantage that machines have over people in many decision situations is that machines exhibit a lot fewer biases in their judgments. If you search Wikipedia for a "list of cognitive biases," you will encounter a list of 105 different judgment biases that humans have been shown to exhibit.[6] Scanning the list may convince you to turn all decision-making over to your computer. Here are just a few of the 105 that have been well documented in humans, but not computers:

• **Confirmation bias** refers to people's tendency to confirm their preconceptions or hypotheses independent of the likelihood that they are true. At least three mechanisms that support this bias have been documented by psychologists: (1) selectively collecting new evidence, (2) interpreting evidence in a biased fashion, and (3) selectively recalling information from memory. These biases have been found to be particularly pronounced when people are dealing with emotional decisions or decisions related to the core beliefs that shape their day-to-day expectations.

• **Mere exposure effect** is the tendency for people to develop a preference for things merely because they are familiar with them. This effect has been shown to occur for a wide variety of stimuli, from Chinese characters to geometric figures to other people. It has also been shown to occur without conscious awareness or thought. People frequently select an alternative simply because they have seen it before, not because it is the best answer.

• **Outcome bias** is people's tendency to judge the quality of a decision by its ultimate outcome instead of by how well the evidence was weighed at the time the decision was made. People frequently fail to consider when information first became available. For example, when evaluating the decision to launch a new product that turned out to be a poor seller, the team carrying out the postmortem often considers market dynamics that only became apparent *after* the product was launched.

• **Availability heuristic** refers to people's tendency to estimate the frequency of an event or object within a population, based on how easily an example can be brought to mind. As a result, people generally overestimate the frequency of vivid, unusual, or emotionally charged events.

• **Actor-observer bias** refers to people's frequent tendency to explain others' behavior by personal rather than situational factors. Beware of conclusions such as, "That's just the kind of person she is." Not surprisingly, just the opposite bias occurs when people provide explanations of their own behavior. Here, you are most likely to hear something like, "I just had to do it. Given the situation, I had no other choice."

• **Illusory correlation** refers to people's frequent perception of correlations when none exist. Often, this occurs when multiple unique events stand out in memory. For example, when someone says, "The only time I forget my pencil is when we have a test," it is most likely an illusory correlation resulting from a few easily remembered pencilless test days. Computers, on the other hand, use a formula, rather than how easily they can retrieve a fact from memory, to compute correlations.

A review of the complete list of judgment biases leaves little doubt that in many situations judgments by computers are much more likely to be dependable than those of their human creators!

One final area in which computers win out over humans when making decisions is stamina. Computers can run 24/7 without wearing down, they seldom stay out late drinking or partying, and they are not prone to emotional swings. As a consequence, not only can they frequently make better judgments than humans, but the quality of their judgments and decisions tends to be much more consistent.

Where Humans Shine

The intent here is not to imply that computers always make better decisions than people. There are clearly times when humans make better decisions than machines—at least up until now.

One area in which humans shine is when a decision must be based on deep knowledge, where the rules are not yet fully understood. One example would be the world of art appraisal. An expert art appraiser's knowledge is so broad and deep that to date no computer program can surpass, or even mimic, an expert appraiser's ability. As Malcolm Gladwell documents in *Blink*, there are instances in which art experts reach conclusions instantaneously, so quickly that they themselves are unable to explain how they did it.[7] But expert advantage may be short-lived, as we will see momentarily in a case related to selecting the next great music hit. Don't be surprised to increasingly see computers prove the experts wrong.

Another related area in which computers struggle to keep pace with humans is when relevant data are not formally available in a digital form at the time the decision has to be made. Despite high levels of automation, many decisions are made in part by humans calling their peers or superiors on the phone, holding impromptu face-to-face meetings, or accessing other data sources that may be difficult to load into a computer in a timely fashion.

To date, computers are also woefully behind humans in their ability to read emotions with nuance and to codify social and body language. Humans seem likely to continue to lead in decision making when emotions play an important determining role. However, Professor Rosalind Picard, founder and director of MIT's Affective Computing Research Group, argues that it is only a matter of time before computers will begin to acquire components of emotional intelligence and be able to read our emotions and adjust their responses accordingly.[8] This may be both good and bad news. At some point, we might have to argue with anxious computers, never mind irrational bosses!

Humans also shine in cases where the participatory nature of the decision-making process itself helps achieve results. It has been widely observed that American executives typically make decisions faster than their Japanese counterparts, but implementing those decisions is another story. The Japanese, on the other hand, tend to be slower at making decisions, given their cultural imperative to build consensus among all those who have a stake in the decision—*ringisei*. When it comes to speed of implementation, however, they typically beat their American counterparts.

Or to choose a more fanciful example, consider elections. Most of us would like the optimal candidate to win, but few of us would delegate our right to vote to some type of election-optimizer software program. Besides abridging a fundamental political right, protracted campaigning—an important, though some would argue painful, part of the selection process—would be eliminated. This would deny citizens the opportunity to vet candidates and to have candidates build coalitions necessary for winning elections—and for governing.

It is also the case that in the right circumstances humans can be much more creative than computers. While computer optimization can make remarkably efficient and correct decisions, it cannot think outside the box. In fact, it *is* the box! Optimization programs are limited in their range of "thinking" by the rules built into the model. Faced with an "unsolvable" problem, optimization programs report back that there is "no feasible solution." Sometimes a brilliant (or desperate) human will figure out which rules can and should be broken and will brandish a creative sword that can cut the Gordian knot. Humans excel at developing state-of-the-art solutions to problems that have not yet been solved or fully understood.

Rapidly changing circumstances that escape the framework of the optimization software designers can also prove challenging for computers that are making decisions. In addition to their day jobs, human decision makers live in a broader environment of information, which includes everything from formal company briefings to informal discussions to simply reading the news. Sometimes, the rules change in a way that is obvious to a person, while a computer could only become aware of such a change if it were reprogrammed. This is especially true for an unanticipated Black Swan event, such as the 9/11 terrorist attacks. A human flight controller could immediately conclude that the best course of action is to clear the skies, while a computer might well continue to instruct planes to take off and land.

What should we conclude from our brief comparison of human versus machine decision making? One conclusion, which we will discuss in later chapters, is that decision making should not be viewed as an either-or situation in which man and woman are pitted, antagonistically, against machines. Humans and computers each bring something to the decision table. The key is finding the best ways in which they can work together to make the quickest and most accurate judgments.

Another conclusion: in certain decision situations, computers are likely to outshine their human counterparts. These include decisions:

- That can be facilitated by comparing or testing a large number of permutations
- Where quickly sorting, screening, retrieving, and synthesizing information from large databases is necessary
- That do not depend on large amounts of inaccessible information, such as a person might build up over a lifetime of experiences
- That require the combining of probabilities
- Whose solution is not heavily dependent on emotions or emotional intelligence
- In which protracted discussion is not needed to obtain buy-in or commitment
- For which stamina or 24/7 monitoring is of value
- That can be modeled or optimally solved through the use of mathematics

Optimization: From Learjets to Hit Songs

Let's look more closely at how a variety of companies have used computers and optimization software to make decisions that have increased the value of their assets and improved their organization's competitive position.

Scheduling: Come Fly with Me

If you have ever been involved in scheduling—even something as simple as a multiparty conference call—you know how quickly despair can set in. Juggling everyone's schedule is the stuff that migraines are made of, but it is a piece of cake compared to the complex schedules of delivery services, trucking companies, railroads, delivery services, and airlines. These companies represent just some of the Main Street industries that can reap enormous benefits from optimization thinking. Let us look at one company that has successfully optimized its major asset: an international fleet of jets designed to transport corporate movers and shakers.

If you're not president of your company or relatively high up on the corporate food chain, you've probably never heard of Argent-Air. When they're not traveling by corporate jet, chances are that many senior executives, their clients, prospects, and guests are being shuttled around by ArgentAir. (The company name has been changed to protect confidentiality.) ArgentAir is an independent business unit of a Zurich-based multinational: a diversified company that operates in a wide range of industry segments, including financial services, technology, aviation, energy, and heavy-equipment manufacturing. ArgentAir operates on the subscription principle: each of its passengers signs up for a minimum number of air miles over a five-year period of time. The benefit: a plane is available to each subscriber whenever and wherever he or she needs it.

At first blush, ArgentAir does not appear to have much in common with, say, Walmart. ArgentAir caters to high-end business travelers, while Walmart serves the lower- and middle-class masses. Unlike Walmart, which rose to the top in a mature industry, ArgentAir operates in a relatively new industry segment. But look beneath the surface and you will see that both companies have the same business philosophy, which is what makes them both so successful.

Like Walmart, ArgentAir's competitive advantage comes from its unparalleled operational expertise. Walmart optimizes every asset decision: what, where, when, and how much to buy, store, distribute, and sell. ArgentAir's primary assets are its fleet of planes and its pilots. To get the most out of these assets, like Walmart it employs Optimization to make critical allocation decisions.

ArgentAir cannot afford to fail the busy executives whom it serves, but unlike commercial flyers, each individual passenger schedules his or her own flight, often requesting arrival and departure times and airports on as little as four hours' notice. ArgentAir completes hundreds of thousands of flights annually, on 500 aircraft, to over 125 countries around the globe. The resulting complexity makes efficient scheduling a major challenge. Yet ArgentAir has become a rapidly growing and highly profitable passenger air carrier by optimizing decisions related to moving its fleet around the world in order to manage complexity and meet the needs of demanding customers.

For any airline, a key statistic is the percentage of capacity utilization. For a commercial airline, 100 percent utilization would mean that every seat on every plane was filled. For ArgentAir, where each customer takes a personal trip on a jet, utilization takes on another meaning.

Because ArgentAir customers can request a trip from a wide number of jet-capable airports throughout the world to almost any other, crews and planes—often empty—must be repositioned to meet the customer, thereby reducing the fleet's utilization. If the customer's stay is short, the dispatcher may choose to keep the plane waiting at the airport until the customer is ready to depart. For longer stays, the dispatcher may instruct the crew to fly the plane to another destination and pick up a second customer. Another plane is then scheduled to pick up the first customer for the return flight.

Moving an empty plane to another airport to pick up a passenger is called a shuttle, and shuttles, or empty air-hours, are expensive! Depending on the size of the aircraft, an empty air-hour of a private jet costs between $1,000 and $5,000, which includes the cost of jet fuel, the crew, and wear and tear on the plane. Similarly, when a plane sits idle on the ground, referred to as lagging, it is an underutilized asset. This makes reducing empty air-hours and lag time primary measures of success for ArgentAir. Each day, ArgentAir publishes and reviews the previous day's statistics. Each 1 percent reduction in empty air-miles saves the company $15 million dollars a year. If the fleet were to grow or the price of fuel to rise—as it has—the prize would be even larger.

Prior to using Optimization, ArgentAir took fairly conventional steps to manage its complex scheduling. First, it divided its large number of jets into smaller fleets comprising similar types of planes. Each fleet was then assigned a scheduler charged with developing a schedule two days in advance of each flight date. The goal: pick up and deliver all their passengers at the scheduled times, minimizing empty air-hours and lag time for planes in the fleet. The smaller number of planes in each fleet helped make the task more manageable compared to scheduling all the company's planes. ArgentAir also developed a software program, Scan, which enabled schedulers to place their flights and crews on a screen that looked something like a Gantt chart on steroids and reposition or replace flights when they found a more efficient route. Scan monitored the action and alerted the scheduler if an international or local-country rule—such as keeping a crew member on duty longer than allowed—had been violated.

The system was efficient, but not optimized. The flight schedules were built by people, not computers. More shuttles than necessary continued to occur, and as many as 35 percent of the flights were empty-air ones. Furthermore, the fleets created organizational "silos" that resulted in inefficiencies. There were times, for example, when it might be much more efficient for a plane from another fleet to pick up and deliver an executive or his or her team. Not only would such a switch eliminate an empty flight; it could result in a free upgrade for the customer. Unfortunately, the fleet silos kept this from happening as often as it should: either a fleet scheduler did not know about all the available planes in another fleet, or schedulers protected the planes in their own fleet to cover late requests. It was a good practice for the fleet, but not for ArgentAir as a whole.

Enter the optimizers. Or more precisely, enter a team of optimizers. At ArgentAir, the team included consultants from our company, an in-house champion who had designed ArgentAir's information technology (IT) system, the head of fleet operations, several subject matter experts from the airline, and a university professor. The goal: develop optimization software to recommend schedules that would maximize utilization while minimizing customer dissatisfaction—no easy task when dealing with executive-suite-size egos.

Early in the discussions, the team grappled with a number of nettlesome issues. For example, during times of high demand the ArgentAir fleet schedulers in Rome, Italy, and Lisbon, Portugal, might find themselves facing the inevitable zero-sum question regarding moving scarce assets to some customers and not to others. What were the rules by which the "Who should get which jet?" decision should be made?

And many rules must be considered. Some are related to the planes: how many passengers they hold, how fast they fly, and so on. Other rules are mandated by in-country aviation regulations. For example, in the United States, the Federal Aviation Administration (FAA) mandates that pilots who are not night certified can fly only during daylight hours, certain airports do not allow landings and takeoffs at certain times of the day or night, pilots can be on duty only so many hours before they must rest. There are union regulations to consider, and company policies: treat all customers as if they were owners—which, during the period of their subscription, they are. If you have recently disappointed a customer, you will want to move mountains—and planes—to avoid a repeat experience.

Another complicating factor: the well-heeled executives who use ArgentAir often think nothing of changing their plans—and the flight they booked—at the last minute, and they are none too pleased if the airline cannot accommodate them. Weather and air-traffic patterns, neither of which is under the control of ArgentAir, are yet another source of constant uncertainty and change. And aircraft, which are maintained to the highest safety standard in the industry, are absolutely not allowed to take off unless the pilot in command gives the green light. With so many constraints, choosing when and where to fly each jet and crew at the moment of truth—when an executive calls and wants a jet *now*—is a challenging decision of Herculean proportions.

The optimization team assembled at ArgentAir was up to the challenge. It realized that the ideal approach would be to develop not one schedule optimizer, but three—to resolve the three distinct aspects of the scheduling problem. The first program was called the IScheduler. It was capable of building an optimal schedule two days in advance of flight day. It took approximately 15 minutes to run and would recommend an optimal schedule for the entire ArgentAir fleet of planes. The second program, Retrofit, was used to "repair" the schedule when late customer requests, airplane maintenance, weather delays, or a sick crew member suddenly required an adjustment to be made. Retrofit would consider the schedule interruption and recommend a dozen prioritized alternatives for making adjustments in ways that minimized shuttles. Retrofit runs in fewer than five seconds, which is required for operational acceptance, and searches for solutions with the highest value and minimal impact on other schedules. The third piece of software—Shuttle Optimizer—ran continuously in the background, reviewing each schedule or asset change to find ways to reduce the number of shuttles even further without stranding any customer. Whenever a scheduler made a request, Shuttle Optimizer would display a list of recommended adjustments to the schedule to optimize it even further.

And the bottom-line results? When the optimizing team first arrived, the number of empty trips each day ranged from 30 to 40 percent of the daily flights. The optimization programs were able to reduce this number by approximately 10 percent, saving the company roughly $150 million a year. But Optimization improved competitiveness in other ways, too. Schedules that previously took hours to construct are now developed in minutes, freeing schedulers to work on other tasks. Furthermore, since the optimization programs look across all the fleets when making recommendations, they see many more opportunities to upgrade customers while eliminating shuttles. It is a win-win situation: reduced costs for the company, improved service for the customers.

Allocating Space: All the Ads That Fit in Print

As the ArgentAir example illustrates, Optimization is a powerful approach to driving up the value yield from a scarce and expensive asset. Space is another asset that can be as scarce as equipment and no less contentious: shelf space, space in shipping containers and freight cars, seats in auditoriums and arenas, and space in magazines and newspapers. Take ad space. It is a precious and limited asset, both for businesses needing to reach a target audience and for those who own the media outlet. Allocating ad space in a publication also represents a decision that has to be made over again each time a new edition hits the street, making it a prime candidate for Optimization. One major metropolitan newspaper with which Princeton Consultants worked provides a case in point.

Like most major newspapers, this one was not a single paper: there were several editions—regional, city, suburban, and so on. A retailer selling exclusively within the city is not likely to want placement in the suburban edition, while a large regional chain of stores would likely opt for wider coverage. To complicate things even more, some advertisers insist that their ads appear in a certain sequence, such as on three consecutive right-hand pages. Others want a campaign in which a single ad runs for x number of consecutive days.

While the paper would like to say yes to every request, doing so is not as easy as it sounds. There are often many constraints and rules that govern the way a newspaper positions ads: competitors' ads cannot be placed on the same page, an ad cannot be run near an article about the advertiser, and certain types of ads are not "appropriate" for placement in the paper's main news section.

Given the complexity of the editions and the number of rules, laying out the paper's ads was tricky business. And as the paper began to expand its use of color, the exercise became even more challenging, since only so much color could be included in each run of the paper.

For many years, placing of the ads was done manually by two employees whose role was so critical and specialized that the two could never be on vacation simultaneously. Over the years, these two individuals had created written scenarios—nearly 64 of them! The scenarios represented alternative preset configurations for laying out the paper, depending on news content, planned inserts, and, of course, the type and number of ads being requested. Each night, the two employees decided which scenario would best accommodate all the requested ads for the edition and proceeded to lay out the paper accordingly. Ads that did not meet the scenario's specs were shelved, leaving advertisers guessing until morning about the fate of their ads. Sometimes, when the newpaper could not immediately assure an advertiser where, when, and how a submitted ads might be published, the advertiser took his or her business elsewhere. The result: lost revenue and lost customers who headed for more reliable advertising venues.

Realizing that it was time to replace this antiquated system, the paper's management asked Princeton Consultants to develop a program that would optimize available advertising space. Our company's consultants worked side by side with the paper's subject-matter experts—the employees who had created the scenarios—and support staff to design software that would rationalize the ad-placement process and drive up the value of available advertising space. Early on in the project, the consultants probed deeply into the experience and judgment of the two layout men, being sure to incorporate into the program every rule and constraint under which they operated.

As you might suspect, the optimization software came up with many more than the fixed 64 permutations that were featured in the scenarios. More important, it could reconfigure the paper on the fly, identifying an optimal layout as each new ad request came in. As a result of Optimization, the paper did not have to buy more presses, hire more people, or discount its rates to increase revenue. Just getting more ads into the paper each day did it. Placing ads with the paper also became much more customer friendly. Now, an advertiser could call and ask for an ad and find out almost immediately if it would appear in the next day's paper, eliminating surprises.

Production Planning: Let a Thousand Flowers Bloom

Next time you admire an arrangement of lilies or some other ornamental flowers, you may say a silent prayer of thanks that you are not in the business of growing and distributing them. Many of the world's ornamental flowers come from Brazil, where competition is fierce, especially since the government began giving grants for the production of flowers to help increase the incomes of small- and medium-sized nurseries and exporters.

One of Brazil's oldest and largest wholesale producers of bulb flowers is the Jan de Wit Company, located in the "City of Flowers": Holambra, Brazil, 160 kilometers due north of São Paulo. The company began growing lilies on a small scale in 1992—one of the first companies to do so in Brazil. By 2000, when the company began to consider Optimization to help in its production planning, it had 18,745 square meters of greenhouses, 1,032 square meters of cold-storage rooms, and a team of approximately 30 employees.[9]

It is difficult to overstate the complexities of production planning at Jan de Wit. As with many businesses, planning begins with an attempt to project demand. For Jan de Wit, this involves two types of sales: auction and intermediation. Auction represents a daily cash market at which distributors can bid on flower purchases. It accounts for approximately half of Jan de Wit's sales. Quantities and prices can vacillate considerably, reflecting such things as fashion trends, economic conditions, and competitors' production volumes. Prices, of course, also fluctuate, affecting Jan de Wit's optimal product mix.

The other half of Jan de Wit's sales are through intermediation, which operates like a futures market. Specialized agents negotiate buy-and-sell contracts between distributors and producers for the short, intermediate, and long term. Based on history—and what Jan de Wit can surmise about the market—the company attempts to identify market opportunities by analyzing weekly sales quantities and prices for each lily variety.

Projecting demand is just the first in a long list of challenges in production planning. To produce the lilies, Jan de Wit needs bulbs, most of which are furnished by bulb wholesalers in Holland. A year's order can include annual imports of 3.5 million bulbs, comprising 50 different varieties. All bulbs must be purchased during the three-month bulb-harvesting season. Thereafter, the Dutch suppliers send part of the order on a predetermined monthly schedule. Each arriving batch contains a set number of bulbs from a specific harvesting year, producer, and variety. Once the bulbs arrive and are sorted, they must be prepared, which means they are held at the correct temperature for approximately two months. Next, the bulbs are planted in a place where they will remain at the correct temperature for two weeks, until the stem roots form. Only then can they be moved to a greenhouse. Of course, temperature, growth rate, and care requirements can all vary at any step in the process. Depending on the variety, the bulb size, and planting week, the production cycle can last anywhere from 6 to 16 weeks.

The bottom line? To produce an optimal production plan, Jan de Wit Company must schedule the correct planting of the right bulbs during the right week in the right greenhouse environment to meet projected market demand, which must include seasonal fluctuations for such holidays as Easter, Mother's Day, and Christmas. Some additional constraints on planning decisions include bulb inventory and production-cycle variations stemming from plant variety, bulb size, bulb origin, sprout length, and planting week. Technical requirements produce yet one more layer of complexity, with such constraints as number of bulbs per pot or box, bulb spacing, and bed-usage limitations associated with each type of greenhouse.

The way in which Optimization first found its way into the Jan de Wit Company illustrates how operations research concepts are spreading to smaller companies. José Vicente Caixeta-Filho, a professor at the University of São Paulo, published a short article in a student journal entitled, "Modeling, Through Operations Research, in Agribusiness." Jan Maarten van Swaay-Neto, a flower-business-management consultant who had not previously heard of Operations Research, read the article and called Caixeta-Filho to discuss possible applications to the flower business. He went on to take one of Caixeta-Filho's classes on linear programming, which was being offered to graduate students in applied economics. At the end of the course, he wrote a final paper entitled "Gladiolus Bulb Production" and extended an invitation to Caixeta-Filho to develop more accurate approaches to applying mathematical models to flower production problems.

This initial collaboration led to further efforts to apply the techniques, first at a company named Terra Viva and then at Jan de Wit. Reflecting today's abundance of computing power, the decision-support system was programmed on a Windows-compatible computer, using Visual Basic and Microsoft's Access database. The team used linear programming to maximize contribution margin (revenue minus variable costs). The actual set of equations in the linear program generated a solution matrix involving 120,000 rows and 420,000 columns.

The results of using optimization software to aid production planning speak for themselves. The first year that Jan de Wit used the software, revenue grew 26 percent, while contribution margin improved 32 percent. Return on owner's equity increased from 15.1 percent to 22.5 percent—a 49 percent improvement. This growth was managed with the addition of a single employee. All this was accomplished in spite of the fact that during that year the Brazilian flower market experienced excess capacity and reduced auction prices. The company also found that by improving its planning and control of production it was able to increase its short-, medium- and long-term supply agreements, locking in prices and profits years in advance.

Finally, there was the saving in planning time. Prior to implementing the optimization software, Johannes de Wit, the general manager and owner of Jan de Wit Company, planned production himself. With the new system, he found that he was able to delegate the planning process, which now takes only a fraction of the time it once required. Clearly, implementation of the planning system has increased the company's competitiveness. De Wit commented, "Companies in the flower business that don't wake up to planning-and-control systems risk almost unsurpassable capital losses, endangering their continuity and damaging the market."[10]

Smart Pricing

Pricing decisions are tailor made for Optimization, for three reasons. First, Optimization can help increase the speed with which prices can be set. This can often produce a competitive advantage, especially in large B2B transactions. How would your customers and prospects react if you could give them a price quote in seconds? What would such agility do for your company's reputation? How many more prospects would call you for a quick quote?

Second, Optimization can help you better understand the true costs of your decisions, thereby allowing you to make better pricing decisions. There are many methodologies to measure operating costs. ABC and other accounting systems help you find the "actual" cost of each element of your business. But what about the *opportunity* costs of business decisions? In its attempt to maximize long-term profitability, Optimization goes beyond looking at the cost of each decision in and of itself to assess the opportunity costs of one decision versus another. It asks, "What will it cost me over the longer term and in terms of missed opportunities if I choose A instead of B, and vice versa?"

Assume that you run a trucking company based in Chicago, and you want to know the cost of hauling a load of freight to Los Angeles compared to that of hauling it to New York. An accountant would calculate the difference by totaling all the direct and indirect costs of each trip: gas, tolls, the driver's salary, depreciation on the truck, and so on, and then comparing the two. Do this and you will probably find that your out-of-pocket costs are not much different in either direction; it is pretty much a toss-up whether to take the business that sends your truck east or that which sends it west.

Optimizers would look at the decision much differently. They would argue that the accountant's calculations are only part of the story. They do not include a calculation of the opportunity cost of each trip. Determining this requires asking a very different question: "If I had a truck in L.A., what could I then do with it compared to what I could do with a truck in New York?" Perhaps there is a large amount of freight in L.A. that needs to be shipped, and people are paying top dollar to move it. Meanwhile, in New York there are only empty shipping containers. In trucking, when planning the outbound trip, or head haul, you always think of the return trip, or back haul. So if it is going to prove more difficult to bring a full truckload back from New York, driving there instead of to L.A. is a far more costly choice—even if the gas, tolls, and other actual costs run about the same. It also suggests that you should charge a different price for heading east than for heading west.

Or, going back to our work with the metropolitan newspaper, if a customer asks for a two-page spread in the middle of the paper, before saying yes, consider the probability that later on you might be able to sell the same space to someone else at a higher price, perhaps as part of a broad package of ads. What is the cost of saying yes to one versus the other? Or more precisely, what are the opportunity costs of these different decisions? That is where the real money is made or lost—and that is why optimizers focus on it.

Third, if you choose to—and if your industry allows for it—Optimization can help you institute yield management, or scientific variable pricing. Yield management is the name for the technique used in many industries to scientifically vary the price of a product or service to maximize the amount of revenue that can be extracted from a marketplace. It exploits the famous supply-and-demand curves that we learned about in Economics 101: namely, that sellers are willing to sell the same product or service to different customers for different prices, and that different buyers are willing to pay different prices for the same products or services. In Economics 101, we learned that this would lead to a *single* "market equilibrium price," where the supply-and-demand curves crossed. In contrast, yield managers set *different* prices for the same basic commodity when selling to different types of customers or at different periods, with the goal of achieving maximum profits.

We see variable pricing designed to improve asset yields all the time: for example, the early-bird special that restaurants give to folks who agree to eat earlier in return for a discount. Yield management differs from this sort of ordinary pricing differentiation by varying prices continuously: repricing daily or even hourly. Yield management started in industries such as airlines and hotels: businesses with essentially fixed capacity that has a limited shelf life. After the plane takes off, the unsold seats are not sellable; the next day, a hotel cannot sell the previous day's rooms.

Not surprisingly, these industries pioneered the use of Optimization to vary prices as seats and rooms filled up. When recommending price changes, optimization software keeps track of how much space remains and the likelihood that it will remain unsold as it reaches its "expiration date."

What makes yield management tricky, however, is that yield managers are not trying to maximize daily revenue; they seek to optimize *long-term profits*. Simply selling to the highest bidder will indeed give you the highest short-term revenue, but it may also drive away customers who, over the long term, would likely spend more money. If you keep calling an airline or hotel, and they never have a seat or room at a price you are willing to pay, eventually you stop calling. Whether in B2B or B2C transactions, people experiment and learn to make repeated purchases from those who can offer them both consistently good price *and* availability. The best optimization software takes multiple factors—including customers' buying patterns—into account when setting a price.

Money Management at Marriott

We recounted some of the story behind Marriott's success in Chapter 1. On May 20, 1927, two young men, J. Willard "Bill" Marriott and Hugh Colton, opened a nine-stool A&W root beer stand on 14th Street in northwest Washington, D.C. Over the next 82 years, led first by Bill Marriott and then by his son, J. Willard "Bill," Jr., those nine stools grew into Marriott International, a global lodging and hospitality company, which by 2010 had over 137,000 associates; more than 3,400 properties in 70 countries; and was processing 75 million room-reservation requests per year across its 18 hotel and resort brands, generating more than $11 billion in revenue.[11]

In 1957, Marriott opened its first hotel in Arlington, Virginia. The 365-room Twin Bridges Motor Hotel rented its rooms for $10 to $13 a night, depending on the number of occupants in the room and whether or not they needed a cot or a crib. Right from the start, Marriott showed an interest in—and talent for—"revenue management." The Twin Bridges had a drive-up registration booth. Whenever the hotel approached being fully booked, the desk clerk would lean out the window and turn away any car that did not have at least four people in it. The result? A lot more rooms were booked at a premium price of $13. In fact, this simple revenue management practice was estimated to generate as much as 44 percent additional revenue at absolutely no cost to the hotel.

Today, Marriott's revenue management practices are far more sophisticated. In fact, in the 1980s, following the lead of the airline industry, Marriott introduced the first computerized revenue management system in the lodging industry. The need for such a system is driven by the fact that "rooms" represent perishable inventory. As with airline seats and departure times, once a room has been empty for a night, the revenue it might have brought in is lost forever. The room cannot be sold twice the next day to recapture the lost income— at least not without creating irate customers.

This initial computerized revenue management system worked extremely well, helping Marriott adjust its prices as needed to improve occupancy rates. However, the system only worked when booking individual travelers. By the second half of the current decade, almost 50 percent of Marriott's business came from catering services and group bookings for such events as business meetings, conferences, and weddings. While the scale of the group business had increased exponentially, how group business was sold had not changed very much. Marriott's booking agents, or sales managers, as they are called, were booking groups using paper calendars and spreadsheets that displayed hotel occupancy levels and rates: "While the sophistication of the systems used to sell to the individual traveler increased substantially, how group business was sold had not changed very much," according to Sharon Hormby, Marriott's senior director of total yield systems.[12]

Given the volume of business that Marriott was facing, this presented multiple challenges for the sales teams. For one, while the spreadsheets were updated weekly, they were obsolete by the time they were distributed. In addition, there was no simple way to evaluate the financial trade-offs for booking a group at a reduced room rate as opposed to waiting to fill as many rooms as possible with reservations from individual travelers. There were simply too many mediating factors, alternative scenarios, and unknown data points to allow the sales managers to make good decisions.

Marriott's answer: replace the spreadsheets, paper calendars, and pricing decisions of the sales managers with a Total Hotel Revenue

Management optimizing software program. Fortunately, Marriott's Total Yield Systems Group could draw on a rich reservoir of data from the company's reservation system. Looking across only two years of data, they were able to examine 800,000 group reservation requests at 200 different hotels, together with 180 different descriptor variables such as group composition, group size, how far in advance a reservation is requested, customer segmentation, audio-visual requirements, offered price, and, perhaps most important, whether Marriott had won or lost the business with the price it offered.

The wealth of historical data allowed Marriott's Yield Management Group to develop price sensitivity curves for each segment of customers, including how different factors influence the group's likelihood of booking a property. Moreover, the data allowed the programming team to develop models for predicting group demand at different hotels throughout the year. When these models are considered together with data that shows hotel profitability at different room rates, the software can recommend an optimal price to ensure profitability while maximizing the chances of winning the business.

Here is how the optimization software works:

1. When a prospect calls requesting a group reservation, a sales manager enters the request into the computer system, along with any available additional information about the group's characteristics.
2. The software then determines the projected occupancy and profitability of the hotel that is being requested, during the desired week, excluding the group's request in the calculation.
3. Next, the computer repeats the calculations, this time including the assumption that the group has been booked and the inventory consumer by the group is not available for sale. The computer then calculates the displacement costs, or the expected difference in profitability for the hotel when the group is booked compared to its not being booked. If this number is negative, the computer recommends a group rate high enough to offset the difference.

Most impressive, the computer calculations are just about instantaneous, displaying the room price to the sales manager, thereby enabling her to provide an immediate price quote. The computer can also make recommendations for other nearby hotels in the Marriott family where the group can book a reservation at a lower price if the quoted rate exceeds the group's budget.

Here's the best part of the Group Price Optimizer (GPO): conservative estimates indicate that the GPO increased revenues by $46 million in 2008 and by $75 million in 2009, even though bookings declined as a result of a depressed economy. Sales managers fully support the system and report that the information that the computer provides allows them to offer alternatives that keep prospective customers from shopping the competition. If you do not want to take time to talk with a sales manager, Marriott has recently developed QuickGroup, a program that allows prospects to shop and make small-group reservations directly on Marriott's website.

All in all, the GPO has helped put muscle behind Marriott's brand promise of providing "the right product to the right customer at the right time for the right price."

Order in the Queue: Don't Stop the Presses!

While most people read magazines, few have any idea how complex the publishing business has become. Your local *Newsweek* that arrives in the mail is not just one magazine. Rather, it is a collection of magazines under a single title. By that, I mean that people in different regions of the country get different inserts, different ads, and different blow-ins: those annoying little cards that flutter to the floor no matter how hard you try to keep them between the pages. Not only regional, but also demographic differences determine an edition's structure. If your age and neighborhood demographics suggest that you have young children, your issue may carry an ad for baby diapers on page 23, while your parents in the retirement community across town are looking at a Depends ad on page 23 of their issue. If your subscription is about to run out, you will even get a different cover alerting you to the fact. Who figures out how to put all these things together and get them shipped to the right address?

The answer: a printing company such as Quad/Graphics, which was started 39 years ago in an abandoned millwork factory in Pewaukee, Wisconsin. Today, it is the second-largest printer in the Western Hemisphere, with 28,000 employees and $4.8 billion in annual sales. Quad/Graphics' big break came in 1978, when it landed a contract with *Newsweek*.[13]

Quad/Graphics' challenge in printing *Newsweek* and many other products is even more daunting than simply putting together a dozen different regional and demographic editions. It is a little-known fact that the shipping costs involved in getting a magazine to your doorstep can be significantly greater than the cost of printing it. The U.S. Postal Service, however, offers a discount if magazines arrive packaged in a way that bundles together those that are to be delivered on a single postal route. Consequently, not only do different editions of a title need to be printed; they need to be printed and assembled in an optimal order, which has them streaming off the presses and saddlestitchers in batches that match specific postal routes.

To add further complexity to an already complex situation, small specialty magazines such as *Dog Fancy* or *Bird Talk* have too limited a circulation to receive significant volume discounts from distributors and the U.S. Postal Service. To survive, they must be produced in a way that allows them to be interleaved with the other magazines for each individual subscribing household. This reduces sorting time by the U.S. Postal Service and entitles the publishers to get discounts. Thus, when Quad/Graphics runs the saddle-stitchers for a magazine like *Newsweek*, it may include other titles that get sandwiched into the correct postal-route bundle.

Quad/Graphics produces all these titles and title versions using a binding line with multiple slots, or pockets, that are filled with different magazine parts needed for a particular run of the title. The binding line can be programmed to pull material from different slots to assemble a specific edition or magazine at just the right moment in time to position it with other magazines headed for the same household. What really makes the process difficult to manage is the fact that often there are not enough pockets on the assembly machines to handle all the different magazine parts needed for complete production of an issue. From time to time, the machines must be halted to reload the pockets—an expensive procedure. To maximize productivity, the pockets need to be loaded in ways that minimize the number of times the machines must be stopped and the pockets reloaded.

Each production center has a scheduler, or planner, whose primary job is to decide how the pockets should be filled and the runs scheduled each day to minimize press stoppages. With so many moving parts, it's not an easy task. Before Optimization, the scheduler would work with a spreadsheetlike matrix, in which the columns represented different press runs and the rows represented magazine components. A dot was placed in each column in the row of the components to be used in that run. A large number of dots next to each other in one row reflected good planning. This indicated that two or more concurrent runs would use the same component, thereby eliminating the need for changeovers. Scheduling involved repositioning rows and columns in ways that grouped dots together to minimize changeovers. Producing a solution was complicated and time consuming and tended to produce suboptimal solutions. Executives at Quad/Graphics were not only concerned with the length of the planning process and questionable solutions, but they worried about having available only a limited number of people who understood the scheduling task. If one of them were to be hit by the proverbial truck, production would suffer.

Enter the optimization team. Because the scheduling challenge was so complex, the team decided that a symbiotic decision process, in which the schedulers and the optimizing software worked together interactively, would be best. The problem was sufficiently complex that no single algorithm or approach could provide an optimal solution in every scheduling situation. This led the team of optimizers to devise an "algorithm of algorithms," which evaluated the situation and decided which of several other algorithms was most likely to produce the best solution, given the production constraints. Once the selected algorithm had been applied, it recommended a scheduling solution for the human scheduler to review and approve. If schedulers saw a problem, they could adjust the constraints and rerun the optimization program to get a quick alternative.

The schedulers at Quad/Graphics did not need much convincing that the software was capable of producing superior solutions. They could immediately see that the run lengths of dots and spaces on the planning grid created by the software were significantly longer than those provided by the human planners. The reduction in machine stoppages and changeovers averaged approximately 10 percent, a significant savings when you think about a $4.8 billion business. The software increased Quad/Graphics' competitiveness in other ways as well. The improved efficiency increased printing capacity without any additional capital investments. The improved bundling generated lower postal rates, which allowed Quad/Graphics to increase the competitiveness of its bids for additional work. Innovations such as this have allowed Quad/Graphics to earn *Newsweek*'s "Printer of the Year" designation for the past two years: an award based on final-product quality, paper consumption, turnaround times, and equipment speed.

Marketing Dollars: Sing a Song of Sixpence

There is no accounting for human taste . . . or is there? Certainly, the world of music appears to represent an eclectic universe impossible to quantify. And in fact, music has traditionally been a "gut feel" industry, not known for data-based decision making or mathematical modeling.

This began to change in a big way in 2000, when Nolan Gasser, a Stanford graduate student, planted the seeds for the Music Genome Project. The project grew partly out of Gasser's doctoral-dissertation study of Renaissance music and a drive to ". . . really understand what made that music tick."[14] His systematic study of the structure of music resulted in his teaming up with two friends, John Kraft (a tech entrepreneur who had already started and sold a company) and Tim Westergren (a composer of music for low-budget films) in an effort to "codify" 20th-century pop music.

Their codification involved decomposing a piece of music into its large-scale aspects of melody, harmony, rhythm, form, instrumentation, voice, and text. Each of these broader categories, in turn, could have as many as 50 elements. Voice, for example, could be decomposed into such dimensions as smooth, rough, gravelly, or nasal—to name just a few. The outcome of the effort was approximately 250 "genes" for every song in the original pop-rock set of tunes. The ratings of each piece of music were done by music lovers who were trained and tested for their ability to listen and consistently rate the dimensions of test songs on a five-point scale. Typically, a trained rater needed around 30 minutes to create a song's complete genome.

So what do you do with a large database of "rated" songs? For one, launch an Internet radio station. In 1999, Tim Westergren founded Savage Beast Technologies, which in 2005 morphed into Pandora Internet Radio. The idea behind Pandora was a radio station that plays only music that each individual listener likes.

Here's how it works. When you log in, you are invited to create your own radio station. You do this by entering the name of an artist, song, or composer that you like. If you are feeling expansive, you can enter two or three more. Pandora's computers then select other musical compositions that are similar to your selection, based on the Genome rating system. Like different types of music on different days? No problem. Pandora allows you to create multiple radio stations, each one seeded with a different type of music. As 2009 drew to a close, Pandora had a database of 750,000 titles, which was expanding at approximately 10,000 tunes a month and which spanned 18 genres—from classical to country to jazz to hip-hop. While the station may not be able to accommodate all your tastes, its software can make excellent recommendations of music that you are almost certain to like. Today, Pandora has 39 million listeners enjoying its optimized recommendations and is reporting the addition of around 65,000 new sign-ups a day, more than half from mobile-device users.

Matching individual tastes in music is one thing, but could a mathematical algorithm make an accurate prediction about the next great musical hit? Mike McCready, CEO of Polyphonic HMI—who was soon to spin off Music Intelligence Solutions, Inc.—believed that it could. In 2003, the management team of this Barcelona-based company was prepared to launch its optimization tool, Hit Song Science (HSS), to do just that.[15]

As you might imagine, picking the next great song has always been an extremely tough and expensive business, particularly when evaluating a new artist's album. The successful marketing of a new album depends on picking the right single release, since radio airplay is the primary advertising vehicle. The goal is to have the single appear on Billboard's weekly Top 40 chart. This ensures wide exposure. Making and marketing a single to give it a shot at the Top 40 can cost $300,000 or more. However, only around 10 percent of the singles released each year make the list. You had better be good at singles picking if you want to survive in the music-promotion business.

Different promoters approach single selection in different ways. It is reported that Antonio "L.A." Reid used to round up kids from the streets of New York and ask them to rate new songs and artists. Another famous record executive, Clive Davis, was known for trusting his own judgment and no one else's. Many promoters use "callout" research, which involves contacting people on the phone and having them listen to and rate 15- to 30-second-long fragments of music. With a mere one-in-ten success rate, certainly none of these approaches could be considered optimal.

Enter McCready and Optimization. Just as Google spurned Yahoo!'s use of human experts to rate Web pages, Music Intelligence Solutions relies only on computers and mathematical algorithms to "listen" to and evaluate songs in 25 different dimensions, such as beat, chord progression, duration, fullness of sound, harmony, melody, octave, rhythm, sonic brilliance, and tempo. Based on the computer-generated scores, each song is then mapped onto a multidimensional grid called the "music universe." When Polyphonic initially evaluated millions of songs, including almost all music labels' releases from 1950 on, it found that hit songs of different genres tended to cluster together in the multidimensional space. New songs could then be evaluated and placed in the universe to see how close they came to a "hit cluster," as represented in Figure 3.2. Each song in the album receives a "closeness" rating, reflecting its distance from a hit cluster, with songs that are rated higher than 7 having a very high chance of becoming hits.

How accurate are the software's predictions? In McCready's initial research, he and his team analyzed music released over a six-month period. The software correctly predicted whether a single would reach the Singles Top 40 8 out of 10 times. Given the current success rate of 1 out of 10, the software certainly seemed promising.

FIGURE 3.2   A Hit-Song-Science Mapping of a New Album to Its Hit Clusters[16]

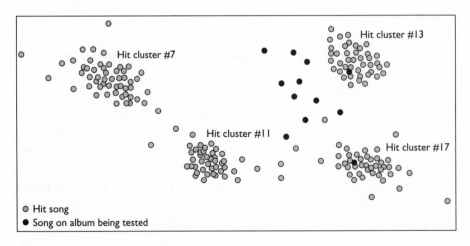

It was now time for reality testing. In 2002 the company tested the first album by a then-unknown artist, Norah Jones. The industry pundits did not give her sultry rendition of "Come Away with Me" much of a chance of success, but Hit Song Science predicted that eight songs on the album would be winners. The album was a runaway success and the winner of eight Grammy awards!

Skeptics remain, but an increasing number of music executives are coming to accept the fact that a computer can improve their decision making. Ken Bunt, an executive with Disney's Hollywood Records, told *Harvard Business Review* that, "This business has always been run by instinct and gut, and even my own colleagues might have a hard time believing this, but my experiences with Hit Song Science have been fantastic. HSS has been extremely accurate on the tracks that we have taken to commercial radio."[17] At a cost of $300,000-plus per miss and a 90-percent failure rate, it is hard to understand why every music executive is not interested in adding the software to his or her toolkit.

Music Intelligence Solutions has extended the HSS service to the individual singer-songwriter through its website: http://uplaya.com. If you log on, you can upload your own creation and assess its hit potential. One satisfied customer of the service is Ben Novak, a New Zealand singer/songwriter.[18] After HSS had given his song a high score, it caught the eye of a record executive, who convinced British pop star Lee Ryan to record the song. It quickly rose on the charts and ended up number 12 in Britain and number 2 in Italy.

Final Note

Whether it is used to manage ad space or schedule planes or pick the next megahit, Optimization is being used to improve asset values and increase competitiveness across the industrial landscape. Wherever complex, repetitive decisions are being made about how to deploy or use high-value assets, Optimization has proven to be a powerful *prescriptive* tool to drive up the value of these decisions. It represents a giant evolutionary step away from pitting humans against machines and toward creating a new partnership, in which the combined intelligence of both are applied to our most complex problems and decisions.

Given its power and wide potential, you would think that Optimization has become one of the very first weapons that corporate leaders reach for in today's war for competitive advantage. Surprisingly, this is not the case. Optimization remains very much an afterthought—or even a *non*thought—in too many management arsenals.

In Chapter 4, we will look more closely at exactly how Optimization is different from other productivity-improvement methods, including typical IT investments. We will explore more closely some of the reasons why quants and their optimization toolkits have often been ignored or unwelcome in the boardroom. We will go inside the minds of quants to understand the ways in which they think differently from the typical manager or executive, and we will examine the differences between good and great optimizers. Finally, we will present a series of questions that you can use to identify barriers to adopting Optimization in your own organization.

PUTTING OPTIMIZATION TO WORK

CHAPTER 4

OPTIMIZATION: PROMISE AND REALITY

We've all been through the "a big storm is headed our way" routine. The local weather pundits take to the airwaves to warn of the impending cataclysm about to descend on you and your neighbors. This sets in motion an areawide stampede to the nearest supermarket. You and just about everyone else in town hightail it down the aisles in a desperate hunt for food not seen since the Paleolithic period. As you emerge from the last aisle, shopping cart loaded with enough provisions to feed the state of New Hampshire, you head for the checkout area, hoping to make it home before the dreaded event kicks in.

Now comes the all-too-familiar decision point known as Morton's choice: which of the long cashier lines to choose, knowing full well that whichever one you select will, inevitably, become the slowest. Resigned to studying mints, tabloids, and home-decorating magazines, you ask yourself: Isn't there a better way for stores to manage checkout lines?

In fact, there is, as optimizers know. Your supermarket experience points to a fact that this book hopes to help change: Optimization is a woefully *underutilized* capability in many industries. A few sectors, such as the airlines, are heavy users of Optimization in a number of areas, from scheduling planes to serving customers, and comparing their efficiency levels to those of industries that don't use Optimization should give the latter food for thought.

Using optimization principles, airline passengers form a single line in front of each airline's ticket counter, while behind the counter a row of agents provide service. As an agent becomes free, he calls the next customer to come forward. Which arrangement do you think works best: the single line feeding into multiple servers used by the airlines or the multiple lines used by most grocery stores? It is a question that an optimizer can answer using queuing theory, a discipline dealing with the mathematical study of queues, or waiting lines. Queuing theory focuses on such performance measures as "average waiting times," or the number of people expected to be served within a given period of time.

What can queuing theory tell us about the comparative performance of each type of line? A comparison requires us to make some assumptions. Let's keep it simple and consider a small grocery store with three checkout lines. Sometimes people arrive at the checkout line close together; in other instances, the time between arrivals is a little longer. However, with the storm coming we will assume that the store is relatively busy and that the *average* time between arrivals to the checkout line is two minutes, with the actual arrival times being normally distributed around this mean. Let's also assume that customers are rational and will choose the checkout line with the fewest people in it; furthermore, customers will not switch lines once they have made a selection and positioned their grocery cart. Finally, we'll assume that the average time a cashier takes to check out a customer is five minutes, again with the actual times of each checkout being normally distributed around this mean.

Question: How much less (or more) time, on average, would customers spend waiting in line if the grocery store were to switch to a single-line queuing system served by the same three registers? The answer: Customers would save an average of one minute and 15 seconds.[1] That may not seem like much time saved during an average day—during a storm, of course, every second that's saved becomes critical—but think about it from the grocer's perspective. Switching to a single-line system represents a whopping 23 percent increase in checkout productivity. Depending on his brand promise, the grocer could use this sizable improvement in efficiency to either shorten waiting time or maintain current service levels but employ fewer staff.

The mathematics for computing the 75-second difference is beyond this book. If you are wondering why the single line is so much more efficient, the answer comes down to how effectively the system uses a limited asset: checkout personnel. Every customer cannot be checked through in exactly five minutes. Some take a little more time, some a little less. Consequently, in a multiline setup some checkout cashiers become overwhelmed, while others occasionally experience an empty queue and downtime. This creates inefficiencies that don't exist in the single-line arrangement, where a customer is immediately available whenever a cashier becomes free. Whether your grocer figures it out by logic or by using queuing theory, making the switch will save you time and aggravation, unless you enjoy thumbing through the tabloids and musing over the mints.

You would think that more grocers would adopt the optimal solution and switch to a single-line system. Alas, they do not—and they are not alone. While the number of businesses that are using Optimization to improve their problem solving and decision making has risen, these forward-thinkers are still in the minority. Optimization could make a far greater contribution to improving the way today's organizations are led and managed—if only it were given a chance.

Let's look at a few of the many examples from across industry segments that point to woeful business inefficiencies begging for an optimized solution.

Curing Health Care

Few industries face as many complex decisions, resource limitations, and inefficiencies as health care. The pervasive waste and inefficiency throughout the health care system are well documented. To cite just a few examples:

- Pharmacists spend 20 to 30 percent of their time playing telephone tag with doctors, trying to make sure they correctly understand the intent of illegible prescriptions.[2]
- One out of every 14 people who enter a hospital contracts an infectious disease while undergoing treatment.[3]

- Studies have found that the percentage of money spent on administration and insurance in the U.S. health care system is double that of Canada, Japan, Australia, and the United Kingdom, and half again as high as that spent by the Netherlands and Germany.[4, 5]
- One-third or more of the clinical procedures performed in the United States are of questionable benefit, with the projected health risks substantially exceeding the expected health benefits.[6] For example, one study calculated that the inappropriate use of spinal fusion results in more than $11 billion in wasted resources each year.[7]

Such waste might be defensible if it somehow produced superior levels of health, but sadly this is not the case. Infant and adult mortality rates in the United States are 30 to 90 percent higher than those in other developed countries such as Japan, Sweden, France, Germany, Canada, Australia, and the United Kingdom.[8]

Poor decisions leading to high costs and poor service—it is a tailor-made challenge for Optimization. Among the many voices calling for the use of Optimization in the health care arena is that of former U.S. Treasury Secretary Paul O'Neill. O'Neill estimates that half of the more than $2 trillion spent on health care in the United States each year is wasted needlessly.[9]

Early in his career, O'Neill worked for the Veterans Administration. As an operations researcher and systems analyst charged with applying linear programming to feed 210,000 veterans across the country each day, he saw firsthand how powerful Operations Research (OR) and Optimization could be in correcting systemic inefficiencies in the health care system. By his estimate, applying OR-inspired solutions to today's health care system would significantly improve outcomes and slash waste by as much as 50 percent.

O'Neill's estimates are supported by the successful application of Optimization by other countries to improve their health care. In Canada, for example, applications of queuing theory have been used to improve ambulance response time, reduce waiting time in emergency rooms, and improve patient scheduling for scarce diagnostic resources such as computed tomography (CT) scans.[10]

In Sweden, an optimization software program called Laps Care is being used by 200 organizations to schedule and route 4,000 home care workers throughout the country's municipalities. The system has increased operational efficiency by 10 to 15 percent and is estimated to be saving between $30 and $40 million a year. In addition, it is reported to have improved home care for patients by doing a better job of ensuring that each home care recipient gets the specialized services and equipment that he or she needs.[11]

In the United States some progress has been made through OR. O'Neill describes how OR techniques were used in a 600-bed Pittsburgh hospital to reduce patient falls from 600 to 100 per year—a reduction of 83 percent. In another example reported by O'Neill, OR techniques were used to reduce infections in a hospital's intensive care unit by 84 percent over a 12-month period.[12]

As mentioned earlier, Optimization has also been used, in at least one instance, to address a pervasive contributor to the high administrative costs in U.S. hospitals: the need to manage hundreds of private and government contractors and payees. Texas Children's Hospital in Houston developed Bayesian forecasting software and nonlinear optimization models to monitor contract performance and make specific recommendations for subsequent renegotiations. The system was credited with increasing hospital revenues by $17 million in its first year of operations.[13]

But despite the tremendous opportunity and demonstrated successes, the health care industry has been slow to adopt optimization techniques. Applications like those described here represent the exception, not the rule. Much of the discussion concerning Optimization in the health care field represents academic research, not field applications used on a daily basis to reduce inefficiencies and improve service.

Paul O'Neill summed up the extent of the missed opportunities when he said, "For me, there is no bigger smorgasbord of potential opportunity for the application of your [OR practitioners' and optimizers'] talents and insights than in the practice of American medical care."[14]

Optimization: Rx for Underperformers

Health care isn't the only area that needs a shot in the arm. Doctors and medical professionals have a long-standing reputation as late adopters of technology, but it is not just the medical profession that has been slow to adopt Optimization. Throughout the business world, companies continue to manage scarce and expensive assets in traditional ways, shunning proven optimization techniques. Two areas that until recently have been stagnant are sales and human resources. In both areas, the success of initial applications gives us hope that the word will spread.

Sales Can Soar

Few functions are bound so tightly to business success as sales, and it was one of Optimization's early areas of focus. Almost 75 years ago, American mathematician Merrill Flood popularized one of the most celebrated combinatorial Optimization problems: the traveling salesman.[15] The problem involves trying to determine the most efficient route for a salesperson to take in visiting a series of cities, without passing through the same city twice. Following this early interest in a sales problem, one might have expected sales departments to be early adopters of Optimization techniques. Yet Optimization is still not widely employed by salespeople. Many have some type of customer relationship management (CRM) software to help them track customer data, but very few use optimization software to make money- and time-saving recommendations about where and how they should pitch business.

This oversight has profound repercussions. The exact number of salespeople in the United States is difficult to determine. Most estimates place the number somewhere above 15 million. Imagine how much more revenue they could generate if, instead of having rah-rah motivational meetings and stale training programs, their managers had provided them with the tools to optimize their sales calls!

Fortunately, Optimization is gaining a foothold. Several pharmaceutical companies have begun using it to instruct their salespeople which drugs to highlight during their hard-won face time with physicians. The recommendations are based on such things as the doctor's prescription history, medical group affiliation, and geographical location.

At UPS, sales reps use advanced analytics software that uses a sophisticated algorithm to alert the sales force when a customer is likely to switch to another shipping company. A UPS sales representative is sent out immediately and often shows up at a customer's door to resolve a potential problem before the customer even realizes that the problem exists.[16]

For several years, NBC has been using optimization software to set prices and draft proposals for the sale of advertisements for its fall lineup. The software balances client requests with the network's sales objectives, taking into account such constraints as client budget, targeted demographic groups, desired program mix, and desired ad length. The software has reduced proposal-preparation time from days to less than an hour, while doing a much better job of meeting client requests. Perhaps most significant, because of the optimality of the software's plans and the reduction of errors, the reworking of proposals has been reduced by 80 percent, saving both the sales force and clients untold hours of unproductive effort. NBC credits the proposal software with generating an additional $200 million in sales over a four-year period.[17]

Such examples are encouraging, but much more can be done. Today's sales environment is far more sophisticated than it was in the good old days, when a "shoeshine and a smile" were keys to successful selling. Sales has become a team sport—and a global one at that. Database management has become pivotal. Increasingly, to convert prospects to customers, sales functions must cut across organizational silos to tap into resources in research and development (R&D) and management information systems (MIS). Optimization can and should be more strategically deployed to provide a competitive edge at every step in the entire sales process, from data capture and analysis to time and territory management to prospect contact.

People Can Be Profitable

Just about every company's annual report trumpets the virtue of people as "our most important asset." Whether this is rhetoric or reality, people are surely an asset that is extremely expensive to acquire, train, retain, and replace. While Optimization is not a widely used tool among human resource practitioners, a number of companies, including British Telecommunications, Continental Airlines, General Motors, Intel, and Schindler Elevator, have begun to use optimization software to help solve complex workforce scheduling challenges.[18] In Chapter 1, we described the development by Intel's Decision Engineering (DE) group of the highly effective Resource Planning Tool to improve the assignment and reassignment of product-design team personnel.

IBM's consulting arm is developing software that scans its worldwide consultant workforce and suggests optimal teams to staff new consulting engagements, based on such constraints as project-required technical skills, budget limitations, profitability goals, and consultant availability.[19]

Hiring and retention are other areas in which Optimization is slowly beginning to be used. According to data from the U.S. Bureau of Labor Statistics, it costs on average almost two times the person's salary to replace a professional worker. Even a frontline service worker costs three-fourths of her salary to replace, and this can climb to two or three times the person's salary, if you add training costs, processing, ramp-up expenses, and lost productivity of the supervisor.

To minimize employee-replacement costs, Walmart has begun using written tests and optimization software to predict which of their potential new hires are likely to remain with the company.[20] By analyzing applicants' responses to questions such as, "Do you agree that there is room in every corporation for a nonconformist?" the software can make much more accurate predictions concerning employee retention than a human interviewer, who is often burdened by judgmental biases. While applicants may not like having a computer turn down their application for a position, the savings from reduced turnover goes right to Walmart's bottom line!

McDonald's, another mega-optimizer, has also begun to rely heavily on Optimization to help manage its human assets. A typical McDonald's restaurant has 50 employees and 30 work shifts, presenting many more permutations than Dantzig's early personnel-assignment problem. By utilizing a computer-based linear-programming model that considers 100,000 variables and 3,000 constraints, harried franchisees are able to cut their personnel-scheduling time by as much as 80 or 90 percent.[21] Not only does the computer program tell the restaurant owner now how many employees she will need based on traffic projections and expected order complexity; it also recommends how they should be positioned throughout the restaurant.[22]

Sports professionals are among the highest-paid human resources. The story of how Billy Beane was able to keep the Oakland Athletics in contention year after year, even though he was paying some of lowest salaries in baseball, has been colorfully documented in Michael Lewis's book *Moneyball*. [23] Beane's secret: OR and optimization techniques. Members of Oakland's optimization brain trust were subsequently recruited by the Boston Red Sox, who in 2004, after adopting similar techniques, captured their first World Series pennant in 86 years.

One might expect that such repeated success—combined with the publicity from a best-selling book—would have propelled Optimization into ESPN's top 10 plays and every front office across the land, but this has not happened. A few football teams, including the New England Patriots, have increased their use of optimization techniques. However, many franchises continue to rely heavily on folkloric selection criteria developed by long-dead scouts. When it comes to voicing his opinion of more rational methods of player selection, John Fox, the head coach of the Carolina Panthers in the National Football League's South Division, does not mince words. "Statistics," he says, "are for losers." [24]

It Never Gets Any Easier

From queue management to sales force deployment to talent acquisition, Optimization has clearly proved its worth in a wide spectrum of applications. Many of these—such as the pricing of hotel rooms and airline tickets—are familiar to a large part of the population. Yet the spread of Optimization often seems to creep along at a snail's pace. Chapter 2 discussed how after Edmond Halley created his table of life expectancies in 1693, a century passed before insurance companies began using the data to offer variably priced annuities based on a purchaser's age. The speed of business may have accelerated since the 1600s, but speaking with Karl Kempf of Intel Corporation, whom we met in Chapter 1, you realize that the more things change, the more they stay the same.

Kempf has led the OR and Optimization effort at Intel since 1987. He has introduced optimization tools to dozens of divisions and departments throughout the company, including the product-design group whose story we have already told. In many ways, Intel seems an ideal environment for the spread of Optimization. The company employs large numbers of engineers, scientists, and mathematicians. It also has a "by the numbers" culture and a tradition of continuous improvement in its operations divisions. And in fact, Kempf and his team have been extremely successful in saving Intel billions of dollars through deployment of OR and optimization tools. Now for the surprising part: Kempf says that today, when he begins working with a new group or function at Intel, it is just as hard to convince them to adopt optimization tools as it was when he started at Intel 23 years ago. "It's an amazing thing," Kempf comments. "George Dantzig introduced linear programming to the world over 60 years ago. Yet I have people in this company using spreadsheets and taking days to make decisions that we can optimally solve in minutes using linear programming."

Lest you think that Karl Kempf and Intel are somehow unique in encountering barriers to their modern-day efforts to proselytize Optimization, similar stories emerge from other heavy users of the discipline. UPS, touted as the "the tightest ship in the shipping industry," has a long and venerable history in the application of OR and optimization techniques. Back in 1957, then-CEO George Smith commented, "If we did not have Operations Research, our rate of growth might have been affected. As we grow in size our problems increase geometrically. Without Operations Research we would be analyzing our problems intuitively only and would miss many opportunities to get maximum efficiency out of our operations."[25]

But sustaining OR takes much care and feeding, and it doesn't always deliver. In the early 1980s, Mike Eskew, a senior engineering manager at UPS, established its first OR group. He was a true believer in Optimization. But by 1994, not long before he became CEO, he was forced to call for a review of the OR department. It had not delivered any measurable business benefit, and he asked some senior managers to decide whether it should be disbanded. Fortunately for UPS, OR passed the review and subsequently went on to add billions of dollars of value to the corporation.[26]

The fact remains, however, that even in organizations that have used it with great success, Optimization often moves like a glacier rather than a gazelle in gaining acceptance. This begs the question, "Why?"

What's Holding Optimization Back?

Conversations with practitioners, optimization consultants, and academicians suggest that there are a number of reasons why the "O" factor has so often been ignored. Lack of familiarity and understanding certainly plays a role. Although modern optimization techniques have been around since World War II, for many years technical expertise and computing power were only available to government, the armed forces, and a few large companies.

Also, OR and Optimization did not evolve as a single discipline that could be easily mastered. There were no licensed professionals with whom you could contract for optimization services. The field was viewed, by the few who knew about it, as a general approach to problem solving and decision making that included a wide range of concepts and techniques emanating from a diverse set of disciplines. Coming as these did from mathematics, economics, industrial engineering, game theory, and computer science, they were anything but easy for someone without a technical background to isolate, identify, or master.

Nor has it been easy for people to determine which problems are—or are not—candidates for Optimization. Most people are not quantitative by nature. They make intuitive, holistic judgments without breaking down every decision into its component parts or into numbers. Only a few unique individuals are driven—as was Francis Galton, the father of modern genetics—to measure reality to its fullest. Very few people would ever think of measuring the characteristics of a piece of music to determine the likelihood of it becoming a hit. Someone who cannot imagine the feasibility of quantifying and computerizing a specific type of decision is unlikely to entertain Optimization as a solution.

Not Always Ready for Prime Time

Adding to the skepticism is the fact that optimization projects haven't always been grounded in reality. To add value, Optimization must not only be theoretically sound, it must solve real-world business problems within an acceptable time frame.

In 1994, when CEO Mike Eskew called for a review of the OR function at UPS, it was because the function had not made a single documented contribution to the bottom line in over a decade. While the management review team did not think that the OR group should be dissolved, it recommended some important changes. Director of process management Jack Levis has been with UPS for 34 years and was on the review team. He understands why executives shy away from Optimization at times. "Executives have every right to be skeptical [of Optimization]," he admits. "In the past, it has overpromised and underdelivered."[27]

One of the key issues at UPS was that OR was seen as a technical, not a business, function. At that time, OR reported to the information services department. After the review, Eskew moved OR under the engineering group. He asked Levis to manage the group and implement the recommendations. The department was given a year to demonstrate its worth.

Other key issues, according to Levis, were that data collection was taking too long, and stakeholders were waiting for the perfect optimization solutions. Collecting and cleansing the data needed to build a perfect model could take three months or more; by then, the business had changed and the model no longer applied. "Once we decided to be satisfied with solving only 80 percent of the problem," says Levis, "we were able to radically reduce data-collection time and get something useful into the field. If you wait for the promise of the big bang—pushing a button to get the optimal answer that solves all your problems—you never get there. We needed to go after the incremental wins."[28] Fortunately for UPS, that is exactly what its OR group began to do.

Optimization's technical and mathematical nature, mixed track record, and the general lack of awareness of its techniques have certainly contributed to its slow growth. But there are obviously other factors holding it back. Today, for every failed optimization project there are multiple successes—many of which have produced a spectacular return on investment. Yet when you talk to practitioners or work to introduce Optimization into a company, you quickly sense that additional barriers exist.

Right Doesn't Make Might

In 2005, lawyer Richard Copaken took down his shingle and founded Epagogix, a British company willing to take on a challenge equal in difficulty to predicting the next great hit song. The company's mission: develop a neural-network computer program to predict how much money a movie would gross, *using only an analysis of the movie's written script as input data.*

The results that Copaken has achieved indicate that the importance of top stars, special effects, and marketing have been vastly overrated as predictors of box-office success. In one test, the neural equation was able to accurately predict the profitability of six out of nine films—just from their script. Although 66 percent may seem like a low level of accuracy, traditional studies have been accurate in their predictions of gross revenue only about a third of the time.

As recounted by Ian Ayres in *Super Crunchers*, the time came for Copaken to hit the road and pitch his software to the movie studios. By Copaken's modest estimates, if a major studio had the discipline to follow the advice of his program, it could net an extra billion dollars a year. While a few studios expressed interest, many did not. In one memorable meeting, in order to pique the interest of the studio Copaken brought with him two hedge-fund managers willing to invest $500 million to make films of scripts recommended by the optimization software. However, the meeting did not proceed well. Finally, one of the exasperated hedge-fund managers asked in frustration, "If Dick's system here gets it right fifty times out of fifty times, are you telling me that you wouldn't take that into account to change the way you decide which movies to make or how to make them?" The studio head's answer?

> No, that's absolutely right. We would not even if he were right fifty times out of fifty times. . . . what if we are leaving a billion dollars of the shareholders' money on the table; that is shareholders' money. . . . If we change the way we do this, we might antagonize various people. . . . Our wives wouldn't be invited to the parties. People would get pissed at us. So, why mess with a good thing?[29]

Clearly, when you are proposing that an executive change how he makes decisions, there is a lot more involved than ROI. And it's not just party-loving movie moguls who think this way.

In 1987, after an illustrious career in Europe—including four years at INRIA, France's preeminent information technology (IT) research institute—Pierre Haren cofounded ILOG, a developer of expert systems and optimization software that he subsequently sold to IBM. During a plenary presentation at the 2009 INFORMS Conference,[30] Haren recounted how ILOG developed and successfully deployed production-planning software in IBM's Fishkill, New York, plant. The software worked so well that the plant's investment in buying and installing the software was repaid in 30 days. With such a quick payback, Haren was convinced that orders would come pouring in. Alas, ILOG was only able to sell one other similar system. Haren's conclusion? ROI is not enough. It makes for great stories, but even if you could cite twice as many high-ROI stories, you would be lucky if you increased your software orders by 20 percent.

When you ask Intel's Karl Kempf why he has to work just as hard to introduce optimization software to a new department at Intel today as he did 23 years ago, he quickly points to how executives view themselves, their jobs, and the process for making business decisions.[31] Most executives believe that they have been successful because of the smart decisions they have made. As Martin Seligman[32] and a number of other psychologists have shown, humans have a strong tendency to exaggerate the correctness of their personal judgments and the control they exert over a situation. It's another one of those human biases. Nothing suggests that executives are exempt from these tendencies. In fact, their history of success indicates just the opposite: they are likely to be more self-assured and more confident in their decision-making ability than most people. Few successful senior executives feel the need to improve their decision-making capabilities.

Over the past 20 years, Kempf has been studying senior executives' decision-making modus operandi. Most, he has observed, ask their trusted advisors to analyze the alternatives and identify the two or three best among them. The executives then ask probing questions, test assumptions, apply the business acumen they have developed through the years, then make—and bless—the final decision.[33]

The trusted advisors may be interested in a tool that can help them explore, understand, and explain options to their executive. However, neither they nor the executives are likely to bet their farm or their careers on a "black box" or mathematical model they don't understand, especially when the recommendations that emerge are counterintuitive and not fully explainable. Given the way in which boardroom decisions are typically reached—together with the high levels of confidence that executives have in their own decision-making ability—it is not surprising that quants and their decision tools are slow to be welcomed. As we will see in the following chapters, this has important implications for how optimization projects need to be introduced and structured if they are to be successful. Kempf believes that one reason OR or Optimization has spread so slowly is that optimizers frequently spend too much time thinking about math models and the optimal way to make a decision rather than about how executives currently make decisions and the human needs these decision-making processes fulfill.

There is one other characteristic of the human decision maker that Kempf believes contributes to the gulf between optimizers and many business managers. When parts of the brain that control emotions are injured, people may no longer be capable of making any decisions. It would appear that our decisions are highly dependent on our emotional intelligence.[34] This bias has been documented: when two alternatives are considered, if one is linked to our emotions, it has a better chance of being selected—regardless of the evidence. Just as Dr. McCoy resisted turning decisions over to the emotionally challenged Mr. Spock, executives are often reluctant to turn decisions over to a mathematical algorithm that is devoid of emotions.

While much of the resistance to Optimization runs counter to reason, one common objection cannot be refuted: computers don't always do as good a job as people. Earlier in this book, when we compared human decision makers to computer programs, we noted that humans have a much broader array of stored knowledge that they can call on when making decisions. Jack Levis uses the following example to illustrate: if you are packing trailers, and you have 10 packages left over, a computer will recommend adding another trailer. A human would call over to the dock and ask if they could pack the load tighter or carry the packages in the cab.[35]

The Mind of an Optimizer

Let's face it, optimizers are the ultimate quants. They and many traditional businesspeople see the world through vastly different lenses. It isn't just their decision-making processes that vary. Both the thought processes followed and the questions asked vary tremendously between the two groups. When presented with the same issue, they would likely come up with radically different solutions, which in turn would have an entirely different impact on employees, customers, and other stakeholders. Understanding this disparity is important for evaluating the potential of Optimization, understanding the type of thinking it involves, and then determining whether or not it is right for your company.

The majority of quants I have met who have left academia to work in business have different goals from most businesspeople. They are not interested in occupying corner offices on executive row, where the focus is on enterprise-defining, big-picture strategic decisions. They prefer to head for the operational area, where they can rivet their attention on day-to-day asset-allocation decisions. Quants know the importance of doing the right thing, but their passion lies in doing things right—and in the process, optimizing value.

In the corporate world, benchmarking is a major preoccupation. Identifying best practices, assessing how well you measure up to them, and closing the gaps is considered the optimum way to improve systems, processes, and products.

Among optimizers, being *as good as others* is never the goal. The goal is always to be *the best possible*. Quants are never satisfied with the status quo. They believe that there is always a better way, and they work continuously to keep generating creative hypotheses, testing them, and moving along smartly to make decisions.

Optimization is about taking an upside-down look at things and moving into unexplored areas. Rather than starting in the boardroom, quants and other optimizers are creative thinkers continuously on the prowl for optimal solutions—starting from the bottom up. A good deal of their time is invested in understanding how a company's line employees make repetitive decisions and coming up with hypotheses about how optimization software might do a better job. Some of these theories seem impractical—even outrageous—but if they test positively against the data, they may be the next big win.

Think about how Google ads work. A traditional marketer concentrates on one ad at a time, saying, "Before we come up with an ad, let us profile the target group, get an idea of what their interests are, and then design ads that work for them." Google marketers proceed more experimentally, asking, "How can we determine which ads are most interesting to any particular viewer?" Because Google is paid not just for placement, but for click-throughs, the greater the response, the more revenue. Google's optimizers avoid being fixated on a single alternative. Instead, they pay attention to the words and phrases keyed into the search bar, which provide data about buyer interest and behavior. They then create an array of related ads, post them, and monitor which ads and which ad variants are most attractive in which situations. That is a quant's view of how marketing should work.

Half Empty or Half Full?

An excellent time to compare the thought process of a typical executive to that of a quant is during a period of extreme challenge, such as the global recession of 2008–2009. At such times, it is not just the economy that heads south. Morale, spirit, hopes for the future—they all plummet along with sales and revenue. As Dr. Gregory Berns, director of Emory University's Center for Neuropolicy, points out, "Work is feeling more and more like a Skinner box. . . . Workers' fear has generalized to their workplace. . . . We are caught in a spiral in which we are so scared of losing our jobs . . . it makes it impossible to concentrate on anything but saving our skin by getting out of the box intact. Ultimately, no good can come from this type of decision-making."[36] As a mentality of fear and scarcity sets in, businesses attempt to rein in spending and do more with less. Cost-cutting becomes the management weapon of choice, just as it did for Howard Johnson's, whose self-sabotage was described in Chapter 1.

Optimizers do not reason this way. They look for opportunities, even as resources become more constrained. Rather than asking, "How can we reduce costs?" optimizers attack a business challenge by taking a long, hard look at each step of an operation and asking, "What is the best way of doing this? How can we add value by getting more from the assets that are available to us?" In other words, "How can we optimize?" Instead of looking to "take away" or impose limits, optimizers look for ways to open up infinite opportunities.

An excellent example of how this shift in mind-set works can be found in a company's call center. When it comes to customer-service calls, the command from management is typically, "Cut call-center costs." But an optimizer, looking at call-center operations, would suggest a very different mandate. To a quant, the objective becomes, "Optimize the way that customer-service calls are handled."

Reducing call-center costs entails lowering the cost per call, which can be done either by employing lower-salaried reps or by reducing the time that reps spend on each call. But when you approach the challenge by looking for a way to optimize service calls, numerous alternatives suddenly become available, and chances are, these will not entail paying lower salaries or alienating customers. If instead you improve the speed and quality of solutions to customer problems, each of your existing reps can handle more calls. Cost per call is reduced, but the solution is optimal. Everyone wins: employees, customers, and the company.

Thus, having a different mind-set and asking different questions can result in a very different outcome. It can also send very different messages to stakeholders. Figure 4.1 summarizes the differences in the messages sent to employees and customers by "cutback" managers and those sent by optimizers. Which company would you chose to work for or do business with?

In tough economic times, leanness is often a virtue. The question is, do you have to get lean by being *mean*? Over time, cutback management decreases employee morale, compromises product quality and innovation, diminishes customer satisfaction and loyalty, and casts a shadow over your brand. If cost-cutting is your mission, then your actions project a sense of scarcity and survival. But if your mission is to be the best, your actions should connote, "We are the best and we can do better." It may even involve—as at L.L. Bean, which is known for the quality of its customer service—incentivizing reps to spend as much time as possible on each phone call. Incidentally, the company found that the longer one spends on the phone with an L.L. Bean rep, the more one buys.

Optimization sometimes ends up cutting costs, as Walmart, McDonald's, and UPS have done. However, the "best" solution isn't always the cheapest. Optimization often improves margins by creating a premium product, which requires a financial investment by the company, as was the case with ArgentAir and the Jan de Wit Company.

FIGURE 4.1   Cutback Management Versus Optimization

What a "Cut-Back" Manager Asks:	What an Optimizer Asks:
How can we reduce costs?	What are we trying to accomplish? Can it be optimized? And, how should that be measured?

What Employees Hear and See:	What Employees Hear and See:
How can we cut or outsource jobs?	How can we be the best?
How can we work people harder?	How can we use everyone more effectively to be better, faster, more cost effective?
Tough times require tough decisions.	It's easier to get through tough times when you're the best.
We want to survive.	We want to be #1.

What Customers Hear and See:	What Customers Hear and See:
Service from the cheapest staff that can be hired	The best way of handling customer calls
Routing through voice-mail hell	A system that avoids wasting customers' time
Interaction with tier-one reps glued to a script	Highly qualified people answering each call
The old heave-ho (e.g., "Why don't you try rebooting your computer, then call me back.")	Well-trained personnel skilled at root-cause analysis and choosing the right corrective action
Killer cycles of being put on hold, calling back, having to repeat their story	Being quickly reconnected to the same rep or to another who has their records

Vive La Différence

Given the unique mind-set of quants, it's not surprising that the projects they develop are sometimes misunderstood by others in the company.

For example, those who don't understand Optimization often view what quants do as "just more IT projects." This attitude can quickly scuttle an optimization plan. True, Optimization uses computers and involves programming, but therein ends the similarity with a traditional IT project. A typical IT project begins by specifying the output or end results. Next, a firm set of requirements and a design plan are developed. From there, it is on to a sequential process of development, testing, modifications, and rollout—sticking throughout to the detailed project plan created at the onset of the project. Application programming and selection of off-the-shelf program modules are common in IT projects. Rarely do such projects involve true R&D.

In contrast, optimization projects tend to be far more fluid and creative. Most do not lend themselves to off-the-shelf software solutions, so they require continuous R&D and experimentation. An optimization project is akin to the development of some type of new material. At the outset, an identified decision may seem right for Optimization, but who knows for sure? So you test a few alternative approaches for generating an optimal answer and assess the results. Your approach must not only generate a good decision, but also generate the decision quickly. If a user has to wait days for an answer, the optimization software will never be accepted. That is the flavor of optimization R&D: "Let us try a few things, see how they work, see how quickly we can generate an answer, and find out if people like it." Because of these unique characteristics, optimization projects often need to be managed outside the traditional IT chain-of-command.

Optimization projects are also distinct from other performance-improvement initiatives. For example, few programs have improved the quality and culture of commerce as much as the succession of Total Quality Management (TQM), Lean Production, and Six Sigma. All three focus on reducing the cost of product defects. Measures are put in place to spot and eliminate deviations from the standard. The resulting uniformity reduces the cost of scrap, rework, and returns. Underlying all such initiatives is the belief that "differences are our enemy." The challenge: ferret them out and eliminate them.

Optimization is based on the opposite premise. Optimizers say, "Differences can be our friends. Rather than presenting us with challenges, they may well offer us opportunities, so let's explore." Optimizers develop ways to measure deviations from the standard in products and services with an eye toward uncovering different situational needs and tailoring unique responses. This reflects the optimizer's bias toward adding value.

Take the automated music-recommendation service, Pandora, which was explained in Chapter 3. It first invites the listener to identify a preferred genre of music by selecting either an artist or a tune. It then plays similar music based on its genome analysis and computerized algorithm. But it doesn't stop there. It invites the listener to rate individual pieces of music. This additional information is incorporated into the algorithm to refine differences in preferences even further. Thus two listeners may both be listening to Beethoven, but given previously rated preferences, one may be listening to a sonata, the other a symphony.

The Times They Are A-Changin'

For the most part, this chapter has focused on Optimization's under-utilization and slow rate of expansion. However, as argued by Thomas Cook, former president of INFORMS, there are a number of reasons to believe that this situation is changing and that Optimization is on the cusp of explosive growth.[37]

First, the data needed to fuel optimal solutions is becoming increasingly available as the result of the Internet and the digitization of extremely large databases. Companies themselves are taking tremendous strides to improve the quality and integrity of their data. As high-quality data become more easily accessible, and the tools for manipulating them become more sophisticated, problems of timeliness such as the one that derailed UPS's early efforts at Optimization are fast disappearing. Data is the fuel that Optimization runs on, and unlike oil, it is becoming cheaper, cleaner, and more abundant every day!

Second, computing power no longer constrains Optimization as it once did. Like data, computing power is also becoming ever cheaper and more abundant. We have already discussed how smaller companies and even individuals are now running optimization programs on desktop computers. As the power and speed of computers increase, many more problems are being solved by Optimization. This is especially true of the many applications, such as those related to customer service, that demand real-time solutions. Applications such as Marriott's Group Pricing Optimizer would not be possible without today's high-powered computers, which can deliver a solution within seconds instead of the once-required days, weeks, or months.

Third, the body of knowledge and number of quantitative tools available for optimizing are exploding. This includes specialty software programs focused on specific tasks, such as deciding when and how much to mark down retail prices as inventory ages. Or you can log onto the Internet and access an optimization program that evaluates the chances that the new song you have just written will become a hit. As businesspeople become increasingly exposed to optimization programs in every facet of their life, they are certain to discover new opportunities to employ Optimization in their own organization.

They are also likely to find an increased number of knowledgeable practitioners to assist them. Years ago, if you wanted to hire OR expertise, funding university research was the only game in town, and it was sure to be a multiyear undertaking. Today, an increasing number of specialty consulting groups like Princeton Consultants are available to provide a range of choices for assistance.

Fourth, promotional materials and ease of access to information about Optimization are exploding. You can Google "optimization software" for instant access to more than 18 million references. Books, like this one, and contests, such as the one run by Netflix—with a million-dollar prize for better movie recommendations—are all contributing to getting out the word about Optimization.

The Institute for Operations Research and the Management Sciences (INFORMS) has played a major role in spreading the word about Optimization/OR. Each year, it holds a competition for the prestigious Franz Edelman Award for Achievement in Operations Research. In Chapter 1, we listed some of the well-known corporations that have received the honor in recent years. For example, Hewlett-Packard (HP) was the 2009 winner, for its application of OR to product portfolio management:

> . . . The breadth of HP's product offering has helped the company achieve unparalleled market reach, however, it has come with significant costs and challenges . . . including increases in inventory-driven costs and order-cycle time; liabilities to channel partners; and costs of operations, research and development, marketing, and administration. . . . complexity in the company's product lines also confused customers, sales representatives, and channel partners, sometimes driving business to competitors. HP developed two powerful operations research-based solutions for managing product variety. The first, a framework for screening new products, uses custom-built return-on-investment

(ROI) calculators to evaluate each proposed new product before introduction; those that do not meet a threshold ROI level are targeted for exclusion from the proposed lineup. The second, HP's Revenue Coverage Optimization (RCO) tool, which is based on a fast, new maximum-flow algorithm, is used to manage product variety after introduction. By identifying a core portfolio of products that are important to order coverage, RCO enables HP businesses to increase operational focus on their most critical products. These tools have enabled HP to increase its profits across business units by more than $500 million since 2005. Moreover, HP has streamlined its product offerings, improved execution, achieved faster delivery, lowered overhead, and increased customer satisfaction and market share.[38]

The fifth, and perhaps most powerful, force likely to accelerate the use of optimization software is competitive pressure. Three decades ago, when American Airlines adopted yield management software, it was a pioneer in its industry. At that point, Optimization represented a competitive differentiator for American Airlines; today, it is a requirement for entry into the commercial airline industry. As Optimization penetrates new industries, early adopters will be capable of making better, faster, and more optimal decisions about how to deploy their assets. Other industry players will need to follow suit: keep up and compete—or perish.

Final Note

Can Optimization add value to your business? If so, will your organization be receptive to it? To find the answers to these questions, take the quiz that follows.

The quiz has two parts. Part 1 is designed to help you assess your need for Optimization and identify areas in which it could add substantial value. The questions in Part 2 will help you determine whether or not Optimization will fit with your organization's culture. In each part, simply select a numerical response for each question. Then total your scores for that part. Positive scores on both parts suggest that you should carefully read the next two chapters to learn how to successfully implement an optimization project.

IS OPTIMIZATION FOR YOU?

Part I: How Pressing Is Your Need? How Big Your Opportunity?

1. Our organization's most critical assets are:

   −5   −4   −3   −2   −1   0   +1   +2   +3   +4   +5
   Unbounded and inexpensive   Extremely limited and expensive

2. Decisions about the use and deployment of our most critical assets must be made:

   −5   −4   −3   −2   −1   0   +1   +2   +3   +4   +5
   Infrequently (once or twice a year)   Frequently (hourly or daily)

3. The decisions we have to make about deploying our assets are:

   −5   −4   −3   −2   −1   0   +1   +2   +3   +4   +5
   Data are not captured systematically   Data are organized and accessible

4. We know how effective the decisions are that we make about our assets:

   −5   −4   −3   −2   −1   0   +1   +2   +3   +4   +5
   After many years   Quickly, in hours or days

5. The ways in which our assets are currently used and deployed are:

   −5   −4   −3   −2   −1   0   +1   +2   +3   +4   +5
   Highly efficient; little room to improve   Inefficient; lots of room to improve

6. In managing their assets, our competitors:

   −5   −4   −3   −2   −1   0   +1   +2   +3   +4   +5
   All use Optimization   None use Optimization

7. In making decisions about deploying our assets, we rely on:

   −5   −4   −3   −2   −1   0   +1   +2   +3   +4   +5
   People without experience whom   Critical subject-matter experts
   we can train quickly

8. Relative to our long-term strategic success, executives consider improving operations as:

   −5   −4   −3   −2   −1   0   +1   +2   +3   +4   +5
   Marginally important   Extremely important

Total Opportunity Score: _____

Add the numerical scores of your answers to the previous eight questions to determine your Opportunity Score. The higher the positive
total, the more likely your organization's ability to compete will be significantly enhanced by Optimization. A lower positive score or a negative one suggests fewer opportunities for Optimization to improve your
competitive position.

IS OPTIMIZATION FOR YOU?

Part 2: How Receptive Is Your Culture?

1. The number of executives who come from an operational background in my organization is:

   −5   −4   −3   −2   −1   0   +1   +2   +3   +4   +5
   Nonexistent   Very high

2. The leaders at my organization generally believe that:

   −5   −4   −3   −2   −1   0   +1   +2   +3   +4   +5
   The important things   If it isn't measured,
   can't be quantified   it isn't managed

3. In my organization:

   −5   −4   −3   −2   −1   0   +1   +2   +3   +4   +5
   Not much has been quantified   We are drowning in data

4. When it comes to documenting and engaging in best practices, my organization is:

   −5   −4   −3   −2   −1   0   +1   +2   +3   +4   +5
   Undisciplined; we all   Disciplined; we follow
   do things differently   standard procedures

5. In my organization, the use of software to help plan, forecast, and make decisions is:

   −5   −4   −3   −2   −1   0   +1   +2   +3   +4   +5
   Nonexistent   Widespread

6. The continuous-improvement process at my organization is:

   −5   −4   −3   −2   −1   0   +1   +2   +3   +4   +5
   Nonexistent   Highly disciplined; all participate

7. The number of our executives who are scientists, engineers, or Ph.D.s is:

   −5   −4   −3   −2   −1   0   +1   +2   +3   +4   +5
   Zero or very low   Very high

8. In my organization, the level of trust among employees and management is:

-5   -4   -3   -2   -1   0   +1   +2   +3   +4   +5

Extremely low   Extremely high

Total Readiness Score: _____

Add the numerical scores of your answers to the previous eight questions to determine your Readiness Score. The higher the positive total, the more likely your organization's culture will be receptive to adopting optimization practices. Lower positive scores or negative ones indicate the need to examine your organization's norms, values, and beliefs—that is, its culture. Pay special attention to whether or not the espoused values and beliefs of the top management team are congruent with their day-to-day decisions and actions.

CHAPTER 5

READY, SET, OPTIMIZE

In 1964, Blue Ribbon Sports began importing and distributing track shoes from Japanese shoe manufacturer Onitsuka Tiger. Blue Ribbon was founded by University of Oregon track athlete Philip Knight, and most of its early sales were made from the trunk of Knight's car at track meets. It was an inauspicious beginning for what has become a world leader in sports apparel: Nike, Inc.

Fast-forward to 1999, when Nike had 500,000 employees working in 55 countries, annual revenues of $9 billion, and over 40 percent of the red-hot athletic shoe market. But Knight and his team were far from satisfied. The new stretch goal: reduce from one month to one week the time needed to change Nike's production schedules around the world whenever market demand for different shoe styles began to change. To help the company achieve this ambitious objective, Nike turned to Texas-based i2 Technologies, a major software vendor whose optimization software was designed to improve sales forecasting, inventory management, production scheduling, and shipping.

Nike and i2 brimmed with confidence. Nike was hardly a newcomer to Optimization; the company was already using a worldwide company intranet and SAS software to help it manage production. And i2 had an extensive stable of satisfied customers who were already successfully using its inventory management software. It seemed like a marriage made in heaven.

Or was it? On February 27, 2001, Nike warned of a profit drop at the end of its fiscal third quarter. Knight, Nike's chairman and CEO, blamed i2 and its software for major production snafus. Apparently, Nike had produced and shipped too many increasingly unpopular shoes. In fact, orders for some of the less-popular shoes had been sent to the factories twice: once by Nike's older inventory management system and once by the new i2 system.

At the same time, key orders for several newer models of shoes that were rising in popularity somehow got waylaid. The interruption in production forced Nike to send shipments of high-demand shoes by plane, at a cost of four to eight dollars a pair compared to the 75 cents a pair it typically paid to ship by boat. The bottom line: Nike announced that the problems would take six to nine months to correct and would likely cost the company between $80 and $100 million. Both Nike's and i2's stock value plummeted by 15 percent after the announcement.

Controversy swirled concerning the underlying causes of the problems. While Nike blamed the software, a spokesperson for i2 blamed the way that Nike had implemented it. Katrina Roche, i2's chief marketing officer, commented, ". . . we recommend that customers follow our guidelines for implementation—we have a specific methodology and templates for customers to use—but Nike chose not to use our implementation."[1]

Jennifer Tejada, i2's vice president of marketing, added that her company always urged its customers to deploy the system in stages, but Nike went live to thousands of suppliers and distributors simultaneously. And a somewhat more neutral authority, AMR Research analyst and supply chain expert Pierre Mitchell, appeared to side with i2 when he commented, "Blaming the software vendor is a very old practice . . . Phil Knight makes it sound like it's a surprise to him . . . . If he doesn't have checkpoints for these kinds of projects, if he doesn't know where $400 million of his company's money is going, then he doesn't have control of his company."[2] The once happy marriage had definitely soured.

Whatever the full explanation of the Nike-i2 debacle, a clear lesson is that optimization projects typically represent a significant departure from business as usual. They cut to the heart of organization life and managerial leadership: how decisions get made, how data gets collected and analyzed, how decisions get implemented. Since optimization projects are potentially game changers, they must be carefully selected, designed, and carried out. This chapter will introduce you to a proven process that dramatically increases the chances an optimization project will meet or exceed expectations.

Before we outline the process, here's an important question to consider: what sets great optimization projects apart from the merely good ones, let alone those that disappoint?

Good Versus Great Optimization

All optimization projects are not created equal. Some, like Nike's, just don't work out. That's the real world. Other projects meet objectives; they get the job done but don't catapult the company to a new level of competitive advantage. Then there are the great projects: those that achieve breakthrough results. Here is what sets great optimization projects apart:

Good Optimization Automates Decision Making; Great Optimization Changes How Things Are Done

Google's Optimization of Internet searches illustrates the point. Google was a late arrival. By the time it arrived on the scene, other search engines such as Yahoo! were using human experts to rate the content quality of Internet pages—a process that might work for a million pages, but for not a billion or a trillion. Google didn't just automate and improve the search process; its PageRank algorithm revolutionized it. First, it replaced human raters with a citation index that ordered pages for relevancy, based on how often they were cited by other reputable pages. Next, it accelerated the lookup process by breaking apart its indexes and distributing them across thousands of computers. With many machines working in parallel, lookup could now happen instantaneously. It's like giving one page of a 30-page index to 30 different people. It takes each person only a moment to search through his or her single page.

Good Optimization Supplants Human Decision Making; Great Optimization Extends the Ability of People to Make Decisions

UPS moves a great number of packages among its own shipping facilities. In a single day, a facility such as the one in Willow Grove, Pennsylvania, can ship 80,000 packages to as many as 150 locations—and Willow Grove is one of the smaller locations![3]

Sometimes, there is no efficient way to get a package directly from point A to point B. Suppose for a moment that Willow Grove needs to send one-and-a-half trailers of packages to Worcester, Massachusetts. Packing and sending out the full trailer is easy, but what about the half-empty one? Hauling a half-empty trailer across several states is expensive. To avoid the cost, Willow Grove will look for a way to send the packages to another UPS shipping facility. For example, it might send the Worcester-bound packages to Washington, D.C., hoping that that facility will be able to combine the packages in a full trailer on the next trip to Worcester. This is a good solution for Willow Grove, but it might be less so for Washington, D.C., especially if there are no partially empty trailers headed toward Worcester from D.C. anytime soon. UPS might have been better off instructing Willow Grove to send the partial load to New York, assuming that New York happened to have had a partially filled trailer headed north to Massachusetts.

The problem is that UPS has over 1,300 facilities in the United States, handling more than 15 million packages per day and loading thousands of trucks. Finding the best route for the entire network is simply too complex for a human planner to handle. So UPS developed a piece of optimization software to find the best routes between locations for partial trailer loads. Here's the *great* part. When the software was being developed, the optimization team built an interface that enables the load planner in Willow Grove to instantly access data about shipments and loads from surrounding facilities. He now has accurate, just-in-time data and a greater range of options with which to make informed decisions. Not surprisingly, the quality of the load planners' decisions improved significantly. They were made quicker and produced more cost-effective solutions. Now imagine the system-wide impact when the optimization software was rolled out to other UPS locations.

Over at Intel, leader of the OR and Optimization group Karl Kempf says this about great Optimization and decision making: "When we develop an optimization tool, we are trying to give people the opportunity to explore the decision space . . . to explore the upper and lower bounds of the choices to help them be better."[4] UPS's software allowed its planners to do exactly that even before it was programmed to make recommendations.

OPTIMIZING GROUP DECISIONS AT MCDONALD'S

McDonald's executives like to say that theirs is a business of "inches, seconds, and pennies." With 30,000 restaurants in 117 countries, serving more than 60 million customers daily,[5] small changes can add up quickly—along with costs. If you are, say, the McDonald's director in a country like Japan, with 3,000 restaurants, some of the toughest decisions that you will have to make are when and how to invest in upgrades.

Why are such decisions so tough? First, restaurant operations consist of many interconnected parts. Expand drive-through capacity without upgrading the potato fryer, and you suddenly have long lines of grumpy customers waiting for fries. Second, the 3,000 restaurants in Japan have as many as 300 distinct layouts and equipment configurations: changes that improve profits for one class of restaurant can drive profits down in another. Third, any changes affect multiple constituents: McDonald's is committed to improving its customers' dining experience, but it is also committed to minimizing stress on its employees. And, of course, customer service and employee working conditions must be balanced against improved profitability and the opportunity for future expansion.

Traditionally, decisions to upgrade a McDonald's in Japan were made by an investment-governance council comprised of a dozen or so people, including country management, franchisee representatives, and technical experts from operations and IT. Because any investment decision

continued

would produce winners and losers among franchisees, debate could easily become lengthy and heated, as different perspectives and self-interest took center stage. Personal experience, "managerial wisdom," and positional authority dominated the decision process.

Enter Mike Cramer, director and founder of McDonald's operations research department. Like other great optimizers, Cramer's goal was not to make decisions himself but rather to enable the management team to make better choices. In the case of Japan, Cramer and his team began with a month-long field study of restaurant traffic flows, order patterns, service levels, and employee behavior. Back at McDonald's research center in the United States, the collected information was used to build two functioning restaurants modeled on Japanese configurations. These were then used to test the impact of different upgrades. Next, data from these experiments was incorporated into a customized software program capable of simulating the impact of different investment combinations on service levels, employee stress, financial performance, and expansion potential for the 300 distinct restaurant configurations found in Japan.

With software in hand, Cramer set out for Japan to facilitate the discussions in a series of governance-council meetings. Rather than argue from personal experience and conjectured outcomes, council members were able to test various investment scenarios, allowing the software to calculate the impact on service levels, employee stress, financial performance, and expansion potential. Among other things, the software was able to clearly demonstrate how some of the investments that were being considered would have little or no impact on revenue growth unless they were combined with additional investments. The software was also able to calculate the optimal sequence in which these additional investments should be made.

The results? Changes to the Japanese investment strategy added an additional $100 million in revenues in the first year. Eight of the 12 restaurant segments that made the investments increased traffic by 10 percent—the precise level projected by Cramer's software. The remaining four have experienced even greater increases. While elated with the success, Cramer is quick to point out that his team didn't make the decisions; they simply provided the tools to help the company's leaders make more optimal choices.

Good Optimization Provides Recommendations; Great Optimization Provides Recommendations—and the *Whys*

"Here is *what* I think you should do"—this is what makes good optimization software stand apart. It goes beyond data analysis to venture into prescription. It offers you a data-driven opinion, based on high-powered analytics. But great optimization software goes beyond prescription to provide the underlying rationale for its judgment. It explains *why* one alternative is superior to others. When you call Marriott to request a group reservation, its Group Price Optimizer displays for the sales manager a recommended price to optimize profits, along with the probability of getting the business. The computer also shows information explaining *why* it is recommending a particular price, including such factors as hotel occupancy rate and what, if any, large events are in town during the requested reservation period. By explaining to a prospect that there is a large convention in town, sales managers report that they can often keep people on the phone to discuss alternative options, rather than having them hang up and shop the competition.[6]

An easily accessible example of decision software that offers an explanation is available on Pandora, the personalized radio station that plays "only the music you love to hear." As you listen, simply click on "Why was this song selected?" Right now as I am writing and listening, Pandora tells me, "Based on what you've told us so far, we're playing this track because it features new-age aesthetics, an overall meditative sound, acoustic sonority, extensive vamping, and major key tonality."[7]

Good Optimization Gives You Good Choices; Great Optimization Searches for the *Best* Choices

The word *optimization* comes from Latin for "the best." Before the optimization team started to work with ArgentAir, each fleet manager was making good decisions scheduling the planes for a small fleet. He or she would define a good day as one when every corporate customer was serviced on time, with an acceptable number of empty miles, or miles flown without a passenger on board. The optimization project enabled the team to ask: "What is the theoretically best possible service and lowest empty air mileage?" "What policies did we have in place that drove up empty mileage or made it challenging to have the right jet in the right place at the right time?" The results: consistently improved on-time service *and* lower empty air miles beyond what experience had suggested was feasible or even possible.

At Marriott, when the hotel behemoth evaluates how good a job it is doing booking rooms, it does not waste time benchmarking competitors. It is not interested in catching up to competitors, but in maintaining market leadership. It evaluates how well its optimization pricing model is working compared to the bookings of its Total Hotel Revenue Optimization Model, which calculates the theoretical best the company could be doing.

When struggling to reverse Alcoa's dismal safety record, Paul O'Neill didn't challenge his organization to get better; in the spirit of Optimization, he challenged it to "get perfect" and hit the theoretical limit: zero accidents. Did Alcoa achieve that? Not quite, but it came a lot closer than it would have if it had simply "benchmarked its competitors."[8]

Good Optimization Is Fast; Great Optimization Is Ultra Fast

Speed *does* matter, especially when you are engaged in complex, time-dependent operations such as scheduling airplanes, getting out a daily newspaper, or shipping packages for next-day delivery. Overnight runs of the computer just do not cut it in situations where the market is changing in real time. At one railroad that our firm worked with, the time needed to quote an intermodal shipping price was reduced from days to seconds; at NBC, preparation time for pricing proposals for TV advertising was reduced from days to hours; and when Google executes a search and selects a dozen Internet pages from a trillion possibilities in a fraction of a second, the speed of Optimization becomes apparent. If time is money, then Optimization stands out as one of the modern business world's ultimate cash generators.

Good Optimization Gives You the Best Choice Based on the Data; Great Optimization Is "Robust" and Resilient in the Face of Change and Data Errors

We live in an inconsistent world, one filled with ambiguous, error-filled data. Great optimization software is designed to sense when something fundamental has changed or when an error in the data has appeared. It then can make adjustments or self-correct. It asks: "How did I do on that recommendation?" and "What, if anything, should I do differently going forward?" It factors the success or failure of previous recommendations into future ones, thereby creating its own experience curve, which improves outcomes. Again, Pandora stands as an example. It invites the listener to report, with a click of the mouse, any recommended song that he or she likes or dislikes. This information is factored into the recommendation algorithm, resulting in increasingly improved music recommendations.

Marriott's Group Price Optimizer (GPO) is also self-correcting. When the GPO recommends a room price, its algorithm computes an "expected win rate," or the percent of time it expects to land the business. Initially, the program was doing an excellent job having its real-world wins match its expected wins. However, when the recent recession struck, the percentage of times that a room rate was accepted suddenly plunged below the expected rate.[9] Prospects had become much more sensitive to even modest price changes, as everyone scrambled to save a dollar. The divergence was noticed immediately, and more-recent data was used to recalculate the price-sensitivity curves. Prices were lowered, and the sales managers' closing ratios were reestablished, allowing revenues to be optimized. To remain optimal, decision makers—human or computer—must continuously monitor performance and make adjustments as circumstances change.

Good Optimization Saves You Money; Great Optimization Makes You a Star

Optimization lets you have it both ways: it can cut operating costs dramatically, while at the same time improving your service or product. For example:

- When the metropolitan newspaper cited in Chapter 3 optimized its layout, it not only earned more money by including more ads, but for the first time it could provide instant feedback to customers by letting them know whether or not it could meet their request. It was a win-win for the paper and its customers.
- At NBC, the Optimization of proposal preparation reduced rewrites by 80 percent, not only saving money and time for the NBC sales teams, but doing the same for customers.

- At Marriott, while the GPO was increasing occupancy rates and margins, it was also allowing sales managers to instantaneously offer customers choices and alternatives, if the price being quoted was outside their budget.
- Optimization at Quad/Graphics not only saves the company money by reducing the number of times the binding lines have to be shut down; it reduces customers' mailing costs by combining the products from a single route.

Great Optimization is not a one-dimensional win. It is not just about service or efficiency or convenience or reduced costs. It is more about winning across the board.

Good Optimization Creates a Winning Project; Great Optimization Establishes a Winning Culture

Optimization may begin as a single project, but once it is successful, changing the way decisions are made can permeate people's thinking and change the culture of an organization. For a start, it can reduce binary, either-or thinking. A thought like "fast, cheap, *or* high quality" is replaced by the thought "fast, cheap, *and* high quality." "How can we make this better?" thinking is replaced by "How can we make this the best possible?" Decision making becomes a systematic and visible process, with clear accountability and measures of success. Optimization's heavy dependence on data—as opposed to personal biases or opinion—pushes an organization toward empirical testing and fact-based decision making, rather than relying on those traditional pillars of flawed organizational judgments: history, hunches, and hierarchy. Companies such as Amazon, Google, Marriott, McDonald's, and SAS—all of which have embraced Optimization—run hundreds of experiments each week to test ideas, sort through alternative suggestions, and choose the *best* road forward. When optimization projects take hold, they lead to a set of norms, values, and beliefs—a culture—that fosters innovative, out-of-the box thinking, along with a bias for rigorous, quantitative analysis.

Beyond keeping in mind these general distinctions between good and great Optimization, don't even consider undertaking an optimization project without a clear, step-by-step process to guide you through its selection, design, and implementation. The process that has proven most successful for Princeton Consultants through the years consists of the following five steps.

1. The Charter: Select Your Project and Team

Designing and implementing an optimization project is hardly a trivial pursuit. It requires commitment, time, and resources. In the first step, you need to:

- Choose the right area of opportunity
- Assemble the right team

2. The Vision: Design Your Project

Develop a clear vision of how the software will operate, what value its recommendations will have for the organization, and the steps to carry out the project. To do so:

- Conduct research and analysis
- Arrive at a final problem definition and "proof of concept"
- Organize the initiative into phases

3. The Early Win: Deliver Value Quickly

To ensure success, carefully select first test users that will give you tangible payback and build project acceptance.

4. The Scale-Up: Extend the Usage

Fully embed the application of Optimization throughout the field operations and establish its use as the default behavior. Build on this platform to further extend the value.

5. The Harvest: Leverage the Benefits

Capitalize on your success in this area, and look for other areas in the organization where similar applications can be implemented.

In the remainder of this chapter, we will look at detailed examples of successful execution of Steps 1 and 2. In Chapter 6, we will take a close look at Steps 3–5.

Step 1: The Charter—Select Your Project and Team

Successful Optimization begins with two elements: selecting the most promising area of opportunity and choosing the best people to work on the project.

Choose the Right Area of Opportunity

In what way(s) do you want to change your game? Optimization is a flexible tool. If you run a business, Optimization is a technology that you can apply at any or all of three different levels to help you change your game.

1. **Operating efficiency.** At the first level, you may want to reach new heights of productivity or reliability that traditionally have been beyond the grasp of your organization. Like UPS or the Jan de Wit Company (the lily grower discussed in Chapter 3), you may want to tighten up operations. You want to do things faster, better, cheaper. This is the blocking and tackling of Optimization that can help you catch up with, or even overtake, your competitors.

2. **New-product development.** On the second level, you are not satisfied with just optimizing existing products or services. You want to create a new product or service that enables you to break away from competitors. Think of Intel's use of Optimization to help it design the next generation of computer chips.

3. **A new business model.** On the third level, Optimization can be used to create an entirely new business. Using this technology, you can stake out a new frontier or reinvent your current value proposition—think Google, Amazon, or Expedia.

Most of the optimization projects that our firm carries out for clients are on level one. We are typically called in by a general manager or director whose focus is on achieving greater operating efficiency through cost reduction, through the reallocation of resources, or by raising performance levels of underutilized assets. The Optimization of line operations is not limited to *physical* assets. It can include optimizing any combination of assets physical, intellectual, human, and intangible.

Company presidents and CEOs, on the other hand, tend to be more interested in revenue growth than cost savings. They are more inclined to think strategically about how the next round of competitive advantage can satisfy future customer demand, as Amazon has done. For these leaders, Optimization is an important ally in high-stakes strategic decision making that relates to the nature, direction, and growth of the enterprise.

In today's environment, improving operating efficiency and cost is an imperative, but changing the business model holds the potential for greatest reward, and it is a ready-made challenge for optimizers. Top professional optimizers compare themselves to music teachers. Most pupils are so-so, and they improve with instruction, but every once in a while a student comes along with the potential to be a world-class musician. And that is what the teacher lives for. Optimizers get plenty of projects to improve a situation, but once in a while they get one that calls for creating a new game—and that is what *they* live for.

Most businesses are target-rich environments for Optimization. There are countless systems, processes, policies, and procedures, along with decision-making patterns and management practices that contribute to underutilized assets.

Imagine what the results would be if you were to improve your organization's performance by 15 percent through better hiring practices, through lower scrap and rework rates, or by increasing the yield from a key asset—be it your planes, trucks, railroad cars, or people. There are almost endless opportunities for asset optimization. Which ones should you pursue? Regardless of the level of an optimization project, a *great* optimization opportunity has certain qualities. Here is what to look for.

The Size of the Prize

Suppose you are considering a key asset as a candidate for Optimization. The question is, what would success look like? In particular, what is the value of optimizing this asset, and by how much will it offset the project cost?

To find the answer, you need to develop a realistic picture of the size of the optimization prize. One quick way to do this is by creating a point-in-time snapshot of the costs and benefits of utilizing the asset during a single week. Then review all the decisions you made during that week that relate to the asset, calculating the results you would have achieved if each decision had been *optimized*: "Here is what it would look like if we had made perfect choices with the data known at the time of each decision." The result is the *theoretical* best that you could have done during that week. The gap between that and your actual results is the size of the prize—your *potential gain*.

This is exactly how the decision to invest in the Group Pricing Optimizer (GPO) came about at Marriott International. When the senior director of Total Yield Systems, Sharon Hormby, and her group first began thinking about where they thought the company should increase its investment in Optimization, they had a solid foundation to build on. For 20 years, Marriott International had been using yield management to adjust rates for the individual traveler. As part of that effort, the company had developed a Revenue Opportunity Model, which compares how Marriott hotels have done each month to the maximum theoretical best they *could have* done. With the individual traveler, Marriott was receiving a grade of better than 90 percent. Because this metric was familiar to the company executives, Hormby and her team decided to expand it to group business, which had grown to more than 40 percent of revenues. When extended to the group business, Marriott's score dropped to a B-rating, closer to 85 percent. The nice thing about this metric—beyond the fact it was widely used and understood by senior executives—was that improvements in percentage points could easily be converted to dollars. Hormby and her team were now in position to make their business case, as well as to discuss the relative return of alternative optimization projects. They could say things like, "If you fund this project for *x* millions of dollars, it likely will result in an increase of 5 percentage points against the model that will return *y* millions of dollars annually. This compares to an alternative project that is only likely to improve our scores by 3 percentage points, or *z* millions of dollars."[10]

At ArgentAir, the optimization team took a similar first step. They began by targeting an important, well-understood metric that was reviewed each day and could be converted to dollars: empty air miles. Each 1 percent reduction in empty air miles could save ArgentAir over $15 million a year in jet fuel alone. Here was the foundation for a powerful business case that any executive would be willing to entertain.

Optimization tools are just like any other business investment: Step 1 is always to gain an understanding of the investment compared to the potential return and then compare it to alternative investments.

How Are Decisions Being Made Today?
When looking for areas of opportunity for Optimization, look for situations in which decisions are highly repetitive over short periods of time, across departments, or in multiple geographical locations. All three can provide big-win opportunities. Marriott makes millions of reservations each year that need to be priced; ArgentAir has an extremely large fleet of planes, and each plane has to be positioned two, three, or four times a day; every day, UPS must make decisions about how to move 15 million packages among its 1,300 facilities. If you are looking for big savings, look for decisions that are being made again and again. Very small improvements in the quality of each decision can add up to big-time savings.

However, when looking for optimization opportunities, don't just look at the frequency with which decisions are made. Examine *how* they are being made as well. Are decisions being made in an uncoordinated, fragmented way? For example, do decisions become separated into numerous subdecisions, each being made by different people working independently? Would value increase by making sure that all decision makers are able to see the larger picture?

At Marriott, the GPO enabled sales managers to look at booking opportunities across multiple hotels—not just in single ones, as the previous business process had. This allowed them to offer many more alternatives to prospects who called with a fixed set of dates and a tight budget.

Similarly, prior to Optimization, UPS planners were focused only on the cost of moving partial loads out of their own location. They gave little consideration to what the cost might be for the next shipping center to move their package to its final destination. Optimization made it possible to "scope up" and consider the impact of each decision on the entire network, not just on a single location.

ArgentAir's decisions were fragmented not only across fleets, but across time periods as well, since some groups of individuals were focused on the daily schedule rather than the longer-term one. These limited, fragmented perspectives were not only generating unneeded empty air miles; they were creating missed opportunities to both reduce shuttles *and* to increase customer satisfaction through upgrades.

REFINING THE SUPPLY CHAIN SAVES TENS OF MILLIONS AT INTEL

After Karl Kempf delivered a lecture at Arizona State University on Intel's supply chain and its operational complexities, one of the faculty members in the audience approached Karl and asked if he could draw on Karl's wall chart of Intel's supply chain, which he had used during the talk. Karl, of course, agreed, and professor of chemical engineering Daniel Rivera rotated the diagram 90 degrees, changed a few of the captions, and said, "This looks to me like the way oil flows through a refinery, and we have been efficiently controlling flow through oil refineries for the last few decades."

There were, in fact, many similarities: every barrel of crude oil has a slightly different composition, just as every semiconductor lot contains chips with a different distribution of operating speeds. Crude oil can take different paths through the refinery, including different packaging routes, depending on demand. Likewise, semiconductor chips take different routes, including packaging, as demand for servers, desktops, and laptops changes. Kempf realized that Rivera's use of Optimization in controlling flow in oil refineries might be the perfect solution to Intel's problems with the flow through its supply chain.

Kempf procured funding from the Intel Research Council to support collaboration with Rivera and his university research team. Three Ph.D. students—two of whom have completed their degrees and now work for Intel—and a U.S. patent later, a substantial part of Intel's supply-chain logistics is optimized in near-real time by the Model Predictive Control (MPC) technique that includes, at its core, an optimization algorithm. The system balances inventory holding at Intel's factories with shipping time and cost between factories to maximize responsiveness to customers, while minimizing supply chain costs.

The new technique has enabled Intel to improve both the speed and quality of its supply-chain planning, and replanning, efforts. The company can respond rapidly either to changing demand in its dynamic markets or to changing supply, as the speed distribution of chips being produced in its factories improves over time, or to both. And on the bottom line: tens of millions of dollars a year saved by Intel, as the MPC technique replaced the weekly manual spreadsheet and telephone technique used previously.[11]

The Degree of Complexity

If you find an area in which decisions require a high level of expertise, it is safe to assume that the decisions being made are complicated and could very likely be improved by optimization software. This was exactly the case at the metropolitan newspaper we worked with, where layout decisions were so complex that only two "experts" could make them; similarly, at the Jan de Wit Company the production-scheduling issues were so complex that the president himself was spending significant amounts of time making market projections and planning production.

In contrast to these types of complex situations, consider a situation in which a new hire comes aboard and pretty much masters the job in a week or two. This area of operation is probably not a good candidate for Optimization. The area may benefit from additional computer resources or you might be able to automate some decisions, but it is probably not a candidate for investing in Optimization. Optimization shines where there are complex decisions with more variables and alternatives than humans can handle.

The Pace of Change

When you enter a department or unit for which Optimization is being considered, ask employees how much—and how often—change occurs. If they tell you that things are relatively stable, with changes few and far between, it is unlikely to hold great potential for Optimization. But if employees tell you that the game keeps changing and getting more complicated—customer complaints are on the rise, competitors and suppliers are changing their policies, new regulations have to be followed, more overtime is required, product development time frames have shortened—you've come upon a high-potential area for Optimization.

Where change is rapid and continuous, rules of thumb—those shorthand truisms that have worked well in the past—become increasingly obsolete. Decision making becomes riskier without the usual parachutes. Planning suffers. Decisions get made on the fly, leading to costly misjudgments. Flux is a marker for the need to optimize. Just such conditions existed at ArgentAir, as corporate flyers called in last-minute schedule changes from around the world. Similarly, at a railroad company we created an optimization program for, the capacity of its trains, as well as the competing prices offered by truckers, varied not just daily but as the day progressed: just the type of situation in which Optimization often shines.

Postscript on Choosing the Right Area of Opportunity

Our firm is often retained by operational managers who are focused on reducing head count. But while overhead reduction is admirable, as consultants we know that the biggest impact on the bottom line typically comes from making better decisions about assets, not from reducing the number of people who make them.

Consider the case in which a company runs three shifts, every day of the year, and on each shift 5 to 15 people are involved in scheduling company assets: at the rail carrier just mentioned, these would be railroad cars; at ArgentAir, private jets; at the metropolitan newspaper, ad space; at Quad/Graphics, available machine time. Suppose for a moment that by installing optimization software each of these companies had been able to reduce head count by an average of 10 people. If each person costs $100,000, that would be $1 million in yearly savings. It's not exactly chump change.

But in each of the companies, savings of just 1 or 2 percent resulting from better utilization of assets—railroad cars, jet airplanes, ad space, and printing-press runs—could produce savings of multiple millions of dollars a year, while at the same time increasing customer satisfaction and goodwill. Which outcome is likely to produce the greatest value for your organization: reducing head count or improving the utilization of assets by a few percentage points?

A final caution relates to the growing reliance on corporate dashboards or scorecards for identifying priority issues for attention. Many executives believe that fixing the "red areas" on their dashboard is the best way to improve the business. But dashboards have real limitations.

In straight and level flight, most airplanes nearly fly themselves most of the time, especially if equipped with an autopilot. True, the pilot is constantly scanning the instrument panel for alerts that something unusual is happening. Corporate information technology (IT) systems with their dashboards are the same: they are designed to give you a thumbs-up in all areas except those where something is radically wrong.

Yet the biggest prizes are often found in areas where nothing is radically wrong. Optimization is not designed for fixing one-off problems that cause dashboards to light up, but for squeezing additional value from assets, either through game-changing breakthroughs or by improving the way decisions are made and the business is managed.

Assemble the Right Team

Zeroing in on the right area of opportunity is important; equally important is putting together the right team to successfully plan and carry out the project. Typically, an optimization team is made up of four different types of people: (1) a project sponsor, (2) subject matter experts (SMEs), (3) support personnel, and (4) optimization advisors or consultants.

Optimization is a challenging, creative endeavor that does not lend itself to a large cast. It is somewhat analogous to making a film. While many people are involved in the final product, the core of the work revolves around a skilled director (the sponsor) and the stars (core consultants and SMEs). The supporting cast (personnel) represents a much larger group, but these individuals are not needed for every scene. Five to ten core people, along with support personnel, would be a large optimization team, with two to three being a small one.

When choosing the right opportunity, look for the *biggest* possible prize; when constructing the right team, look for the *smallest* possible team. Let's look more closely at the members of such a team and the roles they typically play.

1. Project Sponsor

This individual recognizes the potential value of Optimization and often initiates the contact with the optimization consultants to further define the right opportunity. While titles vary, this is generally a person near the top of the reporting chain of the people who will be using the software day in and out. The sponsor is usually a level or two above the SMEs: in most cases a vice president, director, or general manager.

Once the area of opportunity has been selected and the project team is up and running, the sponsor is much less involved on a daily basis than the SMEs are. The sponsor's primary role is to make sure that the project receives the required attention and resources, as well as to make strategic calls at key decision points. Sometimes an effective sponsor needs to change his or her role as the project evolves. As one sponsor told me only half in jest, "I have been known to show up with pom-poms to cheer the team on, with a bulldozer to clear the way, and with free donuts to get the right people to show up for meetings."

When Marriott's Sharon Hormby and her team first put forward a proposal to develop a GPO, a wide circle of people needed convincing. The majority of Marriott's properties are actually owned by independent property-investment groups who contract with Marriott International to manage their properties. To implement the optimization system, Marriott would need to gain permission from these owners, a task made more complicated by the fact that Marriott would need to charge them for the development and deployment of the system. Fortunately, Hormby and her team had a strong project sponsor to support them: Bruce Hoffmeister, senior vice president of global sales and marketing information technology for Marriott International.

Hoffmeister came out of finance, making him exceptionally well prepared to speak about money issues, the value of the project, and key project milestones: in short, to help make the business case. In Hormby's view, he was an ideal sponsor. "Bruce let us develop the problem definition as we wanted to. He is very logical, so if you gave him a good argument he would go with you. More important, he was extremely useful in helping convince the owners to let us roll out the project. Bruce actually came with us on field trips to different hotels to speak with owners about the implementation and its value. He was invaluable."[12]

At ArgentAir, the optimization team also had a very strong sponsor: the executive vice president of scheduling and logistics. What made this individual so unique was his combination of business and technical skills. Although head of operations when the optimization project was launched, he had previously held the position of chief information officer (CIO). He had actually designed and implemented ArgentAir's computerized operations system, which our optimization software needed to interface with. If all that weren't enough, he had an operations research (OR) background. With such strong and knowledgeable support, the project encountered minimal headwinds.

It may be that there is nothing more valuable than a high-level executive sponsor to fly cover for an optimization project, but this is not the level at which such projects are typically conceptualized. Intel's Karl Kempf reports that in the more than 20 years he has been working in OR and at Intel, he has never had a senior executive come to him and request or propose that Optimization be used as a way to make better decisions. At first blush, this may seem surprising, given the widespread diffusion of technological expertise in a company such as Intel. But on further reflection, the fact that Optimization is usually driven from below the top tier should not be surprising. Recall John Kotter's classic delineation of management—which is about dealing with complexity—and leadership—which is about coping with change. As he comments, "Companies manage complexity first by planning and budgeting—setting targets or goals for the future (typically for the next month or year), establishing detailed steps for achieving those targets, and then allocating resources to accomplish those plans." Leading involves dealing with change through setting future vision and formulating strategies to achieve it.[13]

Executives' trusted advisors, who are on the front lines and struggle with complex operational decisions on a daily basis, are generally the first to look for decision-making assistance. At Intel, the first successful project that Kempf ever undertook started in conversations not with a senior vice president, but with a factory shift manager named Bruce who had a degree from MIT and had been contemplating alternative ways of making decisions about his shift.[14] As Kempf reports:

> Working together, Bruce and I designed a series of alternative approaches to making decisions during Bruce's shift. At the time, Bruce's factory was running four shifts around the

clock. Within a few months, the performance on Bruce's shift sparkled, with throughput 10 percent higher than the other shifts. Shortly thereafter, at a shift-managers' meeting, the plant manager asked, "What the heck is Bruce doing that you other guys aren't?" The resulting pressure helped get the other shift managers on board and in time, performance for the entire factory shot up, bringing pressure from above for the other factories to figure out what they should be doing to keep up.[15]

This type of "bottom-up" development is common in successful optimization efforts. Not only are senior executives unlikely to launch an optimization project; at times they can actually represent a formidable roadblock, given their deep confidence in their own decision-making abilities. At Amazon, Greg Linden was leading a software development team and had the idea of presenting recommendations at checkout time based on what was in a person's cart.[16] He began to play with the idea and to test what kind of impact it would have on purchase patterns. Two suggested hypotheses were that (1) it would stimulate additional purchases or (2) it would reduce conversion rates because it distracted buyers and prevent them from successfully completing the checkout process.

An Amazon senior vice president of marketing felt strongly, based on his personal intuition and many years of marketing experience, that the second case was sure to be the outcome. He ordered the tests halted. Fortunately for Amazon, quants are not always the best listeners. Linden rushed a quick prototype test into production and found overwhelming support for the conclusion that making recommendations at checkout significantly increased cross-selling and the size of the "average purchased basket." The rest is history. Today, almost every successful retail website makes suggestions for additional purchases at checkout.

Greg Linden was also fortunate in that Amazon had a strong culture for "letting the data speak." Once the evidence was in, the senior vice president backed down. It's hard to argue with success. The moral of the story: seek the support of senior executives—perhaps even recruit them as sponsors—but don't sit back and wait for them to originate your optimization project.

2. Subject Matter Experts (SMEs)

At the heart of any successful optimization project is the ability to consider and balance a large number of constraints, while reaching the best decision. The individuals most acquainted with these constraints are the people on the firing line. These SMEs have been wrestling with the decisions on a daily basis. They are the ones who possess the greatest knowledge of the detailed, nuanced, day-in-and-day-out operations of the business: how it really works, on the ground level.

Be prepared to invest a significant amount of your SMEs' time in having them brief the other members of the team about how they, the SMEs, make decisions; the constraints they operate under; what the "best" solutions would look like to them; and how they assessed the early prototypes of the software. SMEs are the go-to types whom the consultants rely on for both information to input into the computer program and for feedback on the results of the optimization software. One of the factors we look at to evaluate the readiness of an organization to engage in a successful optimization project is whether its SMEs are willing to spend time taking a deep dive into how they make decisions.

When UPS set out to optimize the movement of packages among its internal shipment locations, the company hardly lacked for SMEs. Each large hub had a "load planner" whose responsibility included planning the route of each package from its location to one of the other 1,300 UPS hubs and centers around the country. In launching the optimization project, director of process management Jack Levis and his team started in Willow Grove, Pennsylvania. His rationale was unassailable: the load planner in Willow Grove was reported to be the best in the company. He possessed a deep understanding of the constraints and how to juggle them to move packages through the system. "The initial goal," recounts Levis, "was to try to program the computer to make decisions that matched the very best decision maker we had. If we could do that, we could then move upward from there."[17]

The Willow Grove load planner was not the only SME included on the UPS team. Levis also included as project manager a 25-year veteran of UPS who possessed a firm grasp of the entire UPS shipping network. In addition, this individual had significant experience doing the planning job. Helping lead the optimization team—and serving as an SME in his own right—became the manager's full-time job for more than a year. At UPS, as in most companies that undertake optimization projects, the SMEs were heavily involved not only in describing constraints, but in testing early prototypes of the decision-making software. Although the UPS optimization team was small—just four individuals—the time commitment required of each member was significant. But it was repaid many times over once the system was up and running.

3. Support Personnel

Although a core optimization team is typically small, as the project evolves there are people throughout the organization who will be called on to contribute the data needed to create, install, test, and tweak the optimization software. Generally, their involvement is much less time-intensive than that of the core team.

Typical functions that possess information vital to the project are the IT and finance departments. Human resources (HR) may have a role as well, especially if the project results in personnel issues such as changes in job descriptions, changes in incentive plans, or possible restructuring of the workforce.

Marriott International's optimization efforts provide an example of the involvement of support personnel. Initially, Sharon Hormby and her team spent time with the individuals in charge of the reservation system to understand exactly what data were and were not available. As the team expanded the Revenue Opportunity Model to include group reservations, it moved into the field to interview executives throughout the system, focusing primarily on the staff of the 24 hotels responsible for 40 percent of Marriott's profit internationally. Team members wanted to hear from the field personnel making group reservations: What did they think about the moderately low Revenue Opportunity Model scores for group reservations? How did they think the making of group reservations could best be improved?

These larger hotels had their own revenue management staff that was only too happy to provide suggestions about how to improve the group reservation process. Optimization team members also needed to spend time with the salespeople who were making reservations, at both regional and individual hotel levels. They needed to home in on the kind of additional information the salespeople needed to do a better job and the type of information typically requested by inquiring prospects. In addition, many hours were spent working with members of the IT staff. They built and maintained all the computer systems that the GPO software needed to interface with to obtain data and make optimized pricing recommendations.

Last, while the optimization pricing programs were being developed, changes in the structure of the sales force were occurring. These involved creating area sales managers who could now—with the support of the optimization program—make reservations across multiple hotels. Such changes in roles and responsibilities, in turn, involved HR. As in an epic film, at Marriott International the core team of optimization stars was small, but the supporting cast was large.

4. Optimization Advisors/Consultants

The last, but certainly not the least, important members of the optimization team are optimization specialist(s). In larger companies, such as Marriott International or UPS, these individuals may be internal resources, although, as we will discuss in a moment, even large companies often bring in an external expert. At smaller companies, the optimization specialists are typically outsiders, as they were with the Jan de Wit Company.

When you are thinking of engaging an optimization advisor or consultant, keep in mind a number of important considerations. Optimization consultants are quants who focus on applying optimization techniques to real-world problems, and they are a unique breed. Think of them as brainiacs on a mission. They are driven to achieve practical results. Their passion is to create software programs that push the limits of computer applications. They could not care less about solving purely theoretical problems. They prefer digging into the nitty-gritty details of running a business and are fascinated by the idea that software can be used to improve operations: from reducing the miles that trucks must travel, to improving the ways planes are scheduled, to finding the perfect price that maximizes both sales and profits. All good optimization consultants want to perform miracles, succeed where others have failed, go where few have ventured.

Just as there are a number of distinctions between good and great optimization software, *great* optimization consultants differ from merely *good* ones in several ways. One of these is the way they think about the "size of the prize." Good optimizers create software to help clients reduce costs. But the best among them know that while cost reduction is a good thing, and you can grab market share by offering a lower-cost product, there are other ways to add value to your enterprise. You can, for instance, command a premium price for the same product by being faster, providing better service, or backing it up with a unique guarantee.

While great optimization consultants engage in hard-core IT and mathematics, their primary mind-set is firmly centered in understanding the strategy and tactics of their clients. They ask their clients: What do you see as the next round of competitive advantage? What is the potential for growing this business or for taking it to a new level of play? How big would the prize be if you could get into a new market or supply a new product to your existing market? And while strategy consultants ask the same questions from their sponsors, too often their deliverable is an impressive PowerPoint presentation that seems to imply that beating the competition is mainly about knowing what direction to head in, rather than digging deeply into the fine points of execution. Great optimizers, in contrast, believe that real competitive advantage comes from driving visionary direction with the best possible Optimization.

The very best optimization consultants differ from good optimizers in yet another way: they excel at relationship-building. They know that to be effective they must win the trust and respect not only of the members of the optimization team, but of others in the company—especially the decision makers they are working to help. Because project success depends heavily on the quality of the information that the consultants can elicit, they are adept at knowing which questions to ask and how to ask them: inquiring without intruding, judging, or accusing. They use straightforward business language, not arcane specialist language such as that used in optimization mathematics. In short, the best optimization consultants are adept at getting facts without friction.

Jack Levis talked about the fact-gathering process at UPS during the load planning optimization project:

> When we first went to Willow Grove, we took along with us a straw man—a possible approach for improving routing and scheduling. This provided a framework for the initial

discussion, and it sent a message that we had a few ideas that might well add value. The person doing the job doesn't want to feel that he needs to do all the directing. The first meeting with the load planner went the way it always does. He was skeptical and did not quite understand what we were attempting to do. Few people believe that a model or computer can do as good a job as they can. We assured the load planner that we weren't there because he was doing a bad job. In fact, just the opposite—we were there because he was a high performer.

Before long, the load planner opened up and began showing us the rule-of-thumb tools he had built for himself to help him make decisions. We questioned the what-why-how of what he was doing and shared our preliminary ideas with him. We learned from him, and he learned from us how he might enhance some of his tools and decisions. It was a win-win.[18]

Your best optimizer may not always be an industry expert. Classes of problems can show up in many guises, spanning a variety of different industries. When we started working with ArgentAir, executives in the company had already spoken with a number of aviation optimization experts. They hadn't been able to solve the airline's problem because they were unable to think out of the box.

When you think about it, even though ArgentAir is all about planes, its challenge is quite different from that facing large commercial airlines that operate according to fixed schedules and destinations set many months in advance. ArgentAir operates more like UPS, where each customer calls to have a shipment picked up and delivered at the time of his choosing.

The key to solving ArgentAir's scheduling challenges was to put aside the algorithms from the airline industry and look for relevant algorithms and solutions from an industry with a similar environment: in ArgentAir's case, the trucking industry. A good consultant knows the client's industry and what solutions have solved that industry's unique problems. A great consultant has experience in multiple industries and when necessary, can skillfully pull solutions from across industries.

Postscript on Choosing the Right Team

When all is said and done, you want the *most valuable* people in the organization on your optimization team. Availability is not a selection criterion; ability to contribute is. UPS, for example, did not ask which load planner had the time to be part of this effort; the company picked the best and brightest among the lot. Once you have the right team in place, you are ready to begin the next step in a successful optimization project.

Step 2: The Vision—Design Your Project

Much more is involved in the designing step of an optimization project than in designing a traditional IT project plan. The former involves *creating a detailed vision* of how the software will work, what kind of value the optimization software can bring to the organization, and the steps by which the software development will be carried out.

One of the quickest ways to scuttle an optimization project is to view it as "just another IT project." True, Optimization uses computers, but therein ends the similarity. Traditional IT projects begin by specifying end results. A firm set of requirements and a program design are set down before the designers proceed through a sequential set of steps, including development, testing, and rollout. Ideally, each of these steps relates to a detailed project plan that was created at the onset of the project. While some application programming is performed, along with selection of "off-the-shelf" components, it is rare for a traditional IT project to engage in true research and development (R&D).

In contrast, optimization projects tend to be far more fluid and creative. Most do not lend themselves to off-the-shelf software solutions; they require continuous R&D and experimentation. An optimization project is akin to developing a new type of material. At the outset, the material seems promising for a number of applications, but you are just not sure. So you test a few alternatives and assess the results. Often the first material tested lacks a critical property that leads to further refinement and retesting. It's a cycle that can be repeated many times.

That is the flavor of optimization R&D: "Let us try a few things, see how they work, see how people like them, see how quickly we can arrive at a solution, see if the solution is the correct one or if more data is required. If it's working, let's build on it; if not, let's revise and try again."

In our experience, successful optimization plans have three important characteristics:

- **Their early deliverables are planned to win over those who will be using the software.** Careful planning of the order of deliverables is designed to demonstrate that your agenda is not to replace people with software, but to put greater power into their hands.
- **They use optimization models that are data hungry, but not data impossible.** The right plan is smart about what information is available, in the short term, on a timely basis. Optimizers know that there is important data buried in the veins of an organization that will be difficult to extract without earning people's trust and respect. Therefore, they build into the plan the ability to continue operating without complete or perfect data.
- **The plan has more of a "skunk works" quality than a "big-project" flavor.** It is positioned more as investment in a high-value initiative than as a finite project. It engages the high achievers who are driven and capable of achieving great things, provided they are not weighed down by bureaucratic entanglements.

The many activities involved in designing an optimization project fall into three major categories:

1. Conducting research and analysis
2. Arriving at a final problem definition and "proof of concept"
3. Organizing the initiative into phases

Let's look more closely at each.

Conducting Research and Analysis

Research and analysis for an optimization project typically include a combination of modern management-science techniques and some traditional management consulting activities. The former ask for a good deal of data and involve rigorous analyses. For example, early on in considering whether to develop the GPO, the Marriott optimization team reviewed years of both individual and group reservation data to uncover important customer groupings and variables that could help predict the likelihood that a particular group would make a reservation. Rigorous, multivariate statistical analyses were carried out to distinguish between reliable predictors of behavior and noise in the data.

Qualitative data can also be important. Typically, optimization teams conduct traditional management consulting interviews with executives, line personnel, sales teams, customers, and even competitors. The goal of the interviews is to uncover the best opportunities for Optimization and calibrate an organization's readiness for it—a very important factor in deciding how to design and schedule project deliverables.

When it comes to optimization readiness, a variety of attributes influence the design of a good implementation plan. For example, large organizations like Marriott International and UPS may already have a lengthy history of using Optimization. They are also likely to have internal OR and IT professionals who can provide project support. On the other hand, smaller companies such as the Jan de Wit Company not only lack internal resources, but the scarcity of optimization users within their industry makes it hard for them to find appropriate external consultants. Even large organizations with substantial IT resources often find it advantageous to bring in an external specialist. For example, as I will discuss in a little while, in developing its proof of concept for the GPO, Marriott International employed two external consultants even though the company had internal experts that it used for the actual software development and implementation.

Other important organizational attributes should be considered when designing an optimization project plan. One is whether or not the organization "runs a tight ship." If an organization has 20 schedulers and each day randomly assigns them to different clients or subgroups, the organization likely runs a tight ship. Interchangeability requires a common, consistent pattern of operation. But if each scheduler is always assigned to the same client or area, and there is no interchange among them, then count on variations among the processes that the schedulers use. For example, if a truck dispatcher always works with the same drivers, he or she may know that one driver avoids a particular route, while another prefers it. So the dispatcher factors these preferences into the scheduling, building artificial constraints—rules that depend on this personal knowledge—into the process.

In loosely run organizations such as the trucking company just mentioned, the optimizer's job is much more challenging because process-reengineering or procedural changes must be made before the optimization work can begin. At Intel, for example, after Karl Kempf had worked with his colleague Bruce to optimize the decisions being made on one shift, the other three shift managers—at the urging of the plant manager—became interested in adopting some of Bruce's methods. Kempf recounts, "After lots of resistance and machinations we got all four shift managers to agree to use a common set of decision policies. That was important because Bruce and I figured out (at 2:00 A.M. one morning, in our little booties and hairnets) that if every shift made decisions in different ways, we would have no idea how to debug this thing. . . . One of our big breakthroughs was getting all four shifts to follow the same decision policies. Then we could move on and improve how decisions were being made."[19]

The best way to determine the extent of process variance is to conduct interviews, early on, with the various shifts or groups. The finance and quality functions of an organization are often good information sources, as is IT. IT departments typically know how planning is done across the organization: on spreadsheets, on a whiteboard, or in a standardized or ad hoc manner. They know how different areas solve problems and make decisions. Because every function and unit inputs information into the company's computer systems, IT is aware of daily usage patterns and the accuracy of data entry. For example, as a rule, customer-service departments are required to register levels of satisfaction of all customers with whom they interact. But all too often the "satisfied" box is checked, even when complaints occur. IT is a good place to start to learn about the frequency and magnitude of the problem.

An additional important factor in planning an optimization project is the level of trust between management and workers. When Quad/Graphics began developing software to schedule its binding runs, it could easily have been viewed as a threat by the schedulers.

This, however, was not the case, and the schedulers quickly jumped on board, doing an exceptional job as SMEs helping the optimization team. When asked why the initiative was so well received by the workforce, Simon Lee, one of our firm's consultants on the project, offered, "Quad is very family oriented. It seems to have a culture of trust and lots of programs that support its employees. It also has a cultural value: 'We build and make things ourselves.' Everyone in the organization is very open and willing to try new things." The more open an organization is to innovation and the higher the level of trust between management and employees, the easier it is to introduce new decision-making processes.

Organizations that are accustomed to doing things "by the numbers" and that have computerized many of their operations are typically more open to accepting optimization solutions than nonquantitatively oriented companies. First, there is less suspicion surrounding the use of computers to assist in management of production; second, such organizations have often already digitized significant amounts of data—the fuel that propels Optimization.

But just because your organization is computerized and quantified, don't be lulled into a false sense of security that it will embrace Optimization. In many organizations, computers have been relegated to low-level database-management tasks. The computers sort through, manipulate, and organize information, but decision making continues to be viewed as a job for humans. The step of entrusting machines with decision making can be a big one and may be fiercely resisted regardless of the degree to which computers have permeated the organization. The amount of anticipated resistance will determine how much education you will need to include in your implementation plan and the degree to which your early prototypes will need to be positioned as "assistants" for helping human decision makers, as opposed to preemptors of the decision-making process.

Arriving at a Final Problem Definition and Proof of Concept

If you have reached this point in the evolution of an optimization project, chances are that you have a good idea of where improved decision making could strengthen your competitive position. During development of the vision, the problem definition is refined further and a proof of concept is developed and discussed with the organization.

Early on in the visioning process, optimization team members work to identify key project objectives, along with those features of an optimization program that would add the most value. The optimization consultants steer the group, providing the SMEs with an array of options and then gauging their responses. Typical questions posed by the consultants include:

- What factors are changing the way business is conducted, and what is driving the need for a better model?
- How are decisions currently being made: by whom and with what data and guidance? How do you determine whether or not a decision is a good one?
- What sorts of decisions are largely out of your hands—such as those based on long-term contracts?
- What does the flow of information look like when decisions are made? What currently unavailable information would help people make better decisions?
- What are the economic and service consequences of poor decisions at each point?
- Where do you believe optimization technology can systematically improve the way you make decisions?
- What would be the economic benefits of optimal decisions in the areas you just identified?
- How would optimal decision making in these areas improve your ability to serve existing customers and gain new ones?

The result of the questioning is an understanding of the best optimization opportunities: what decisions Optimization could help most and what information is needed to make them. In Step 1, exploratory thinking would have identified an opportunity area for Optimization, such as airplane scheduling. In the vision step, this initial thinking is refined into a final problem definition, such as minimizing empty air miles. This refined definition of the problem will evolve as the team thinks more deeply about the objectives and delves into the available data, exploring ideas and opportunities through give-and-take dialogue.

There is a high level of frankness at these design meetings. In every organization, there is a "party line": the politically correct answer to the question, "What drives this business?" The answer is often a string of platitudes such as, "We treat all customers the same," "Quality is our number-one concern," and "We will do anything to satisfy a customer."

Optimization consultants are truth seekers. They slice through the platitudes to uncover what the organization really values and how it actually behaves. What is most important to the owners or managers? What do they really want to achieve: the highest customer-satisfaction ratings or the greatest profits? Quality awards or new accounts? The best optimization consultants excel at getting people to open up and provide them with a window into reality.

Getting employees to give you clear, measurable objectives—gaining agreement on the relative importance of these objectives and how they relate to one another—puts consultants' brainpower and intuition to the test. When we first interview SMEs and support personnel, we often find ourselves wading through fuzzy objectives and the all-too-familiar rah-rah statements, such as, "Quality is job one," and "Our job is to exceed our customers' expectations." The hard rocks of reality have a way of imposing a check on such excess. Posing tough trade-off questions is a great fuzz buster. If customer satisfaction is an imperative, how far would you fly an empty plane to pick someone up in Los Angeles? Would you fly it from Chicago? From New York? From Europe? Such questions set the "pain point"—the *real* cutoff—in customer service. This information can be programmed into the software that will be used to make allocation decisions.

Conversely, if the company is willing to go beyond the pain point for "special" customers, the consultant must explore the exceptions and why they are made. What makes those accounts so important? Where, compared to others, is the cutoff point for them? Once the consultant has that information, it can be factored into the model.

The relative importance of objectives is in the eye of the beholder. The folks in operations tend to be more efficiency and cost driven than those in sales and customer service. The project sponsor plays a pivotal role in making sure that the optimization project reflects the right balance of objectives and that the project team is aligned around them.

One way of learning about how decisions are really made in a company is to act like a Supreme Court justice: spend your time looking at decisions at the boundaries—situations that can teeter in one of several ways. Early in my career, for example, I was working with a nationwide moving company to optimize the scheduling of its truck fleet. The president of the company had recently published a 10-point vision statement that appeared on every computer in the company whenever they were booted up. The eighth point in the vision was, "We will never turn down a load." This simple statement had the potential of scuttling the entire optimization project, since deciding when *not* to go after a load was key to developing an optimal schedule. Someone had to go talk with the president to find out if it was really the case that a load could never be turned down. Although young at the time—and possibly because of it!—I got the assignment.

The president seemed to sense my nervousness and made an effort to put me at ease. However, when I told him that I needed to speak with him about point number eight in his vision statement, the air turned noticeably chillier. I explained to him that I needed to explore some situations when his folks might need to turn down a load to make sure that the software would be able to do what he wanted it to. As we talked about various scenarios, the president loosened up and actually canceled his next meeting to continue sharing his views with me. I laid out various scenarios, pushing the president to make tough decisions about whom to service first when resources ran low. For example, if he had only one truck available, would he send it to a loyal, highly valued, long-term customer or to a new customer who was thinking of switching hauling companies: someone who was testing the company's responsiveness?

During the meeting, the president took time to explain to me the thinking behind his vision statement. For many years, trucking had been a regulated industry. Employees had taken little initiative, acting much like government employees, simply waiting for customers to come to them. The president felt that more than anything the company needed a major change in attitude and culture—thus his insistence on adhering to the new vision statement.

In the end, the president became a champion of the new optimization software, or Operations Planning System, that did indeed occasionally turn down a load. But he kept the vision statement, including the eighth point, to set a customer-focused tone. To really understand how decisions are made—or should be made—optimizers cannot be afraid to push the limits, even at the risk of making a CEO uncomfortable.

One of the most important ways in which the definition of an optimization problem is refined is by deciding how to measure its payback, or return on investment (ROI). In many cases this will be expressed in dollar savings, although there may be some "softer" benefits as well, which are related to improvements in product or service quality.

At Marriott International, Hormby and her team measured the payback as a percentage-point improvement compared to the theoretical best, as defined by their Revenue Opportunity Model. Each percentage point of improvement could be translated into a dollar amount to help executives evaluate exactly what the projected return for investing in the project would be. In the case of ArgentAir, a key metric was minimizing empty air miles, which also had an associated dollar value. At Quad/Graphics, the focus became the number of times the presses had to be stopped for a changeover, since the cost of downtime could be quantified in dollars.

Once the payback measures are identified, the next question is whether Optimization can improve it—and if so, by exactly how much? In short, what is the likely "size of the prize" from optimizing? Not only must optimization team members convince themselves that they can program a solution to the problem after taking into account the relevant decision constraints; they must also convince their business partners that the project is feasible and that the resulting payoff will be worth the investment. This is what proof of concept (POC) is all about.

At Marriott, internal optimization team members actually hired two external consultants to help them test their ideas about the GPO program. One consultant was an expert in traditional airline revenue management models; the other came from a supply-chain-pricing background. What the Marriott optimization team was testing was whether both individuals—coming from different perspectives and working independently—would be able to spot the same revenue savings opportunities that the Marriott optimization team had seen. Optimization projects typically represent major interventions that have a widespread impact on an organization. It's important to be able to demonstrate the value before beginning full-scale implementation.

At ArgentAir, the POC step was particularly important, since we were recommending the use of truck-routing algorithms to optimize the plane schedules. Not only did we need to demonstrate that such algorithms could produce schedules that significantly reduce empty air miles; we needed to show that they could do so *quickly*. Often, when an ArgentAir user calls to reschedule a flight, the company has hours, not days, to get a plane there. In addition, the schedule adjustment can impact multiple flights, some of which may be scheduled even earlier than the pickup time being requested. A new schedule needs to be generated in minutes, not hours.

An important part of any POC is confirming that the right data is available when it is needed. As noted earlier, optimization models should be data hungry, not data impossible. When UPS first began working on a computer program to generate optimal delivery routes for its brown package trucks to arrive at your door, it ran into a big problem. The publically available street maps initially used by the program to generate solutions had too many errors to provide an accurate solution. POC had to await a lengthy investment of time and money to upgrade the street maps.

Early on in the POC process, the Marriott team was searching for characteristics that would help it predict the likelihood that a group would accept the offered room price. Searching through mounds of data, the team found that one of the best predictors was a group's need for audiovisual equipment. A group was much more likely to reserve a room regardless of price when it had a significant need for audiovisual equipment.

When the Marriott optimization team sat down with its business partners to discuss its model and the variables it was considering using to set prices, team members met initial skepticism and a few wry grins. It seemed that even though sales managers were supposed to note audiovisual needs when a prospect first called for a reservation, in most cases this need was not discussed until *after* the reservation was made. With the data being entered only after a reservation had been made, it was not surprising that audiovisual needs correlated so strongly with the making of a reservation.

This incident illuminates an important requirement for successful Optimization: not only does the right data need to be available; it needs to be available at the right time. It also illustrates why it is so important for an optimization team to work closely with its business partners. They are the ones that best know the realities of what's happening on the front line.

As the optimization team works on developing the proof of concept, it invariably holds multiple meetings with the business sponsor to talk about progress. These include numerous exchanges such as, "Here are a number of projects we can tackle, each with different levels of impact, resource commitments, and time to completion. Which do you want?" Or "You asked for x. We can't do that. You asked for y. That is more realistic. It seems to us that project y would have the best return on investment for reasons A, B, and C. What does it look like to you?"

There is one sure killer of optimization initiatives that must be addressed during such give-and-take sessions: unrealistic expectations. All too often, our consultants encounter executives who have had a great experience with Optimization in the past or have heard about a successful application. They see it as a magic bullet that will save the company. This is a danger signal that will send any reputable consultant running. As always, it is better to underpromise and overdeliver.

Organizing the Initiative into Phases

In the chapter that follows, I will describe in detail the first deliverables of several optimization projects. Here I merely want to mention that planning the deliverables—and the rate at which they will be produced—is an important final element in the design of any optimization project. The best plan will depend to a large degree on the readiness of the organization. Nevertheless, bear in mind some important concepts as you consider how to schedule the deliverables:

• **Get something useful into people's hands quickly.** The quicker you can develop "must have" tools—those that create user dependency from the outset because of their usefulness—the quicker you will develop a cadre of champions for the optimization project. You know you have arrived when users, especially SMEs and other thought leaders, proclaim, "Wow, this helps me work much faster and smarter. It's dynamite."

• **Avoid black boxes.** Steer clear of "big black box" Optimization: creating a big software solver that produces a megasolution in some mysterious way. Big black box Optimization is a favored alternative of some academics who, in effect, say to businesses, "Trust me, I have a Ph.D." and "We can optimize your decisions in this area. Just give us all your data, and we will run it through our solver and then send you the results. All you have to do is make sure your IT system is ready to install it."

Unfortunately, such megasolutions are invariably launched with errors, which leads to a great deal of back-and-forth rework, reconfiguration, and loss of credibility. The people who are being asked to use the software are not trained mathematicians, so it is unlikely that they understand how or why the software is making a certain recommendation. Furthermore, if and when an error does occur, you have no idea why. Was it bad data? Was it an inappropriate algorithm? Perhaps it was a problem with the user interface?

However seductive the idea of solving all of an enterprise's problems with a black-box optimizer, it is far better to opt for a series of incremental, transparent solutions. Users do not need to understand the intricacies of the software, but they must be given insight into *why it is making the recommendations it makes*: the rationale behind its recommendations.

- **Collect extensive user feedback.** It's not an exaggeration to say that you can't get too much user feedback. In every step of the project, from conceptualizing the problem area to deploying the final piece of software, show the users what you are doing in incremental steps and get their feedback. We like to refer to the process as Rapid Action Delivery (RAD): do some development, deliver some value, collect lots of feedback, create more value with additional development, collect more feedback, and continue executing the cycle.

- **Plan an effective cycle time for deliverables.** Here rhythm is the key. Cycle too quickly and users become fatigued; cycle too slowly and you wind up solving last year's hot problem. Striking the right balance in terms of timing for a new deliverable entails pegging it to situational dynamics. Should you aim to produce a new deliverable monthly, quarterly, or annually? You need to find the happy medium, which will vary with every organization and project.

At ArgentAir, for example, two separate groups did the scheduling: one that laid out the schedule for the following two to three days and another that handled daily scheduling emergencies as they occurred. When our firm first began working with the company, we decided to focus our efforts on one of the two groups: the longer-range planning group. We promised members of the group a quick solution that they could modify to improve their three-day plans, and we delivered it within six months.

Since then, every three to six months we have provided additional software that continues to refine their planning. There has been ongoing improvement at a comfortable pace. The project has been so successful that the original sponsors have been promoted, which is a nice fringe benefit for properly executing an optimization project.

To summarize, upon completing the design step in an optimization project, you should have accomplished the following:

- In-depth research and analysis—both quantitative and qualitative—of the problem area
- Final problem definition
- Identification of key decision constraints and how decisions are currently being made in the absence of optimization software
- Agreement on how success will be measured
- The testing of algorithms and alternative approaches for finding solutions in an acceptable amount of time
- Estimates of the benefits—the size of the prize—to be gained by Optimization of the decisions
- Assurance that the data needed for a solution can be captured in a timely fashion
- A proposed first deliverable
- The generation of an increased number of supporters and champions of the project

In the next chapter we will discuss the remaining three steps in the planning process of successful optimization project:

- Step 3: The Early Win—Deliver Value Quickly
- Step 4: The Scale-Up—Extend the Usage
- Step 5: The Harvest—Leverage the Benefits

CHAPTER 6

READY, SET, EXECUTE

Technology can have unintended consequences. Years ago, an anthropologist by the name of Lauriston Sharp studied the effects of the introduction of the steel axe on the Yir Yoront, a group of Australian aboriginals.[1] Technologically, the Yir Yoront culture was of the Stone Age or Paleolithic type. In this environment, the polished *stone* axe—a tool carefully fabricated, owned, and jealously guarded by the male members of the group—was a pivotal economic tool used for hunting, fishing, gathering vegetables, chopping wood, and the like. But beyond economic utility, the stone axe was an important piece of cultural equipment: it helped define and clarify sex, age, and kinship roles. It was a key for building male-to-male relationships outside the group, and it was an important symbol of masculinity and male dominance.

Things changed with the arrival of a group of Anglican missionaries who, in an attempt to win over souls and make life easier for the Yir Yoront, indiscriminately—and in large numbers—introduced the *steel* axe into the group. The consequences were unintended and severe. The males' sense of self-reliance was compromised, since the missionaries dispensed the new technology to men and women alike. The now-universal possession of axes led to a radical change in sex, age, and kinship roles, while compromising traditional ideas and values. Ultimately, Sharp reports, this led to "a mental and moral void that foreshadowed the collapse and destruction of all Yir Yoront culture if not, indeed, the biological group itself."[2]

Talk about the unintended consequences of technology! Whether it involves aboriginal people in a subsistence economy or those of us who live in today's wired, postindustrial society, avoiding the unintended consequences of even the best technology requires carefully integrating it into the prevailing order. Success requires adept change management.

Optimization is no exception. As a growing number of organizations are beginning to realize its potential for breakthrough performance, leaders need to understand that Optimization, like any new technology, requires careful attention to managing its introduction and consequences: in other words, to *managing change*. Like the steel axe that touched the heart of the social life of the Yir Yoront, Optimization touches the vital core of organizational life: how decisions are made and problems are solved. When you think about it, decision making has profound symbolic and cultural meaning to everyone in an organization, reflecting as it does the organization's norms, values, status, roles, and patterns of behavior. Make a significant change in how decisions get made and implemented, and you make a change that is potentially as profound as what the Yir Yoront experienced. Given Optimization's impact on decision making, its introduction within an organization must be undertaken with great care and within the context of an effective change management process.

Optimization: A Framework for Change

At the end of Chapter 5, I indicated that this chapter would take you through Steps 3, 4, and 5 of the process behind a successful optimization project. Because the notion of change management is so critical to each of those steps, I first would like to say a bit more about it before getting into the details of each step.

Based on my consulting experience, here are six points that, taken together, serve as framework for managing the changes associated with Optimization:

1. Optimization Must Address a Compelling Business Issue

Executives and managers don't move to acquire optimization technology because they suddenly have an Aha! moment. Don't expect a bolt of lightning to descend on your leadership team and everyone exclaim in unison, "We gotta have Optimization." More typically, a significant business issue presents itself: the business is becoming more complex, assets are underutilized in the face of growing competition, the time it takes to bring a new product to market is getting longer and longer, or decision "hang time" is increasing. There is a prevailing sense that the old ways are no longer sufficient.

Unless you can make a solid business case for Optimization, tying it into these or similar issues, it will likely go the way of most initiatives: plenty of initial rah-rah, but not much in the way of concrete results. Nor will you be able to command the attention and active support of senior management, which is key to project success.

2. Pacing Is Crucial; Avoid the Big-Bang Syndrome

The last decade of the 20th century might be called the era of big-bang change. It was a time when many organizations were busy restructuring, reengineering, renewing, right sizing, and TQMing. Initiatives both grand and modest were cascaded down through organizations in the hope that enterprisewide fixes would lead to greater competitive advantage.

Some of these changes were undoubtedly successful, but in many organizations employees began to tire of all the hubbub, and a widespread case of initiative fatigue set in. Besides, most of the initiatives sought to improve the "what is," when what was called for were new hypotheses and new knowledge that would allow organizations not only to catch up with, but also to break away from the competition.

Optimization does not work well as part of a high-voltage change initiative designed to radically and quickly alter an entire organization in a single bound. It works best when you (1) position it against a specific business issue, in a discreet problem area, (2) work within the optimization framework to develop and test new hypotheses for managing assets, and (3) allow the emerging software and knowledge that it imparts to take hold and demonstrate value before looking for other deployment opportunities.

At the rail carrier we mentioned earlier, Optimization eventually revolutionized the pricing of intermodal shipping by moving sales online and allowing customers to bypass the sales team altogether: selecting themselves the shipping route that best met their budget and schedule requirements. But that's not where the change began. The first step was to provide the sales team with software that helped it evaluate feasible loads, container availability, and pricing constraints. Only after the sales team and senior executives gained confidence in the accuracy of the software's recommendations could they consider revolutionizing their business model by moving it online.

3. Anticipate the Unintended Consequences of Optimization

We have already discussed the need to think through the unintended consequences of technological adaptation. Here I simply want to highlight two key perspectives that must be examined when embedding Optimization into an organization. One is the organization's internal environment; the other is its external one.

Internally

In what ways will Optimization affect the structure, systems, culture, and capabilities of your organization? What, if any, actions must be taken to manage any likely unintended consequences? Over time, a natural rhythm develops within an organization. Different functions and departments learn to work in sync with one another's decision-making processes. If one department suddenly becomes a super decision maker, how will it impact the departments around it? At UPS, for example, Optimization of the network planners altered the flow of packages into the sorting hubs, causing the hubs to reevaluate whether they had the correct personnel to handle the load. Whether or not you optimize, decisions tend to have a cross impact. Change the way decisions are made in one area of the business, and you will likely affect the decision-making processes in other areas as well.

Externally

Focusing solely on the impact of Optimization on the internal environment is not enough. What about the impact on customers, competitors, and suppliers? What unintended consequences can be anticipated in these areas, and what, if any, actions must be taken to address them? For a number of years, the Piedmont Triad Airport in Greensboro, North Carolina, was one of the fastest-growing airports in the state, outstripping its facilities as well as the infrastructure that supported it. One of the primary causes? The revenue-management computer program designed to optimize revenue in the U.S. Airways hub in Charlotte, North Carolina, was pricing flights from Charlotte to the Northeast Corridor higher than those from Greensboro. When heading northeast, many people living in the northern suburbs of Charlotte were willing to drive an additional 30 minutes to fly out of Greensboro, which saved them hundreds of dollars.

In this case, Optimization had an impact not only on customer behavior, but on highway congestion, airport crowding, regional infrastructure strains, and eventually, competitors who adjusted their services as a result of the differences in the ticket prices.

4. Pay Attention to the "Soft Side" of Organizational Life: The Cultural Patterns and the Psychology of Human Decision Making

Psychologists tell us that beneath the conscious life of human beings lies the hidden zone of the unconscious, which can have a decisive influence on our behavior. So, too, with organizations: beneath the visible pattern of decision making lies an area of tacitly held values and beliefs that can exercise a kind of gravitational pull on the choices the organization makes. Many organizations are unknowingly risk averse, are intolerant of ambiguity, or operate by "seat of the pants" choices. Such cultural traits can have a hard-to-discern influence over strategic and operational decisions. Senior executives shape the values of their organizations. Sometimes they do this explicitly by crafting vision statements—recall the trucking company president I spoke about in Chapter 5, whose new service imperative to "refuse no load" ran up against operational realities that at times required managers to turn down business. More often, executives do it implicitly, by the actions they take. The end of Chapter 4 provided a questionnaire to test "How Receptive Is Your Culture" to Optimization? If you look back at that instrument, you will see that many of the questions relate to your organization's senior executives. Review carefully the answers that you gave, paying special attention to those that reveal values in action, rather than those expressed in annual reports or mounted on plaques in corner offices.

Beyond analyzing your organizational culture, pay special attention to the psyche of the individuals who make up your workforce. Technophobia and fear of job loss need to be addressed head-on. "I was born the twin of fear," 17th-century philosopher Thomas Hobbes wrote in his *Leviathan*.[3] If Hobbes were alive today, he could readily point to the contemporary workplace as an extension of his condition. The modern organization has become a holding pen of fear, given the end of "guaranteed for life" employment and the never-ending whiplash of economic cycles, global competition, outsourcing, and cost containment—hardly have we scratched the surface.

Even the most progressive organization can harbor hidden pockets of neo-Luddite technophobia. Not that there's much rioting in the streets and smashing of equipment, as was the case in Britain between 1811 and 1816, when workers destroyed labor-saving textile machinery. But the ongoing and unrelenting introduction of new technology—computers, robots, and, in our experience, Optimization—inevitably causes workplace stress, fear of job loss, and an assault on one's view of oneself as a valued contributor.

In terms of Optimization, there is a natural tendency to see the technology as a rival of human beings, given its decision-making speed and power. To allay such fears, it is important to carefully position Optimization: in the short term, not as a job killer but as a job aid; in the long term, as a career advancer. Employees need to understand that Optimization puts extra oomph in the hands of decision makers; it doesn't replace human judgment, but informs it; it opens up the very real possibility of achieving levels of performance previously thought to be unattainable. And while there are no guarantees, isn't superior performance the best insurance policy for job security, especially in times of volatility and resource constraints?

5. Make Sure That Employees Have the Right Capabilities

Those who will be using optimization technology need not take a deep dive into the intricacies of the algorithm "brain" of the software. What they really need to know is how, when, and why to use the software. This requires that anyone "touching" the system be clear about the objectives and what constitutes effective performance; that the right resources are in place to do the job, including a user-friendly interface and ongoing system support; and that there is a balance of positive and negative consequences in place to reinforce desired behavior.

Here are some questions to test whether or not the right capabilities are in place for your optimization project:

- Are all users of the system clear about the goals *and* the behaviors needed to achieve those goals?
- Have users acquired the skills they need to operate the software correctly?
- Is there a feedback loop in place that is timely and geared to users' "teachable moments?"
- Is there the right balance of positive and negative consequences for individual performance?

Finally, as we have noted, not all the skills needed for success are necessarily related to the use of the software. Marriott's senior director of total yield systems, Sharon Hormby, and her team included in their training for leaders a seminar on change management. They had the wisdom to recognize that the biggest challenge would not be the mechanics of using the new software, but rather getting people to do things in new ways.

6. Keep a Tight Focus on Progress; Insist on Feedback Measures to Share with Users, as Well as with Management

I remember being told about a study of charitable giving in small towns. The study compared those towns that had a visible display of the money collected—we've all seen those posterboard thermometers indicating progress toward a goal—with those without a visible measure of success. Towns that measured progress and shared the results with the community outperformed the others. There is truth to the axiom that what gets measured gets done.

Put your optimization project to the measurement test by asking:

- Do we have clear, measurable objectives that define the overall success of the project?
- Are there mileposts and related measures in place, throughout the life cycle of the project, to track ongoing progress toward the project goals?
- Have clear measures of success been established for each of the five steps in Optimization (selection, design, identification of deliverables, scaling up, leveraging benefits)?
- Are there mechanisms in place to collect feedback on the soft issues? How do employees perceive the innovations: as a threat or a job aid?
- Is measured progress being shared with all of the right people?

Management gurus tell us that effective feedback has a number of common characteristics: it is timely, direct, never personal, and it focuses on observed behavior. Rather than accentuating the negative, effective feedback focuses on specific behavioral issues and positions the feedback as an opportunity for dialogue and discussion.

When providing feedback, timeliness is next to godliness. At UPS, Director of Process Management Jack Levis likes to program into all his software a small scorecard displayed in the corner of the screen. The scorecard provides the user with immediate feedback on the decision he has made compared to the computer's recommendation. Levis has managed to harness the natural competitiveness of UPS workers to draw them into using the software and self-evaluating as they compete with the software.

We are now ready to look at the remaining three steps in the optimization process in detail. As we do so, think about each step in light of the change framework just described.

Step 3: The Early Win—Deliver Value Quickly

A 2006 study of 500 speed-daters in Edinburgh, Scotland, found that 45 percent of the women and 22 percent of the men came to a decision within the first 30 seconds of their interaction.[4] In his book *Blink*,

Malcolm Gladwell documents even faster conclusions reached at a subconscious level by experts making complex evaluations about such things as authenticating a master's painting.[5] No doubt about it, whatever the situation, first impressions count for a lot. They certainly do when a person evaluates new software.

I Believe It. Not!

It's not just first impressions you need to worry about when introducing an early optimization prototype. In many cases, users come with a built-in censor that prompts them to think, "No way." Bill Boga recently retired from UPS. While working for the company, he was called in by the operations research (OR) team to evaluate its new feeder-scheduling software. He walked into the meeting convinced that the software would not work.[6] Boga was a feeder scheduler for many years and knew firsthand just how complex the job could be. Feeder schedulers are not only responsible for scheduling large tractor-trailer trucks to carry newly received packages to sorting centers, but they often have to schedule en route load transfers. These take place at truck stops and involve one truck transferring a partial load to another vehicle that is headed for the same destination as that partial load.

At the time that Boga was asked to evaluate the optimization software, as many as 22,000 tractor trailer loads were being generated each day, headed for 200 different hubs and 1,100 delivery centers. The challenge was to design schedules that would minimize the trucks' road time, get all packages to their correct destination, and keep all the trucks as full as possible. To further complicate the situation, everything could change in an instant if a load was cancelled after the schedules had been developed.

Back in the 1970s, Boga had actually been involved in evaluating a piece of software designed to help with the feeder-scheduling task. Although promising in concept, the software proved excruciatingly slow and the solutions it generated were unimplementable. When Boga arrived to evaluate the new load-scheduling software, it wasn't an issue of first impressions; it was an issue of a preformed, strong, negative impression that went back to his 1970s experience. Boga was also worried that a computer program—even one that somehow could miraculously be made to work—would not have his personal interest in mind. The program was designed to look across UPS districts and find the cheapest routes. As Boga told us:

> The computer might turn around and say that the cheapest solution was for me to add a couple of drivers, with the promise that some other district would cut drivers. That wouldn't necessarily be in my interest, since we'd incur additional costs. My manager would ask why I allowed this to happen, and I'd have to tell him that I was following computer orders. It wouldn't go over very well.[7]

When it comes to giving up decision-making power to a computer, Boga's experiences and attitudes are hardly unique. More often than not, people come in with a strong bias that the work they do is too complex for a computer to handle or with a concern that the computer will put their job in jeopardy. To overcome this resistance, the first deliverable of an optimization project must be carefully planned to provide users with quick success, making believers out of them as soon as possible.

What's the Real Objective Here?

Academicians and theorists sometimes seem confused about the true purpose of the first deliverable of an optimization project. They act as if the most important thing is to demonstrate that the computer can make better decisions than its human counterpart. In most cases there is really no contest. The computer has multiple high-powered processors with incredible calculating speed; it has the capability to rapidly search gargantuan databases in the blink of an eye; it is loaded with mathematical algorithms that can combine and weigh information much more accurately than humans, especially when probabilities need to be combined; and it will work tirelessly 24/7 without demanding overtime pay. But it is counterproductive to point all this out to a new user. The main purpose of the first deliverables is not to prove how smart the computer is—that is a given. Rather, it is to prove that the computer can be *a valuable assistant that can make the new user a superstar.*

Planning the first optimization deliverable is somewhat analogous to climbing Maslow's hierarchy of survival needs: for greatest success, begin by providing solutions to basic problems that are causing people pain. Once you are successfully meeting this basic need, you can move up the ladder and tackle more sophisticated needs.

At Quad/Graphics, Princeton Consultants took just such a go-slow approach. The optimization team's first deliverable did not attempt to schedule the equipment. Rather, they simply developed a program that could calculate the associated cost of the schedules being developed. This allowed the human schedulers to compare and evaluate alternative schedules that *they* had developed to make an easier choice among them. In essence, it helped them be better schedulers.

Once the schedulers felt comfortable with the costing program, the optimization team took another baby step by developing a program that could generate a production run. In this initial scheduling program, all of the parameters describing the constraints were entered by the Quad/Graphic schedulers. This allowed the schedulers to retain control and to use their knowledge and experience in developing the schedule. In essence, the optimization team positioned the computer program as needing the schedulers' help, not the other way around. Only after the schedulers were comfortable with the computer-generated schedules did the team take the next step: having the computer begin to calculate most of the parameters and constraints, rather than having the schedulers enter them.

In similar fashion, when Jack Levis and his OR team at UPS took an early prototype of their load-planning program to Willow Grove, Pennsylvania, they had designed the program not only to make recommendations about where to send partial trailer loads, but also to display the data that the program was using to generate its recommendations. This included shipments being planned from other package centers around the country. The Willow Grove planner could use this data to make better decisions himself, even when he chose not to follow the program's recommendation. This helped depersonalize his concerns about the program and gave him an appreciation of how both he and the program could make better decisions using the additional information.

The planner at Willow Grove was not asked to accept the computer's recommendations. Rather, Levis and his team cleverly asked him to merely evaluate the appropriateness of the computer-generated routes. They also asked him what additional information would help him create even better schedules and how the computer's recommendations might be improved. Not a word was uttered to suggest that the computer's recommendations were somehow superior. In fact, from the beginning the stated goal was simply to see if the computer could begin to match the quality of the planner's efforts.

Keep 'Em Talking

Apart from being useful, the second most important objective of a first deliverable is to elicit feedback. The feedback can be of several varieties. One type of feedback is designed to test the speed and accuracy of the software's algorithms, in real time, under field conditions. Decision-making computers, like their human counterparts, must negotiate between the competing demands of response speed and accuracy. While the ideal solution is an optimal one, in the real world of applications the optimal solution may need to be sacrificed for a very good solution that can be computed within an appropriate time frame.

As Intel's Karl Kempf explains, ". . . even though we spend a lot of time trying to figure out the optimal answer using some fairly sophisticated math, that's not what the people who use the tools want. They want it to run fast and give them answers that are 95 percent accurate."[8] Feedback during field testing of an early prototype provides the programmer with a test of whether speed and accuracy have been appropriately balanced.

Surely the most important feedback captures the user's opinion about the utility and accuracy of the software. Often, the user has valuable suggestions about how both can be improved. This not only helps improve the program, but it can create a sense of "mine" on the part of the user. High involvement does indeed equal high commitment!

At Marriott, it was user feedback from the sales managers during early prototype testing that led to the idea of displaying market information on screen. This enabled a salesperson to justify the offered rates, thereby discouraging the prospect from shopping the competition. You can bet that the salespeople suggesting these modifications were enthusiastic early adopters.

Kempf believes so strongly in the importance of feedback that he includes in all of his optimization programs a code that tracks how users are using the software. Of most interest to Kempf and his team is whether a user is correctly applying the software to explore and expand knowledge of the decision space or is misusing the software by playing with different variables to justify a decision that the user has already formed before interacting with the computer. "There is no decision tool we have ever made that a person couldn't 'game.' We want to know if this is what's happening or if users trust the software enough to help them make better decisions."[9]

Building "Big Mo"

A final important goal for an early deliverable is to continue building support for the project throughout the organization. Although the proof of concept (POC) established during the design step is important for gaining initial funding, a working prototype that has measurable value for the business and is embraced by grateful users is the best way to ensure continued funding for any project. At ArgentAir, for example, once it was apparent that the computer-generated routes were significantly reducing empty air miles, with associated dollar savings, funds were made available to develop the additional programs to handle schedule changes and to continuously search the schedules for additional ways to eliminate shuttles.

But don't be surprised if even a successful prototype fails to win over every doubting Thomas in the organization. At UPS, for example, once the load-scheduling software was working well in Willow Grove—matching the decisions of the best planner in the company—Levis and his team went back to senior management to request funding to expand the program to more locations. Levis reports what happened next:

> At that point the skeptics began crawling out of the woodwork. Several of the top executives were not convinced that the program would translate to a larger and more complex location. Our next stop was Mesquite, Texas, where UPS had one of its largest—and less efficient—distribution centers. The executive challenge? "It's one thing to make it work in Willow Grove, but if you can make it work in Mesquite, then you've got something."[10]

Fortunately, the software was up to the challenge; it helped transform Mesquite from one of the least-best-scheduled centers to one of the best in the country. The lesson: even very successful prototypes may require additional evidence of their capability before project expansion funds are approved.

The Virtues of Transparency

Early prototypes should exhibit a high degree of transparency. I'm not suggesting that they must reveal their complex mathematical formulas for decision making, but that they display a user-friendly interface that provides users with insight into why the computer is making its recommendations. Bill Boga often shows two slides to management groups when he is speaking to them about Optimization. The first shows a complex mathematical formulation known as Lagrangian relaxation. As soon as eyes begin to glaze over and executives look like they've gone beyond relaxation into full-group coma, Boga flips to a second slide with a simple 20-word layman's description of what the equation and computer program are doing. As he says, "Leave the mathematics to the mathematicians, and leave the business to the businesspeople. People want to know what's going on, but not in mathematical terms."[11]

The transparency that I advocate typically involves providing users with a *clear explanation of the data* being used to make a decision and a *simple description of the rules* being used to generate a recommendation. One reason that such transparency is important for early deliverables is that it builds trust and confidence. Users are much more likely to trust a recommendation if they understand the logic behind it. In addition, users know that they will most likely have to explain and justify a decision to a boss, a team leader, or even a colleague. "Because the computer told me to do it" is seldom a career-building explanation!

There is another important reason for displaying the data and the rationale behind a recommendation in an early prototype: being able to view the basis for the computer-generated decision helps users and programmers identify incorrect or missing data or rules. Even when users make an effort to share all their decision rules, they invariably omit some key information, which only comes to light when the computer misses the mark on a recommendation and they have to explore what went wrong. User-programmer dialogues need to happen early, frequently, and at length for a successful software-development process.

The type of give-and-take dialogue around the first deliverables that is needed to create and deploy great optimization software requires a strong and trusting relationship between the user and the optimization team. Kempf believes that the best way this kind of relationship can develop is for the optimization team to demonstrate in-depth knowledge of the decision process. He comments:

> The most critical factor in every one of our projects—the factor that is the best predictor of success—is the relationship between the decision-science team and the intended users of the decision-support tools. The businesspeople must believe that we have a deep understanding of their decision or problem, including the organizational dynamics that they face and their success indicators. We have to include them in the model-building process so that the decision-support tool is not a "black box" to them, even though they probably will not develop a deep understanding of our mathematics. We have to be there for them over time, as the business changes and the decision-support tools are updated to keep pace.[12]

Beyond transparency and dialogue, here are a few additional ways to ensure that the first deliverables build a solid foundation for the successful deployment of your optimization software:

- Start with a respected leader. This was the UPS strategy at Willow Grove. Your organization's leaders can become exceptional salespeople as deployment accelerates and expands.
- Introduce the prototype into a situation in which it can be repeatedly tested in a relatively short period of time. The quicker and more frequent the feedback, the easier it is to identify needed improvements.
- Introduce the prototype with an open mind, and expect to change, revise, and improve it. Kempf reminds his team of the admonishment of George E. P. Box, a famous mathematician and model builder: "Essentially all models are wrong, but some

are useful."[13] Your optimization team should not become so wedded to a single model that it becomes incapable of considering modifications or changes.

- Explore the impact of the optimized decision process on surrounding divisions, departments, and individuals. Whose work flow will change and by how much? Boga recounts that at UPS the most difficult and time-consuming part of introducing the feeder-scheduling program was getting all the different parties affected by changes in the decision process involved in implementation. "Most people don't say anything until you go to implement," Boga observes. "Then, it seems like you have gotten everything wrong. You need to identify the people who will be impacted and get them involved early."[14]

- Communicate and celebrate successes. One final important goal for the first deliverables: create such a big splash that the success reflects back on many "parents"!

Avoiding the Pitfalls

Developing and testing to provide early wins can be tricky business. Pitfalls that need to be avoided include the following.

The Objectives, Rules, and Constraints Tangle

Programming an early prototype requires untangling the multiple objectives, constraints, and decision rules discovered through interviews with subject matter experts (SMEs). Unfortunately, SMEs are not generally trained to differentiate among the three or to articulate clearly all of the constraints that guide their decisions.

For example, dispatchers at a trucking company might tell you that when someone calls to arrange for the shipment of a load, they send the closest truck and driver. If so, the dispatchers are following the "first pig to the trough" rule of choice, sometimes referred to as the "greedy algorithm." It entails picking the cheapest, quickest, or easiest option. However, while this may be the operating rule of choice—and an SME may even articulate it—there are likely to be some situations in which another rule takes precedence. For example, suppose that the closest truck can pick up the load, but its driver does not have sufficient hours left on his shift to drive to the destination. Or the load may require special certifications—such as those for transporting hazardous materials—and the closest driver does not have them.

Successful optimizers start with the simple rules that are given to them by SMEs and then dig for the underlying rationale behind those rules. Ferreting out this rationale requires careful questioning of the SMEs and often many hours of investigation. Using and experimenting with an early prototype can help crystallize an SME's thinking and bring to the surface additional rules that prevail in special situations.

UPS's Bill Boga feels that the complexities involved in unraveling objectives, rules, and constraints are so challenging that you need a "person in the middle." By this, he means someone with sound knowledge of both the business decisions being made and the technical side of building an optimization program. This person, Boga argues, needs to become the "voice and conscience" of the project. He must be prepared to overcome resistance from both operations and the optimization development group. Such a person's business knowledge can prove invaluable in helping a programming team understand a SME and tease apart issues creating problems for the program code. The middle person's combined business and computer knowledge can be used to encourage programmers to try alternative approaches.

Dumb Rules

Decision makers in every organization are guided by rules of thumb. Think of such rules as standardized shortcuts for choosing among competing alternatives, especially under time pressure. But not all rules of thumb are created equal: some are "smart" and others are "dumb."

Smart rules help employees make good decisions because these rules are based on reliable data that have been recently validated. Dumb rules tend to be rules that were smart in their day but have not changed with the times. For example, a car dealer needs finely tuned antennae to size up a prospect to determine which model to pitch to that particular individual. An error in judgment can lead to an offended customer and a lost sale. At one time, a car dealer could look at how a customer was dressed and assess his financial situation fairly well. Nowadays, knockoffs and credit cards can make paupers look like royalty. The "pitch the top of the line to a guy in an Armani suit" rule has now become a dumb rule that is based on outmoded data.

Rules incorporated into an early prototype need to be simple, but not simplistic; otherwise, they risk becoming dumb. Remember the example of Walmart's competitors shipping air conditioners indiscriminately to all stores? Managers were following a dumb—and costly—rule.

Some dumb rules were designed to remedy yesterday's problems. "This must never, ever happen again," employees are sometimes told, "so make sure that you follow this rule from here on in." Unfortunately, such rules tend to outlive their usefulness and become nothing more than a drag on the organization. The process of developing and reviewing the prototype needs to shine a light on *all the rules* that employees are following so the rules can be examined, one by one, to determine whether they are smart or dumb.

Data Disconnects

Perhaps no challenge is as great as obtaining the data needed to drive the early prototype. An initial investigation of data availability typically occurs in the design step described in Chapter 5, during development of the POC. However, development of the first prototype represents the moment of truth for data collection. It is not unusual to find that data that initially seemed readily available cannot be found or that although they exist, they are riddled with errors.

The first challenge is uncovering important missing data. Operations—where many optimization projects originate—is a function that is well-known for keeping daily work logs: materials costs, equipment downtime, scrap rate, overtime, rework, and so on. These records are intended to capture everything that has been done, but there are always unrecorded data gaps. For example, a jet-charter company might not record dead-end inquiries. "I want to fly out of Milwaukee," a prospect might say, and the response might be, "We do not fly from there." The conversation ends with no one recording the transaction. Yet information of this kind can be critical to making optimal decisions. If records show that callers consistently inquire about flights out of Milwaukee, maybe there's an unmet demand that the company could benefit from filling.

Likewise, if I can sell 100 flights at $50 each, I know that there are at least 100 people out there who will pay $50 for a flight. But how many people would pay $45 or $55? I don't know because I've never bothered to gather those data. As Marriott can attest from its experience during the economic downturn, when pricing curves suddenly changed, information related to unmet demand is essential for making optimal pricing decisions.

Optimizers are trained to uncover relevant data gaps. Do not be surprised if they spend many hours grilling SMEs and support personnel to determine the location and quality of data that they believe should be factored into their decision-making software. The best optimizers suffer from Missouritis: they never accept without scrutiny the data that they are given. They ask clarifying questions to discover and eliminate the gaps: What do these data mean, and what are they intended to measure or convey? Do the data really capture what is important to the decision? When do the data become available? How much noise, or error, is there in the data? Do the data fully capture the results that are important to you? In our experience, when important data are missing or unreliable, the probability of project success is reduced by 50 percent.

Optimizers use two basic strategies for dealing with missing data. The first is a go-low approach, where rules are put in to replicate or estimate the missing data. This is done by using rules of thumb or by surmising what the data would be *if they were available.*

Going back to the example of ArgentAir, every airport in the United States has restrictions, one of which involves nighttime takeoffs and landings. ArgentAir keeps information on all of these airports, but between 10 and 15 exceptions do not subscribe to the standard definitions of "night" and "day." Aspen, for example, does not open until 7 A.M., so you cannot land there at 6 A.M., even if it is daylight. Santa Monica allows night landings, but not after midnight.

When Princeton Consultants first began working with ArgentAir, these exceptions were not recorded; they were lodged in people's heads. The optimization team started out with a go-low approach, simply ignoring the exceptions and classifying each airport as allowing or not allowing night landings. After the team discovered the exact hours of each of the exceptions, through use of the software and discussions with the schedulers, they added these to the database.

The second approach to dealing with missing data is a go-high strategy, in which finding and automating the collection of missing data becomes part of the project. For example, until quite recently retail stores had no way of tracking the buying habits of shoppers. Then optimizers realized that point-of-sale scanners held the key, and the entire consumer products industry started using scanners to capture data about who buys what, where, when. Optimizers have done the same in pharmacies. Today, every time a druggist fills a prescription, he enters the name of the doctor and the drug prescribed. This enables drug company marketers to know which doctors are prescribing their drugs. Before they began capturing this data, marketers had an incomplete picture of how much of the marketing effort was working or which doctors they should be targeting, with which drugs.

The added costs involved in the go-high approach of automating data-capture can often be offset by the value created. The data that supermarket scanners provide, for example, are worth far more in terms of inventory management and marketing opportunities—those dreaded targeted coupons—than their installation cost, and so is the fee that pharmaceutical companies pay to druggists to capture and send them previously unavailable data on doctors' prescription practices.

Apart from availability, other important data questions must be addressed during prototype development. One is, "What data should be ignored?" Information overload is surely the bane of our wired generation. Companywide networks, enterprisewide software, computerized reports, Internet searches, and e-mails by the dozen have created Everest-sized mountains of information too daunting for most of us to scale.

Optimizers question SMEs and other knowledgeable personnel to identify which data can be ignored, discarded, or reinvented. It can be as straightforward as paying attention to the concerns being expressed by employees who feel that a monthly report is not worth looking at because the data it provides are inaccurate or not actionable. If employees receive reams of information but cannot tell you how it has helped them make decisions, then how useful can the information be? There is a kind of Gresham's law of data: too much data drives out—or more aptly, drives under—useful data. Thus it can be just as important to identify and eliminate nonproductive data as it is to fill data gaps.

Once the important data have been identified, the next pressing question is whether the data are "dirty" or "clean." Dirty data contain errors. Data can become dirty in a number of ways, ranging from transposed numbers to data-entry errors resulting from "best guessing" by typists trying to decipher barely legible scanned images or handwriting.

Optimization consultants are skeptics. They assume that perfect data are as rare as identical snowflakes. It is common for them to recommend specific actions: allocating project time to writing programs that can validate and clean existing data, improving the training of those who are gathering or inputting data, and investigating the payback from devices that automatically collect reliable data.

For example, when UPS set out to optimize the routes of its delivery trucks, it got through the POC step with flying colors. However, once the company started building and testing a prototype, the results were inconsistent. Investigations revealed that the publicly available maps being used as input data were replete with errors. The project had to be put on hold for almost a year while the maps were scrubbed.

Even with cleanup, some dirty data is bound to get past the sharpest eyes. And people often muddy the data to serve their own purposes. In sales forecasting, for example, reps are known to lowball or highball revenue production to serve their self-interest. Which is why optimizers know that the real solution to this challenge is to create robust systems: systems that are not vulnerable to dirty data. A system that gives you a fantastic result provided that you give it perfect data is not as robust as one that gives a great result even with some bad data.

A final important issue concerns the *timeliness* of the data. I already mentioned Marriott's challenge of having data about audiovisual equipment requirements entered *after* rather than *before* the reservation was made. This is just one example of a very common problem. Sales departments, for example, typically look back to last year's revenue-production figures as a source for sales planning. These are, after all, available and most recent. But probe more deeply and you will often find somewhere off to the side a two-to-three-year forecast that has not been entered into the computer system. This may well have been developed with more forward-looking statistics, such as demographic cohort growth or projected changes in economic growth. Such data might well provide a better starting point for projecting sales performance than simply looking at last year's results.

Optimizers are constantly seeking the most current and reliable data, which is why they prefer to look at the hard numbers, in real time, whenever possible. By comparing these against similar historical values, they can identify breaking trends and then adjust the projections and actions of their software accordingly. The focus of Optimization is to find forward-looking indicators that help identify trends as they are happening, avoiding rear-view metrics that merely relate what has happened. "Look ahead" is the operative injunction. The goal is to search for data that bridges to the future, allowing executives to anticipate events, forecast trends, and predict outcomes.

At Intel, Karl Kempf summarized the data challenges as follows:

> A lot of interning graduate students visit us. They are surprised by how we spend our time. In school, the professor gives you the problem and the data. Your job is to figure out the math. All my people can do the math. What we spend most of our time doing is working with the businesspeople to define the real problem and then—the really hard part—rounding up all the data. It's not the way they teach it in the classroom.[15]

Wrong Answers

A common pitfall to avoid in the first deliverable is the tendency to do unsystematic butterfly thinking to interpret and isolate the cause or causes of a computer-generated recommendation that is either in error or counterintuitive. The challenge? There are multiple possible sources for any apparent miscue: a problem with the math, the data fueling the program, or the interface communicating with the user. It may even be that the *human* decision makers are using inappropriate decision rules.

Once the optimization team at UPS had cleaned up the maps it was using to optimize its delivery truck routes, it returned to developing a prototype routing program. The program worked great—*sometimes*. At other times, even with the new maps, the program generated a route that simply did not make sense to the UPS drivers. The recommended routes were feasible but inconsistent with the rules of thumb being used by drivers to load their trucks and deliver their packages. There was a good deal of head scratching, checking of algorithms, recleaning of data, and reviewing of the interface. The programmers simply could not find a cause for the inconsistency. Things dragged on so long that Levis issued an ultimatum to his group: solve the problem in nine months, or the project will be abandoned. Finally, one afternoon, after a long and difficult session spent reexamining the computer algorithm generating the routes, one of the team members asked the question, "Suppose the rules of thumb that we are telling our drivers to use in planning their routes are wrong?"

UPS had a unique history in the package-delivery business; it started as a ground delivery business and then added air deliveries into its network. UPS now has "all services on board": a single UPS driver delivers and picks up air, ground, residential, and commercial packages and runs them through a single network. This differs from the way other companies, such as FedEx, operate, running each commodity through a different network, with separate drivers.

Because UPS started as a ground company, the rules of thumb that it taught its drivers and the measures that it used to gauge effectiveness were based on making air packages fit into the ground business. When Optimization tried to mimic the rules of thumb, the results were inconsistent. The pattern of inconsistencies was a result of the "ground company" paradigm, not the software. Optimization pointed out that the rules needed to change.

It took Levis, together with one of the company's top executives, an afternoon in a delivery truck before he was able to convince the top brass that they should be listening to the software and changing the rules that they were giving the drivers. Eventually, UPS not only changed its training methods, but it moved to adjust its performance reviews to reinforce use of the new planning rules. The lesson: when your optimization software does not seem to be working, double-check to make sure that your humans are not the ones in need of reprogramming!

One final source of error in prototypes, which our team encountered firsthand at a specialty publishing company, involves interfaces with other computer systems. When Princeton Consultants worked with this company, it was undertaking two system-development projects simultaneously: our firm's development of the company's optimization software, and the redesign of its core operational system, which did everything from designing page layouts to calculating bonus checks. Both systems were interconnected and, unfortunately, changed continuously, making it extremely challenging to isolate programming problems. Whenever possible, isolate the development of your optimization prototype from other system changes. After the prototype is working well, then go about integrating it with other systems in the business.

Postscript on the Early Win

I have discussed the fact that optimization projects are more akin to R&D projects than to traditional IT programming efforts. One key difference is that during development of the prototype—and its subsequent deployment into the organization—the initial problem can often morph considerably. Consider Marriott, for example. When its Group Pricing Optimizer (GPO) project was first initiated, the challenge was to maximize revenue in a booming economy. This meant charging full rates for the most part, discounting only in a limited number of situations in which demand was light. Once the downturn struck, the focus was much more on occupancy: how far did the pricing curves need to be adjusted downward to achieve the occupancy levels needed to maintain the property—while still covering as many of the costs as possible?

UPS's optimizers experienced an analogous problem shift as they worked to optimize the schedules of their next-day air flights with their Volcano computer program. Initially, the primary focus of the software was to optimize the flow of aircraft around the country. Because UPS was rapidly expanding air delivery, but its fleet was not properly balanced to meet the expanding demand, its most pressing need was to improve scheduling in ways that required fewer aircraft. The main focus was on routing the aircraft in ways that could "save a tail," as opposed to worrying about the flow of individual packages—beyond making sure that each package eventually reached its correct destination, on time. However, as the fleet matured and competition increased, and as economic conditions deteriorated, cost containment became a priority. This led UPS to redefine the problem as getting each package through the network as economically as possible. This required looking not only at the routing of aircraft and at aircraft size, but also examining how packages were routed through the network.

As your optimization project evolves, continue to verify that your going-in assumptions remain valid and that the problem has not changed. The speed of business can create moving targets that may make it necessary to adjust your optimization sights.

Step 4: The Scale-Up—Extend the Usage

At this point, you have a working optimization prototype program that has been tested and embraced by one or more users under field conditions. Now it is time to roll out the program to the organization and be sure that the right people are using it on a daily basis. Because the best optimization opportunities address decisions that are made repeatedly across the organization, scaling up often means motivating and training a large group of people dispersed across the organization.

At Marriott, for example, it meant introducing the program to thousands of sales managers who were making group reservations in hundreds of hotels. For Bill Boga at UPS, it meant spending a year on the road, giving weeklong workshops to introduce the software used in the Feeder Scheduling Optimization System (Feeder SOS) in more than 65 UPS districts. Getting software to make smart decisions can be a challenging task; getting large groups of people to use that software correctly can be just as challenging, if not more so.

There are three major challenges in the scaling-up step:

1. Igniting initial program adoption
2. Managing the expansion
3. Institutionalizing the changes and any associated adjustments to work processes

Let's take a closer look at each of these challenges.

1. Igniting Initial Program Adoption

Any student of change management will tell you that leverage is crucial. During World War II, the Germans taught field commanders to focus attention and resources on the *schwerpunkt*: the decisive point in a battle. The lesson for leaders of optimization projects: begin at a point that maximizes your chances of success and expand from there.

At Marriott, it was a select set of hotels that had computer systems that produced the data needed to fuel the GPO. At Intel, it was other shift managers at the factory where Optimization was first introduced; they had received a nudge from the plant manager to investigate why they were lagging behind. At UPS, when Bill Boga set out to expand the use of the feeder-scheduling software, he initiated the project in Chicago because that district had called and invited him to visit. In each case, the first introduction was characterized by a timely intervention in a situation where minimum resistance was expected.

Typically, the introduction of the software requires significant education, which may include topics beyond merely how the software works. Managing change along the lines mentioned earlier in this chapter is one such topic, especially for leaders of an organization. At Marriott, Sharon Hormby understood the importance of equipping leaders with a framework and skills to drive and support change in her organization. She knew that the GPO was going to require significant changes in how sales managers did their job. Presumably, this would be less challenging for the younger salespeople, who had grown up in a wired age and had come to trust the "power of the computer."

For many of the senior sales managers, however, the challenges would be greater. To mention just one hurdle, the optimization software required sales managers to enter prospect information into the computer during a reservation call. Previously, this information had been recorded by hand on paper forms. Truth be told, a number of the senior sales managers did not know how to type. They were now required to multitask—type while they talked and fielded questions on the phone. Hormby and the team knew from early conversations during prototype testing that there was going to be some push-back.

To meet the challenges, the team decided to begin rolling out the system by immersing the company's leaders—hotel managers, regional directors of revenue management, and regional sales directors—in a two- to three-day training program, rather than by training the sales managers who were going to be the actual users of the software. In each geographical region, Hormby invited the regional sales leaders to be involved in delivering the training. "This was really big," she reports, ". . . because these were the top sales leaders, who got the big bonuses each year. There they were, up on the stage with us. With them on board, it made it a lot harder for others to resist."[16]

The training was designed to immerse the leaders in the software so that they could understand—and support—what the sales teams would be doing. But software was not the first agenda item. Hormby and her team had developed a half-day workshop on change management principles. Change, after all, was what the company's leaders had to think about and focus their attention on. The message to them was clear: introduction of the software represented a significant change and needed to be managed accordingly. Once the company's leaders were on board, Hormby and her team turned to training the salespeople.

UPS's Boga also knew that he was going to face resistance when he and his team introduced the Feeder SOS, even though top management had issued a mandate stating that every district must use the software. Mandate notwithstanding, Boga would be hard pressed to convince seasoned UPS schedulers, many of whom had started their career driving trucks, that the software could schedule the routes more effectively than they could. He did not expect many easy converts.

An additional challenge that Boga faced was the quality of the data that the scheduling program needed from each district. They were chock-full of errors. A great deal of work was going to be needed to clean up and correct each district's data before the routing program was going to be able to generate good solutions. The "junk-in, junk-out" state of affairs created a perfect opportunity for new users of the software to dismiss its recommendations and stop using the program.

To address the problem, Boga structured a weeklong workshop that he eventually led in all the UPS regions. At each stop, Boga asked the district schedulers in the region to bring real data with them and to be prepared for a challenging working session. At the beginning of each workshop, Boga introduced the software and then instructed participants to use their own data to generate solutions. This included teaching participants how to clean and tweak their data to improve the solutions that they were generating. The night before the final day of the workshop, Boga reviewed every set of schedules generated during the week and put together a spreadsheet that displayed each participant's solutions, including what the software suggested were the minimum and maximum cost savings that could be achieved.

In the final session, Boga reviewed every district's data on an overhead screen, asking whether the district scheduler thought the new computer-generated schedule was workable. If the answer was yes, Boga responded, "Great! When will you be able to implement it?" If a scheduler answered no, Boga asked for an explanation. If the scheduler continued to resist, Boga suggested that the reason the solution wasn't correct was because the scheduler's data were in poor shape and needed to be cleaned up. Boga let the scheduler know that he would be meeting with her after the cleaning had been done. This put the onus on the scheduler, not the software system.

In thinking about such educational activities, keep in mind the many reasons that people resist turning their decisions over to a computer. Beyond job insecurity, there are issues of self-esteem, role definition, self-interest, and a common need by almost all of us to maintain control over our environment.

Remember, also, that the people being introduced to the software during this phase of a project typically have not been involved in its development or testing. Low involvement often leads to low commitment. During the rollout, project teams must be wary of the dreaded "kiss of yes": employees who say yes but mean no and continue doing exactly what they have always done.

2. Managing the Expansion

Once the system has been launched, the next challenge is to sustain the deployment at a rate that can be effectively managed. Ideally, you have created "pull" during the launch, so that others in the organization will begin asking about the software, as the schedulers in UPS's Chicago district did. At Marriott, the number of hotels requesting installation of the GPO actually became one of the success metrics used by Hormby and her team. Once the pricing optimizer began to be used out in the field, word quickly spread among the hotel sales teams. One of the highs for the optimization team occurred when franchise hotels began requesting access to the software, especially since Marriott could not mandate the software's use in these establishments.

One of the things that heightened the appeal of the Marriott system was the friendliness of the interface. The long hours spent with sales teams, showing them early prototypes and listening to their suggestions on how to improve the display, paid off big-time in the scaling-up phase. The importance of ease of use to encouraging adoption of optimization software across large work groups cannot be overstated, especially if the workforce includes seasoned workers who have been doing things the old way for many years.

Momentum isn't created by chance. Hormby and her team spread the excitement by carefully tracking and publishing statistics on the successful adoption of the software. Initially, it was not possible for them to measure booked revenue, since reservations are commonly booked six months to two years in advance of the stay and payment. Not to be deterred, team members turned to measuring such usage statistics as the percent of leads being priced using the GPO software. They also calculated and summarized dollars of business being booked through the pricing system, as well as actual closing ratios compared to the ratios predicted by the theoretical pricing model. The close match between the predicted and actual numbers sharply increased confidence that the pricing curves were working as intended: maximizing profitable business, rather than filling hotel rooms at any cost.

The various statistics collected by the Marriott team were summarized, graphed, and distributed in regular reports to regional and top management to ensure that everyone could see how quickly the system was being accepted without complaints by users. David Marriott, head of global sales at the time of the system rollout, would stop Hormby every time he saw her and ask how much revenue had been pushed through the GPO to date. Such buzz from senior leaders was exactly what was needed to help ensure a rapid and successful rollout.

Success is a powerful impetus to expansion. However, expansion must be paced by the availability of properly trained support resources. As the software is tested in an increasing number of situations, new problems inevitably crop up and need to be dealt with.

During the installation of the optimization program at the metropolitan newspaper discussed earlier, the optimization team worked with the paper's staff to identify the rules that were going to be used to lay out the pages in an edition. An example of such a rule would be, "Only two-color ads can be included in a section." Once the rules had been codified, people needed to stick to them. There were consequences to violating a rule, such as running out of space in the paper. But it was difficult to get people to understand this. Someone would suddenly figure out a way to get three-color ads into a section and decide it was perfectly acceptable to do so. The optimization team had to spend time convincing people that they could not violate the agreed-upon rules with impunity. But people can be extremely ingenious at creating situations that "game" the software, so the team decided to develop a second software program to check that no rules had been violated.

At Marriott, a number of ongoing educational and support mechanisms were created to continue to provide advice to sales teams around the country. One was a two-hour, online educational program that was initially presented to 1,600 sales managers in the United States and Canada. Each presentation was led by an online facilitator.

In addition, for three months after the program had been introduced in a city, the optimization team set up "office hours," or set times when people using the system could call in with questions or problems. Finally, during the rollout, Hormby and her team asked revenue management leaders to visit sales offices and spend time capturing on flip charts questions and recommendations for improving the system. These sessions also gave people the chance to experience the enthusiastic collaboration of the revenue managers and sales managers during the sessions, a powerful facilitating force for organizational change.

When Jack Levis finished successfully testing the UPS Load Planner in Mesquite, Texas, and finally got permission to roll it out to the 31 largest UPS distribution centers, he laid out a cautious plan to ensure success. As Levis explains:

> When we deployed the software, there were two sides to the planning problem: the human side and the computer-program side. We visited one site at a time and did not let the planners use the optimization engine until they had demonstrated proficiency making decisions themselves with the new data that the program was providing. This did two things: first, it afforded another check that the program was working correctly; second, it made certain that the planners' capabilities and performance were enhanced at each site.[17]

It took Levis and his team 15 months to install the program at the 31 sites. This was three months longer than planned, but Levis and his team were unwilling to move on to a new site until the planners at the current site were using the program effectively. Both the Marriott and UPS experiences illustrate the high priority that successful optimizers give to training and support.

Finally, as was noted earlier, during the scaling-up step it is important to monitor how the software implementation is impacting other parts of the organization. At the metropolitan newspaper, for example, once the system that recommended section layouts was up and running, one person could do what three people had been doing previously. The others needed to be redeployed. At UPS, when the airplane-scheduler software, Volcano, began to focus on optimizing not just airline schedules but package flow as well, it meant that planes had to be loaded with different-sized containers.

In most cases, when decisions become faster and better, the impact waterfalls through the organization. The optimization team needs to anticipate collateral impact, warn the organization, and help make adjustments.

3. Institutionalizing the Changes to Work Processes

Recidivism is the bane of organizational change. Old habits die hard and are quick to reemerge. There is always a risk that employees will revert to using their stone axes in spite of the benefits of a new tool. Institutionalization involves making sure that the new decision tools become the default behavior: the way of doing business day in and day out.

Sometimes, the actions taken to institutionalize the use of new optimization tools are fairly straightforward. At Marriott, for example, following three months of training on the new system, Hormby and her team removed rates from the systems that were used to communicate the old, manually defined prices. They knew that as long as the old system was available there was a risk that people would continue to use it and not fully commit to the new one. Hormby hoped that out of sight would equal out of mind.

At UPS, once senior managers were convinced that the Feeder SOS worked well, they mandated that every district run the program at least once a quarter to evaluate the efficiency of its schedules. Mandates, of course, can be ignored and need to be supported by education and oversight. However, mandates can demonstrate the commitment of top management to a process, thereby helping make sure that new tools are at least given a chance.

On rare occasions, the tools can be constructed so that there is no choice but to use them. This is what happened at the metropolitan newspaper, where the optimization software was embedded into the paper's larger IT system. If people were using that system, they would be using the optimization engine as well.

It always helps when use of the optimization software is tightly linked to the self-interest of employees and to the evaluation of their performance. This is very often the case with sales-support systems, such as the one installed at Marriott. Two things that salespeople value highly are time savings and accurate information—both of which were provided by these optimization systems. Furthermore, the members of sales teams are generally careful record keepers who are evaluated by outcomes, not just activity. Competitive by nature, they also tend to be aware of how others on the team are performing. Once word begins to spread that a new tool adds value and improves results, sales teams are typically the earliest adopters.

Schedulers are not always so results focused. But they can be, if encouraged. This was the case at UPS for the load planners. Each planner was given a scorecard that included such measures as average number of packages per trailer and number of partially filled trailers departing. Displaying the scorecards allowed the load planners to quickly and easily see improvements in their performance. Like sales-people, the planners were quick to adopt a new tool that made them look better.

An important area in which organizations can institutionalize new behaviors is the selection and training of new hires. Take hiring, for example. Nearly all younger workers are comfortable with computers, so this is no longer a requirement that is difficult to meet. However, finding workers with knowledge of math modeling and optimization principles is still a challenge. Perhaps of greater significance are the criteria for hiring and promoting new managers. Karl Kempf was initially brought into Intel by an executive who directed all Intel's fabrication facilities and had previously been a materials science professor at Stanford University. When he approached Kempf with a job offer, his comment was, "OK, it's time to get a little science into this black art of running our factories."[18]

Initially, Kempf was a lone soldier stalking the factory floor. Few people showed much interest in asking the new Ph.D. how to run their shift. However, Kempf eventually ran into a shift manager, with a master's degree from MIT, who was interested in trying some of Kempf's suggestions. The lesson is clear: one way to encourage the infusion of OR and Optimization is to hire—or promote—individuals who are comfortable using computers, algorithms, and mathematical models to solve problems.

One important transition that often occurs during the institution-alization stage of an optimization project is a shifting of focus away from R&D to more traditional software-maintenance activities. In fact, it is often the case that maintenance and the development of new capabilities are passed back to IT. This is what happened at ArgentAir. Initially, the optimization team reported to a senior vice president of operations. This made sense for a variety of reasons: it put the optimization team close to the problem and the people who would use the software; it also allowed the team to develop and test new ideas quickly, without being slowed by the control procedures that are generally in place in an IT department.

Once the optimization program is up and running, it is sometimes more appropriate to hand it over to IT for maintenance and incremental enhancements, as was done at ArgentAir. IT has procedures in place for quality control. It also is likely to have longer-term planning procedures. While the optimization team reported to operations at ArgentAir, the plans were mostly short-term. The team never quite knew what it would be doing six months out and whether funding would continue to be available. Once the optimization team began reporting to IT, however, planning began to be extended, giving the team a clearer picture of the longer-term road map.

The big disadvantage of moving Optimization to an IT department is that development is often slowed. While the team operated as a "skunk works" within operations at ArgentAir, it took only a month or two for it to put together and test program modules. Once the team came under the wing of IT and had to comply with its planning and control mechanisms, that period extended to six months or more. Speed is not an uncommon casualty of the institutionalizing process.

Step 5: The Harvest—Leverage the Benefits

Most modern enterprises comprise portfolios of businesses. Success with Optimization in one line of business can often be extended into others. When this shift in thinking begins to emerge, you are entering the leveraging phase. This step is ripe with opportunity—but also with danger.

The challenge facing a successful optimization team at this point is analogous to what can happen when a relatively unknown movie actor creates such a memorable role that he is forever after "typecast." Once an executive witnesses the power of Optimization in her line of business, the executive may well want to acquire the talent that delivered it and place it under her own control on a permanent basis. While this benefits one area of the business, it keeps the overall organization from reaping the full value of Optimization. It also can discourage and drive out the very best optimizers, who—like the best Hollywood actors—want to expand their craft with fresh and new challenges.

Reaping a bountiful harvest from a successful optimization project demands both an effectively paced career progression for the best optimizers and an integrated blend of short- and long-term project objectives for each line of business. As always, the most important axiom is *underpromise and overdeliver*.

An Effectively Paced Progression

As was pointed out earlier, Karl Kempf was brought on board at Intel in 1987 by Craig Barrett, then head of the company's fabrication facilities. Fortunately, Kempf was smart enough to know that being well connected meant little. Success hinged on achieving it the old-fashioned way: working hard, one step at a time. He began working with a single shift manager, at a single factory, to produce a 10 percent improvement in throughput. The next step was to get the other three shift managers at that plant to adopt the same techniques as the first shift, to optimize the entire plant's production. The result: hundreds of millions of dollars per year in increased production. Once this plant began to outperform its sister plants, the next logical progression was to spread the gospel to them, which Kempf accomplished over a three- to four-year period.

As Kempf facilitated and watched the transformation, it occurred to him that his team needed to think through how the plant had been designed in the first place. All the changes that the team had introduced had resulted in the plants being run much differently than had been intended by their designers. Kempf's next project? Embed Optimization into the design of the company's plants, which ultimately resulted in additional savings of hundreds of millions of dollars on each newly constructed factory.

The next logical step, given improved plant designs, was to find a quicker way to build the plants and bring them on line. When Kempf and his team first began working on this challenge, it took well over a year to build and ramp up a new plant's production. With better decision making and a good dose of management science, that time was reduced to under a year.

Thinking about plant design next led to looking for ways to optimize procurement of the equipment that needed to be installed in the plants. Looking at procurement, in turn, resulted in an examination of the entire supply chain and ways to optimize production around the world, across all of Intel's plants. This included—in sequence—production planning, materials procurement, inventory planning, and logistics planning.

Kempf was not finished yet. He next cast his net toward Intel's sales and marketing group. The new challenge: come up with improved market forecasts. Next was Intel's product design and development group. The goal: faster and better decisions about what features to include in new products planned for three to five years in the future.

Karl Kempf has been at Intel for 23 years—almost a quarter of a century. During that time, he has avoided being lured into big-bang traps. He preferred to progress incrementally from one contained challenge to the next. This approach led him to deliver anywhere from one to three new decision tools a year. Depending on whether you count the savings over a 6- or 12-month period, he has been recognized as impacting Intel's bottom line by $2 and $4 *billion* over those 23 years. That works out to something in the neighborhood of $130 million a year, not counting the additional savings that each optimization effort has yielded after its first 12 months of deployment. By moving slowly and deliberately, at a pace that the organization could absorb, Kempf has assuredly created a financial revolution by taking carefully measured evolutionary steps. His remaining goal? To create decision tools for every group in the company before he retires!

In 2009, Craig Barrett—now chairman of the Intel Board—accepted, for Karl Kempf and his Decision Technology Group, INFORMS' international prize for outstanding integration of OR and management science into a company's decision making. One reason that Karl Kempf has been so successful at Intel is that he has not let his group's reach extend beyond its capabilities. Another is that he has kept a clear focus on the immediate needs of the business. You might say that he has been focused on Operations *Results* rather than Operations *Research*. Academicians and theorists can at times become enamored with a single model or approach and set out in search of a problem to apply it against. Not Kempf. He and his team are "method agnostics." They start by observing and trying to understand the problems and decisions that the people on the front line are wrestling with. "Only after we thoroughly understand the business problem do we look in our toolkit and try to find an approach that will let us build a quick prototype to improve the business decisions that people are grappling with," says Kempf. "It may be a Monte Carlo simulation; it may be linear programming; it may be something else. We'll use whatever works best."[19]

Just One Metric

A highly visible and successful optimization project can generate an abundance of harvest opportunities. Beyond the projected payback or return on investment, is there another way to set priorities when faced with such abundance?

Maurice Schlumberger, former Cap Gemini chief technical officer and ex-practice head for ILOG's Optimization Consulting Group, believes that there is.[20] Schlumberger emphasizes the presence of two distinct forces in any optimization or IT project: the size of the prize and the time required to achieve it. In general, the bigger the prize, the longer management is willing to wait for results. But the more time that goes by without payback, the more jittery investors become—and the more opportunities arise for execution problems.

This has led Schlumberger to focus on a metric that he calls time to payback, or TTP. The metric is designed to measure the time that it takes a project to break even after its launch date, taking into account all benefits and costs. Schlumberger and his team have spent time investigating the measure and have found TTP to be the best predictor of project success of any metric they have studied.

It is important to recognize that TTP is different from time to delivery, or TTD, a more commonly used metric that represents the time between contract signing and the point at which the software is deployed. In what Schlumberger refers to as "super projects," TTP can actual be *shorter* in duration than TTD—if early completed pieces of the project begin to generate immediate financial returns. This was the case during the optimization work with ArgentAir, where early software-generated schedules created significant savings well before the three software modules that comprised the final deliverables were completed and deployed.

In more-typical projects, TTP exceeds TTD. As long as the TTP is kept relatively short—say, 12 to 18 months—Schlumberger has found that the chances for project success remain high. The client can see the value of the investment relatively quickly, and the returns accumulate at a rate capable of sustaining enthusiasm. The picture begins to change, however, as the time to break even extends out beyond two or three years. In such situations, a project faces increasing risks from either development problems or from shifts in the economic winds, which can disrupt funding. Schlumberger advises companies to look for opportunities in which TTP is shorter than two years.

Blending the Long and the Short

One person who clearly understands the value of a short TTP is Marriott's Hormby. As she put it:

> You need to start small, improve the metric, show what you can do. This is especially true with groundbreaking, innovative projects. If I have a big program, I like to slice it into pieces that each take no more than a year. If you can get some value early and some proof that you are on track for the payback, it's invaluable.[21]

The GPO described in Chapter 3 is only one small piece of a larger Marriott project labeled Total Yield Management (TYM). The long-range goal of TYM is to optimize all the hotel assets—sleeping rooms, dining facilities, meeting rooms, recreational facilities—across both individual travelers and group reservations. To achieve this ambitious goal, several different optimization programs will be needed.

One piece of the puzzle is the GPO that is already deployed and creating value. A second piece—currently under construction—is a forecasting program capable of anticipating demand far into the future. The third piece is a Total Hotel Optimization Model, which when setting reservation prices would take into account not just occupancy rates, but utilization of all of a hotel's facilities. All three programs were envisioned from the beginning. They simply represented too big an undertaking to tackle all at once, so Hormby and her team divided them into manageable pieces, each with a more acceptable TTP.

A similar blending of long-term vision with short-term objectives can be seen in other successful optimizing organizations. At UPS, Volcano, an air-traffic-scheduling optimizer, has been developed. Scott Abell is UPS's air domestic network planning manager and has been involved with the Volcano project for many years. Abell has a clear vision of where he wants the project to go. Eventually, he wants all of his schedulers to have easy access to the system, and he wants all UPS flights to be handled by the system. "Our long-term goal is to have any one of our 60 or so planners come in and say, 'OK, I've got this problem. Let's turn it over to the system and let it fix it.'"[22]

But that day is still far in the future. At the moment, the system is only being used to develop schedules for next-day air flights, not two-day air or international flights. Furthermore, the interface is insufficiently friendly to be turned over to the schedulers. Abell currently has a small technical team with strong analytic and computer skills who are responsible for inputting data, adjusting parameters, and interpreting the output. Once this is done, they huddle with the schedulers. Today, the program is used more to stimulate thinking and create dialogue among the schedulers than it is to generate final solutions. The program is creating tremendous value by improving flight schedules, but it continues to need a great deal of help from the technical team.

Over time, it seems likely that Abell's long-term vision will be achieved. However, as at Marriott, the project has to be separated into digestible bites. UPS knows the value of keeping projects manageable. Abell describes it this way: "With every project at UPS, we have to have deliverables that create value in the short run. With longer projects—say, anything over 18 months—you start to lose your focus."[23] UPS eats its elephants like other successful optimizers: one bite at a time.

Final Note

Some of the early descriptions of Optimization in this book paint scenes in which computers make decisions better and faster than people, replacing them at tasks long thought to be the exclusive province of human beings. But this "machine versus human" dichotomy is far from a complete and accurate picture. Far more commonly, as described in our many examples of Optimization, symbiotic relationships are evolving between people and computers. Humans help computers define problems, identify constraints, and chronicle decision rules. Using that powerful computer that sits atop our shoulders, it is up to humans to assess the environment around them to make sure that the assumptions programmed into the computer continue to remain valid.

The computer, on the other hand, uses its incredible digital computational power to sort through massively large data sets, evaluate voluminous lists of rules, and then instantaneously compute complex conditional probabilities to arrive at recommendations for its human masters to weigh and evaluate. No doubt the relationship will evolve as more problems succumb to the computer's power of optimizing. However, the strong partnership will likely be a long-lasting one. For decades to come, the best decisions seem certain to be generated from human-machine partnerships that rely on each entity pivoting off its unique strengths to help solve the increasingly complex problems of the world around us.

PART 3

THE OPTIMIZED WORLD OF TOMORROW

CHAPTER 7

THE CHALLENGES AHEAD

I remember watching, as a boy, a TV show called "The Jetsons." For those too young to remember, the program was a Hanna-Barbera cartoon about a family living in the year 2062. As I watched "The Jetsons," I often wondered which of the futuristic whimsical inventions featured on the program would become reality during my lifetime. The personal flying saucers that carried George Jetson to work and his kids to school didn't seem too far off. Then there was Rosie, the talking robot. I was certain that before long Rosie would be happily employed vacuuming my living room floor and bringing order to my chaos.

There was one invention, however, that seemed way too far-fetched to ever come true. The futuristic gizmo involved Jane Jetson, matron of the family, pushing a tray through a sliding door, pressing a few buttons, and in just seconds—voilà!—out came a fully cooked meal. As the other characters complimented Jane on her incredible skills as a button-pushing chef, I remember thinking, "Now that's an invention I will never see in my lifetime. You can't cook a meal that fast. It defies physics."

There are two lessons to be learned from my recollections of "The Jetsons." First, the future is sure to surprise us. Do not be too quick to rule out what's possible. If you are, you might wind up like Henry

Morton, president of the Stevens Institute of Technology, who back in 1880 pronounced the electric lightbulb "a conspicuous failure"; or the IBM engineer who in 1968 asked skeptically about the microchip, "But what . . . is it good for?"[1] or the sender of the 1876 Western Union internal memo that declared, "This 'telephone' has too many shortcomings to be seriously considered as a means of communication. The device is inherently of no value to us."[2]

Second, while you can't eliminate from the future the element of surprise, it is important to look ahead to think about "whither thou goest." If you invest time in thinking about the shape of things to come, lay out your expectations, and then make decisions and draw up plans to bring about some desired outcome, chances are you will be less surprised when the future arrives. The future that you inherit may well be one that you have helped invent.

This chapter raises a periscope to look over the horizon at the future of Optimization. What are we likely to see in the years ahead? The future, St. Augustine once observed, is a present expectation. Early in this chapter we will focus on the here-and-now and look at current expectations and research to paint a picture of Optimization's immediate future. Later in the chapter we will look further out to imagine what we might see as we move closer to the year 2062.

In both the short and long terms, the future of Optimization will continue to be connected with developments in the field of computing and data management, which is why we will begin our look ahead with what is likely to happen in these two fields.

A Surge of Smart Computing?

In today's competitive, fast-changing environment, there is a surprising amount of agreement among diverse individuals on the likely immediate future of computing. A recent global survey of 444 information technology (IT) executives by McKinsey & Company found that in spite of continued pressures to reduce spending in practically every area, a majority of executives foresaw a likely increase in IT investments in the immediate future.[3] Among the private-company executives who were surveyed, 73 percent expected their investment to increase.

When the Gartner Group, a leading IT consulting and research company, unveiled its list of the top 10 strategic technologies for 2010, it listed Cloud Computing and Advanced Analytics in positions one and two, respectively. As the report stated:

> We have reached the point in the improvement of performance and costs that we can afford to perform analytics and simulation for each and every action taken in the business. Not only will data center systems be able to do this, but mobile devices will have access to data and enough capability to perform analytics themselves, potentially enabling use of optimization and simulation everywhere and every time.[4]

Andrew Bartels is a longtime student of technological change. At American Express, he held a variety of vice presidential positions in the chairman's office, overseeing technology change, strategic planning, and reengineering. He also served as a technology consultant to the U.S. House of Representatives' Committee on Banking. Today, he is a vice president and senior analyst at Forrester, a publicly traded research company that consults with businesses on the implications of technology change. Bartels foresees a new era of accelerated IT investment driven by what he labels Smart Computing.[5] He provides evidence that the United States has undergone three major cycles of IT technology investment and digestion between the years 1960 and 2008, each lasting approximately 16 years:

1. Mainframe computing from 1960 to 1976, which automated frequent, standardized transactions
2. Personal computing from 1976 to 1992, which brought computing to white-collar workers
3. Network computing from 1992 to 2008, which drove process automation through large systems such as SAP's R/3 enterprise resource planning (ERP) and Siebel's customer relationship management (CRM) software

Each period, Bartels argues, began with the experimental adoption of a new form of IT, followed quickly by a period of rapid and widespread adoption as the technology proved its ability to solve critical business problems. During these rapid-adoption periods, IT investment grew at approximately twice the rate of the overall economy. The acceleration in investment lasted 8 to 10 years, after which investments leveled off, as organizations worked to absorb the technological changes. The periods of tech digestion and refinement typically lasted 6 to 8 years before a new cycle of investment began. These historical cycles of investment are shown in Figure 7.1.

There is evidence that the next wave of IT investment has already begun, illustrated by the acceleration of tech purchases that started in 2008, before being temporarily interrupted by the financial crisis. U.S. Department of Commerce data show that investment in technology from the fourth quarter of 2007 through the first two quarters of 2008 averaged 8.4 percent, almost twice the growth rate of nominal gross domestic product (GDP), which was 4.6 percent.

While the economic downturn dampened the growth spurt, Bartels believes that the brief acceleration in spending shows pent-up demand, which will reappear once economic conditions improve.

FIGURE 7.1   Cycles of Tech Introductions[6]

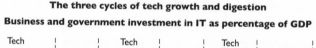

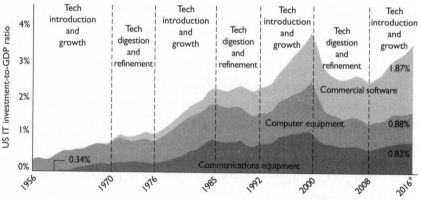

Source: US Commerce Department for 1956 to 2008; Forrester Research forecasts for 2009 to 2016
*Forrester forecasts

As to where this surge in investment is likely to be directed, Bartels envisions ". . . a new generation of integrated hardware, software, and network technologies that provides IT systems with real-time awareness of the real world and advanced analytics to *help people make more intelligent decisions about alternatives and actions that will optimize business processes and business balance sheet results* [emphasis added]."[7]

Forrester identifies five defining characteristics of the new wave of Smart Computing:

1. **Awareness:** New technologies for the pervasive interactions with the environment and the capturing of real-time data such as radio frequency identification (RFID), global positioning systems, chips, and smart cards

2. **Analysis:** Special analytical software for data mining and predictive analysis; decision algorithms to help business and government decide whether to act on emerging data patterns or anomalies

3. **Alternatives:** Although Bartels believes that the basic role of "business rule engines" and work flow analysis will remain, he predicts a seismic leap in the ability of software to handle extremely large sets of real-time data and to adjust its analysis on the fly to evaluate alternative courses of action and make recommendations on the optimal response

4. **Actions:** Smart Computing will not stop with analysis. Rather, through integrated links to process applications—be they manufacturing switches or alerts sent to cell phones—Smart Computing will take the next step of initiating action on its own or through a human intermediary.

5. **Auditability:** Finally, the next generation of systems will include an increased number of ways to monitor and evaluate their own activities in regard to compliance and improvement opportunities.

It seems certain that optimization software—software that reviews a complex set of alternatives and constraints and makes a recommendation—will be an integral part of all five aspects of Smart Computing. Figure 7.2 presents a slightly different perspective on the components of Smart Computing from SAS, a leading developer of statistical analysis, optimization, and Smart Computing software.

FIGURE 7.2   SAS's Hierarchy of Computing[8]

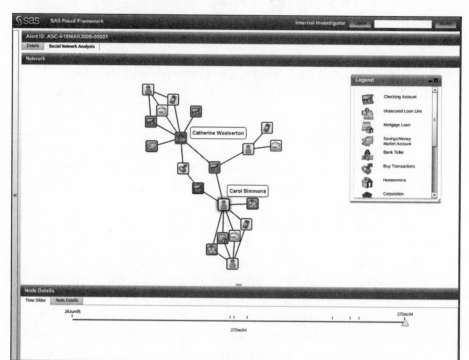

Driving Forces of Optimization

The fact that cycles of IT investment have occurred in the past is no guarantee that another is about to begin. History often repeats itself—but not always. However, in this case there are three powerful forces that seem likely to propel a surge of investment in Smart Computing and Optimization: (1) omnipresent—and superpowerful—computing power, (2) a growing tsunami of digitized data, and (3) pressing business, if not world problems, begging for improved asset management.

1. Omnipresent, Superpowerful Computing

The last 60 years have witnessed an astounding evolution of computing power. We've progressed from a room-sized calculator designed to compute artillery-firing tables, which required 160,000 watts of electrical power, to handheld smartphones running on small lithium-ion batteries, with real-time access, to networks of computer servers and their worldwide databases. As impressive as this transformation has been, it is only a taste of what lies ahead.

Consider for a moment computational power. Depending on how you measure it, today's computers possess approximately the same amount of raw computing power as your family dog. Before the decade is out, some are predicting that personal computers costing $1,000 or less will have the raw computing power of a human brain (although perhaps not the software to think as we do).[9]

Such astounding levels of computing power, in a single machine, are only the beginning. As mentioned in Chapter 2, people are increasingly using the Internet to link together thousands of computers into vast networks. For example, one company, Intelligence Realm, was linked at one time to more than 14,000 computers around the world to create a giant neural network with the goal of "reverse engineering the human brain."[10]

The coming revolution is not simply a story of massive processing power, however. A super number-crunching machine is less useful if only a brainiac can interact with it. As I discussed in Chapter 6, a friendly interface is critical to a successful optimization project. Fortunately, a revolution is also under way concerning the size and shape of computers, as well as new and easier ways for people to interact and communicate with them.

First, computers continue to shrink in size. We are not just speaking of smartphones, but of smart chips—low consumers of electricity, smaller than a thumbnail, that are being embedded in everything from automobiles to home appliances to singing birthday cards. Some of these microcomputers have the capability of connecting wirelessly with the Internet, thereby multiplying their power. The diminishing size of computers has already allowed them to assume alternative shapes and forms, including some that are being woven into clothing. The Military Operational Medicine Research program is developing uniforms with embedded sensors that can monitor soldiers' physiological well-being. In addition to monitoring a soldier's or a unit's physical health, the devices can be used to gather and transmit additional types of information such as weather conditions that the military can use in predictive models of a mission's success.[11]

As for human-machine interaction, it would appear likely that new interface technologies are about to make it almost as easy to interact with a computer as with another human being—perhaps easier, given people's moodiness and unpredictability. Today, anyone with a smartphone can use voice commands to search through a database of thousands of contacts. Voice training is no longer required. Voice commands, however, are only one means of human communication. What about hand gestures, facial expressions, eye contact, and body language? Work is under way to open up all of these channels for human-machine communication.

Gran Turismo has long been recognized as one of the most realistic computer automobile-racing games on the market. The newest version of the game, Gran Turismo 5, will include new body-tracking capabilities. The PlayStation's camera will track a player's head and adjust the cockpit view on the screen to match the way in which a player has turned his or her head. With a quick glance to the side, a player will be able to see what is happening alongside the car without entirely losing sight of the road ahead.

On another front, Pattie Maes, an associate professor at MIT, and her student Pranav Mistry are working to develop a computer system that responds to simple hand gestures, much as the scientist characters were able to do in the movie *Avatar*. The system involves a small camera that hangs around the wearer's neck with software driven by a smartphone in the user's pocket. The system is capable of interpreting hand gestures made by the wearer in front of his or her body. In one demonstration, the wearer needed only to make the iconic hand gesture of taking a picture—a square formed with the thumb and forefinger of each hand—and the camera took a picture of what appeared inside the square.

Maes and Mistry have also included a small computer projector on their camera necklace. The projector allows the wearer to use any surface as a computer screen, again operated by hand gestures. So for example, in one demonstration the user faced a wall and projected onto it an image of the pictures he had just taken with his computer projector; he then began arranging the pictures in groups on the wall screen. Maes and Mistry have labeled their efforts the Sixth-Sense Project, since their intent is to find ways in which a person can easily access or "sense" digital information, wherever they are, to help them make decisions. To demonstrate this capability, Mistry visited a grocery store, picked up a roll of toilet paper, and held it in front of his chest so the camera could see the bar code. Immediately, information about the brand drawn from the Internet, including its environmental-friendliness rating, was projected onto the roll.[12]

Transforming walls and rolls of toilet paper into computer screens is one way of interacting with the digital universe. Another is via a retinal display called the Tele Scouter, currently being developed by NEC. The device is mounted on the frame of a pair of eyeglasses and includes both a display projector and a microphone. One potential use of the Tele Scouter: language translation. Speech picked up by the microphone is transmitted via the Internet to a central server for translation. Subtitles are then sent back and via the retinal projector are displayed in the user's peripheral vision in such a way as to allow the user to maintain eye contact while reading a translation of what the speaker has just said. The next step in the evolution appears to be in the development pipeline at the University of Washington: contact lenses with built-in LED displays that are wirelessly powered by radio frequencies. It is envisioned that eventually the lenses will contain hundreds of tiny LEDs that can display images, words, or other information that can be read without unsightly eyeglasses.

These examples illustrate the emergence of a remarkable world in which we will be able to access astounding amounts of computing power wherever we are, 24/7, with a simple verbal command, turn of the head, blink of an eye, or wave of the hand. In some cases, this power may be used to access information to help us make a decision; in many others, it will allow us to access superpowerful optimization software that can sort through an almost infinite number of alternatives to recommend the best course of action. In doing so, Optimization will move beyond maximizing the value of a few key business assets to maximizing the value of assets in everyday life, including those related to our very biological makeup.

2. A Tsunami of Digital Data

Optimization, combined with ever-increasing computing power, will be needed to deal with the second major driver of Smart Computing: the growing tsunami of digital data. A recent study found that 80 percent of business leaders report that they are making major decisions based on missing data or data that they do not trust.[13] It's not that the data do not exist or even that they cannot be retrieved; more likely, it is because the data cannot be accessed *efficiently*. According to researchers at IDC and storage infrastructure provider EMC, by the end of 2010, 1.8 zettabytes of digitized information will have been created[14]—a number more difficult to comprehend than our national debt and 129 million times more information than is contained in all the books in the Library of Congress.

As you contemplate these numbers, consider that the same study concluded that only 18 months are needed for all the information in the digital universe to double. I am reminded of an elderly friend who once told me, "My memory is still good. It's just that the retrieval has slowed significantly." With so much data to search, it's little wonder that the study also concluded that 85 percent of an organization's unstructured data goes untapped. In the future, to tap and manage such massive amounts of data, companies will need to follow the example of Google and begin to optimize procedures for data search and retrieval.

Computers and the Worldwide Web are not merely digitizing search engines; they are helping to generate entirely new forms of data. One, "social media data," consists of all the chatter generated in online forums such as Facebook, Twitter, and YouTube. Hidden in the megapile of conversational junk is a potentially rich mother lode of information related to current sentiments about products, services, and organizations.

The numbers are difficult to fathom. Facebook alone counts more than 400 million active users worldwide, 50 percent of whom log in on any given day. The average Facebook user creates 70 pieces of content each month and is connected to 60 pages, groups, and events. There are 100 million users who access Facebook through their mobile devices, and these users are twice as active on the site as are nonmobile users.[15]

Then there's the social networking site Twitter. In 2007, the world was "tweeting" 5,000 times a day; by 2008, that number had grown to 300,000 tweets a day; by 2009, to 2.5 million per day; and by February 2010, 50 million tweets a day.[16] That's an average of 600 tweets per second! How can anyone possibly keep up?

The answer to this exploding world of information is Optimization. Adding more hard drives to the data center is merely the modern equivalent of adding more filing cabinets. Optimization holds the key to efficiently combing through exploding volumes of data—and it is opening new doors. SAS, a developer of analytics software, recently introduced a service that it calls SAS Social Media Analytics. Until recently, computers were not as skilled as people in reading text and interpreting whether the message reflected a positive or negative view. (Slang or colloquialisms can be very confusing to a machine.) And the best computers have only been approximately 70 percent as accurate as a human in rating sentiment.

SAS's sentiment-analysis software, however, has been rated as high as 92 percent accurate.[17] The software can also generate an influence score to help marketers identify people, blogs, and websites that carry the most weight in generating a sentiment score for an industry, company, or product. Now, using the SAS service, a company like Marriott can identify the people on Twitter who have the highest percentage of tweets related to the hotel industry in general or to Marriott in particular. It can also look at how often others respond to this person's tweets, allowing the software to identify a group of top influencers whom Marriott should target with information about its hotels and services. The sea of social data is so vast that the only way it can be accurately analyzed is through the use of optimization software.

The combination of vast stores of digitized data and optimization engines is generating new ways of solving old problems. In the 1950s, a heated debate raged as to whether it would ever be possible to "decode" language in the way that a computer program might be decoded. Noam Chomsky, for one, argued that human language was too complex to be decoded. In fact, over the years computer programs that have used a decoding approach to develop language translators have fallen woefully short.

Google, the consummate optimizer, has taken a different tack in developing its language translation program. Rather than decode or translate a phrase word by word, Google relies on statistical translation technology. Type in a word or phrase from one language into Google's translator and ask for a translation, and Google proceeds to search databases of parallel translations from organizations such as the United Nations and European Parliament proceedings to find a translation of your word or phrase. The technique is not particularly accurate when based on only a few hundred, or even a few thousand, parallel translations. However, when based on millions of comparisons, the translations become quite accurate. The rapidly increasing volume of digitized data suggests many future applications. As Peter Norvig, Google's director of research, states, ". . . it certainly seems like there's lots of tasks for which this approach will work. You can approximate human performance if you can get enough examples."[18]

3. New Solutions to Pressing Problems

The coming wave of IT investment is certain to include investments in a number of areas other than Optimization and Smart Computing, such as Cloud Computing, or heavy use of the Internet for data storage and processing. However, Bartels believes that Smart Computing will outstrip other investments for the simple reason that it helps solve problems that could not previously be solved. Historically, each wave of investment has been driven by this problem-solving ability rather than by the ability to simply execute tasks quicker and less expensively. Mainframe computing automated high-frequency, standardized transactions such as invoice generation and claims processing. Personal computing helped automate individual transactions such as memo writing, presentation preparation, and basic financial analyses. Both technologies have had a tremendous impact on the income statements of companies by creating new solutions to existing problems of productivity.

Cloud Computing, which can provide businesses with high-availability, low-maintenance, on-demand storage and computing, is tailor made to help take Optimization to the next level. With it, businesses can explore the potential of CPU-hungry optimization programs without having to make large capital expenditures.

Apart from managing the rapidly building tsunami of data, Bartels argues that the next big set of issues that business will face relates to the balance sheet. How do we go about finding ways to optimize the value of—and return on—assets, while minimizing the costs and risks of liabilities? It's a top-of-mind question for every senior executive, especially in an era of volatility and pullback. The new Smart Computing tools are expected to provide businesses and governments with far better real-time awareness of the status of their assets and liabilities, together with analyses that will help maximize their use.

As portrayed in this book, the initial focus of Optimization has been on optimizing physical assets such as trucks, airplanes, buildings, machinery, and inventory. Today, however, its use is rapidly spreading to managing intangible assets—such as customer contact time, suppliers, brand equity, intellectual property—and knowledge workers—such as salespeople and consulting teams. Bartels anticipates that, "The abilities of Smart Computing to optimize the management of the balance sheet will meet a ready audience because the current recession has heightened CEO awareness of the importance of the balance sheet. The 2008 to 2009 recession was in many ways a balance-sheet-driven downturn."[19]

The need to extract every ounce of performance from assets and the balance sheet extends beyond business to governments and philanthropic organizations around the world. In Chapter 2, we discussed the challenge of meeting the desire of the developing world to follow the model of consumption of already developed countries. There are simply not enough global resources for this model to be extended to the undeveloped world. Concluding that the rest of the world cannot live like the United States, Western Europe, and Japan, however, does not necessarily preclude everyone from achieving a high standard of living. It simply means that the world cannot continue to consume assets in the same suboptimal fashion as in the past. No one knows how many people planet Earth could support comfortably if resources began to be used in an optimal fashion.

Optimization techniques are now being used to better manage global assets. One interesting application is yield management. As described in Chapter 3, revenue or yield management addresses the challenge of optimally using perishable assets such as airplane seats or hotel rooms by adjusting prices. Pay $550 for an airline ticket and then find yourself sitting across the aisle from someone who has paid only $149, and you're apt to think that yield management is little more than a corporate swindling technique. But there is another perspective: yield management can be viewed as a means of fully utilizing assets by opening up markets to people who possess fewer resources. The person sitting next to you may never have been able to fly without a discount ticket. Offering the seat at a lower price seems preferable to simply having it fly empty. It's a win-win-win situation: the company earns more money, a person gets to fly who might never have been able to do so, and the price of your $550 ticket is unlikely to go up, given the airline's ability to generate greater value from an empty seat.

Walmart has recently announced that it will begin to use the same yield management principles to help fight world hunger.[20] The megaoptimizer has announced that it plans to donate $2 billion to the nation's food banks over the next five years. The gift comes in several tranches. First is a $250 million grant to buy refrigerated trucks to help transport fruits, vegetables, and meat from Walmart stores to charity centers. The second tranche will involve donating 1.1 *billion* pounds of food that cannot be sold because it is approaching its expiration date. Estimates are that the food will provide one billion meals to the food banks. Finally, Walmart has also announced that it will donate its logistics expertise to help food banks operate on a larger scale and run in a more optimized manner. No single organization can solve world hunger, even if that organization is the size of Walmart. But Walmart's world-hunger initiative is a good example of what might be achieved by applying proven asset-optimization techniques to intractable problems. Imagine what would happen if networks of organizations worked in concert to optimize their attacks on world challenges such as hunger and disease.

Ubiquitous Optimization

The triple dynamic of always-on computing power, staggering amounts of digitized data, and mounting pressure on many traditional assets such as energy, land, water, and food seem certain to propel Optimization forward into a multitude of new areas. As illustrated in this book, from music selection to lilies to transportation vehicles to sleeping accommodations, an almost limitless number of assets exist that could be managed in a more optimal fashion. Opportunities abound. That said, we will next look at three areas in which societal pressures and current trends suggest especially rapid advances in Optimization: (1) security, (2) health care, and (3) consumer products.

1. Security: Optimal Vigilance

Even in ordinary times, security—for individuals, organizations, and nations—is very basic in Maslow's hierarchy of needs: just above breathing, nourishment, and water. But these are not ordinary times. We live in an age of hyperanxiety. In this post-9/11 age of apocalyptic terrorism and rogue nuclear states, a sense of existential threat has become our constant companion. We not only feel more exposed to threat; we simply feel more exposed. Video cameras in public places, availability of private information on the Internet, companies tracking consumer-spending patterns, and hackers invading information-rich sites—all this can be unnerving. The home movies of our soul have become public theater.

What can an individual, organization, or government do for protection?

Optimization is one answer, and there is evidence that it is becoming a major enabler of enhanced security. The Centre for Secure Information Technologies (CSIT) is located at Queen's University in Belfast. The Centre has brought together under one roof a unique set of resources that possess cutting-edge expertise in data security, network security, wireless network systems, and surveillance intelligence systems. The Centre's mission is "converged security," which it describes as the use of IT systems to improve people's physical security, while protecting the systems themselves from being compromised.[21]

One area on which CSIT is focusing attention is the use of closed-circuit television (CCTV) to not only catch criminals, but also prevent crime. Despite massive investments in CCTV systems across the United Kingdom in recent years, their ability to prevent crime has been minimal. It has proven tough to zero in on dangerous, developing situations before they come to pass. This is primarily because the amount of data fed into the control room is simply too massive for humans to monitor and evaluate intelligently. Rather than hiring increasing numbers of human monitors, CSIT is investigating new optimization software that, in combination with massively parallel processing, analyzes all the video and audio information captured by the cameras. The software gives each situation a "threat" score, based on such factors as time of day, crime statistics for the location, threatening or fearful actions of people in the video. Scenes with a high threat score are then fed to monitors in the control room for human evaluation and the selection of an appropriate response, such as alerting a nearby police car.

CSIT is also using its supersystems and optimization software to improve Internet security. Again, the volume of Internet traffic has grown to such an extent that it has been impossible to monitor in real time. However, with CSIT's new optimization techniques, Internet traffic can be monitored and analyzed at a speed fast enough to allow every suspicious online conversation, virus-bearing e-mail, and request from a "bad" website to be detected and blocked automatically. The project's leader, Dr. Sakir Sezer, comments:

> The combination of next-generation content-processor technology and more sophisticated rule sets will improve Internet security beyond recognition, ensuring more threats and attacks are prevented or mitigated at a much earlier stage. That means less online bullying and harassment, less identity theft, fewer viruses, and less Internet misuse in general for users to contend with.[22]

Monitoring of video and the Internet is one way in which optimization software can improve security. At SAS, John Brocklebank and his team in the SAS Solutions On-Demand Division are moving in a different direction to improve security: uncovering fraud through the analysis of transaction anomalies and social networks.

To understand the revolution that Smart Computing and Optimization are bringing to fraud detection, it helps to understand typical practices. Traditionally, organizations such as banks, insurance companies, and companies that process warranty claims have relied on manual adjudication. This is simply a fancy way of describing the use of hand labor to sort through and review thousands of accounts, looking for anomalies that suggest that some type of fraud may have been committed. Sometimes the adjudicators use simple business rules to help them flag suspect transactions: for example, "Pull anyone with more than three claims in the past year" or "Review the account of anyone completing an internal transfer of $10,000 or more." Once the account has been flagged and carefully reviewed, it may warrant a field visit.

This traditional approach is both time consuming and expensive. Making things even worse is that the business rules often do not do a good job of flagging fraud, causing the hand reviews to be misguided. At one SAS client, for example, each of 30 investigators had a large stack of folders on his or her desk for review. While each folder represented a flagged account, there was no system for prioritizing the order in which each should be investigated. You can imagine the amount of time required to uncover the 10 or 15 percent of the folders that represented a real case of fraud.

That was before the SAS optimizers came along with their Fraud Framework. It features a suite of software solutions that go beyond simple business rules to using an array of different analytic techniques to ferret out fraudsters. As the software zips through years of bank transactions, insurance claims, or warranty submissions, it looks for anomalies or perturbations that have been associated with fraud in the past. Advanced statistical techniques and probability modeling are used to generate "fraud scores" for the folders; the scores can then be used by investigators to set priorities for following up.

The application of such techniques can quickly yield tremendous savings. When the appliances division of General Electric (GE) launched a pilot project, using SAS's tools, to identify fraudulent warranty claims, its auditors estimated that $5 million in false claims was saved in the first year.[23]

One of the more interesting aspects of SAS's work is its heavy reliance on finding errors in data sets. Typically, optimizers abhor error-filled, or noisy, data. They will go to great lengths to clean up "fat-finger" errors, such as a clerk entering 255 instead of 25 in an address line. However, many types of fraudsters exploit data errors by recycling names and addresses. They open an account and then quickly open another account using a slightly altered name, phone number, or Social Security number, knowing that a person, or even a computer, will have trouble finding the discrepancy. The second account may then be used to fraudulently acquire additional free services, to recycle funds, or to illegitimately acquire additional credit.

Rather than requiring a clean data set, SAS's optimizers search for and use "close matches" as one of the keys that fraud is occurring. But how can SAS's software tell the difference between a legitimate fat-finger entry error and an intentional error that suggests fraud? One way is by not relying on just one marker. SAS's Fraud Framework looks at an individual or a set of transactions through multiple lenses. If each of the different perspectives suggests fraud, the probability of fraudulent behavior increases greatly.

One lens or perspective that SAS has been a leader in developing is the social- network lens. Like the rest of us, criminals do not live in a vacuum. They have mothers, families, friends, and workmates. Analyzing a person's network of contacts can be very useful in developing a picture of evolving fraudulent behavior.

Figure 7.3 presents an illustration of SAS's social network-analysis tool. Of interest in this analysis are Carol Simmons, at the bottom of the figure, and another woman, Catherine Woolverton, in the top cluster. The social analysis uncovered two accounts for which the women had been cosigners, represented by the red and green squares with pictures of checkbooks in them.

This link between the two women and the accounts—plus a suspicious number of credits being granted to the accounts—quickly allowed investigators to uncover fraudulent account activity. Historically, such a discovery would have required an investigator to spend days searching through a bank's customer-information data. SAS has found that by incorporating social-network data into its fraud

FIGURE 7.3   SAS Example of Social-Network Analysis[24]

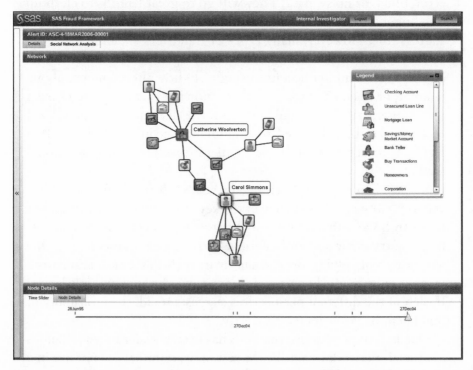

(Copyright © 2008 SAS Institute Inc., Cary, NC, USA, All Rights Reserved. Used with permission.)

analyses, it can increase detection rates tenfold. Only the power of the computer could bring together in a timely fashion so many different perspectives to help increase fraud-detection rates.

Like the scientists at CSIT, SAS researchers are moving away from what is called the pay-and-chase model, in which investigators try to uncover and catch a perpetrator after a crime has been committed. The model of the future is one of rapid, real-time monitoring of transactions as a fraudster is opening an account, making it possible to halt an inappropriate payment or service before it occurs. In security, as in other aspects of life, an ounce of prevention is worth a pound of cure.

2. A Healthy Dose of Optimization

Not surprisingly, one area in which Smart Computing and fraud detection are beginning to have an impact is health care. The amount of fraudulent claims paid by Medicare alone has been estimated to be between $60 and $100 billion a year.[25] In a recent case, SAS's Brocklebank reports that by using the company's fraud-detection tools, his team was able to detect almost $30 million in illegitimate provider claims 24 months before SAS's client, a government agency, would have spotted them. The early detection was estimated to have saved the agency approximately $20 million.

Health care seems destined to experience a heavy application of Optimization beyond the fraud detection and support for complex contract negotiations that were described in Chapter 4. Optimization is also increasingly being used to create breakthrough disease treatments.

Prostate cancer has surpassed lung cancer as the most common form of cancer among men in the United States and is now the number-one cancer killer of men. Between 10 and 15 percent of the approximately quarter-million new cases diagnosed each year are eventually terminal. The two major treatment regiments are surgery, to remove the tumor, and radiation, designed to shrink it. Because of the frequency of severe side effects from surgery—incontinence and impotence—an increasing number of patients are choosing radiation, which for certain cancers has a survival rate equal to that of surgery.

The challenge in using radiation is to deliver a sufficiently strong dose of radiation to shrink the tumor, without harming surrounding healthy tissue. There are two approaches used to do this. One is teletherapy, which involves using external beams of high-energy gamma rays; a second approach, brachytherapy, involves using needles to implant radioactive seeds in and around the tumor to deliver the prescribed radiation dose. Brachytherapy is becoming an increasingly popular choice. The treatment can be compressed into a single-day surgical procedure, as opposed to the repeated visits over a two-month period that are required by teletherapy. And brachytherapy does a better job of confining the radiation to the target area, thereby causing less damage and associated side effects on surrounding organs, such as the rectum and bladder.

Implanting 60 to 150 radioactive seeds into a prostate, in exactly the correct geometric pattern to radiate a tumor but not the surrounding healthy tissue, has its own set of unique challenges. Traditionally, to design a treatment—or seed-placement—plan, a patient undergoes an ultrasound or CT scan several days prior to the implantation procedure. The cancerous area is mapped onto a grid, and the placement positions of the seeds specified. However, because the CT pictures are two dimensional, the physician-planner must rely heavily on intuition and past experience when designing the seed-placement scheme. Then, based on another set of images taken during the surgery, the surgeon may revise the scheme. In spite of all the planning, a host of problems and constraints may arise.

First, since development of the plan requires manual inspection of multiple two-dimensional images, the plan takes several hours to complete and even then takes into consideration only a small fraction of all the possible seed-placement configurations. Next, the images taken at the planning session differ from those obtained in the operating room, often resulting in difficult and inaccurate comparisons. For example, an anatomical structure, not visible in the planning CT, may block the placement of a needle. Or as often happens, the prostate volume measured during planning may be different from the volume encountered in the operating room, again requiring a change in plan. When this happens, the surgeon and the team must revise the plan on the fly.

Faced with the complex set of decisions that need to be made when carrying out brachytherapy, Memorial Sloan-Kettering Cancer Center (MSKCC) turned to Optimization.[26] Many aspects of the problem appeared to make it an ideal optimization project: the dual goals of delivering the correct dosage of radiation in a predetermined area, while avoiding other areas, creates a complex set of three-dimension constraints that must be balanced; the almost infinite number of possible configurations creates an extremely large set of possible solutions within which to seek an optimal solution; and when unanticipated problems arise during surgery, there is a need to quickly adjust the presurgery plan in an optimal fashion.

The calculation complexities turned out to be so great that optimizers from the Department of Medical Physics at MSKCC and the Georgia Institute of Technology in Atlanta had to develop a number of new approaches to solving the large set of mathematical equations. But once they had, the results produced an impressive win for Optimization. Their optimization program returns solutions in seconds rather than hours, making possible real-time solutions in the operating room. This eliminates the need for a preplanning session, saving both patients and medical staff hours of work. Producing plans on the spot, in surgery, also eliminates discrepancies created by changes in position on the viewing table or changes in the size of the prostate. If an obstruction is encountered during needle insertion, an optimal reconfiguration of the insertion map can be generated immediately, thereby eliminating guessing on the part of the surgeon. The result has been an improvement in accuracy of the radiation field from 10 to 20 percent, despite the fact that the optimized solutions typically use 20 to 30 percent fewer seeds. Undesirable side effects such as urinary-tract toxicity have been reduced by 45 to 60 percent.

As for dollar savings, the elimination of the preplanning session alone saves approximately $5,000 per patient. When the system is deployed nationwide, the savings are projected to exceed $300 million from prostate surgeries alone. It will be many times more when the optimization procedure begins to be used in brachytherapies for other cancers such as those of the breast, cervix, esophagus, eye, and brain. MSKCC's successes are a harbinger of things to come: the future of Optimization in medicine will improve treatment, lower costs, enable less-invasive procedures, and reduce the number of side effects experienced by patients.

One final, likely future application of Optimization in medicine is worth mentioning. Although the figures are controversial, some have argued that evidence suggests that 90 percent of prescription drugs work less than 50 percent of the time.[27] Worse yet, conservative estimates have put the number of U.S. deaths from conventional medicine mistakes at more than 750,000 a year.[28] Whatever the exact number, it is clear that taking prescription drugs is a lot less effective and safe than your doctor and pharmaceutical companies want you to believe.

In many ways, this is not surprising. Each of us is biologically a one-of-a-kind package—a unique combination of many factors, including genetic makeup, size, weight, metabolism, and the like. And each of us may be on a specialized drug regimen. It is unrealistic to expect that a single medicine and dosage would work equally well for each of us. High-powered computers and optimization techniques are poised to usher in an age of effective, personalized medicine.

One example is Eli Lilly & Company's recent introduction of the cancer drug Alimta. During clinical trials, the drug showed remarkable effectiveness in combating tumors in a particularly virulent form of lung cancer. However, a series of unpredictable, life-threatening reactions to the drug threatened its chances of approval. In an attempt to understand the side effects, researchers began analyzing a large number of possible "markers" from a group of 246 patients. The research question under investigation was which, if any, of the markers, considered alone or in combination with others, might be able to predict the toxic reaction?

Among all the combinations, the optimization software was able to identify two culprits that caused severe reactions: a deficiency in folic acid and one in vitamin B_{12}. Using advanced multivariate statistical techniques, the software was able to quantify the risk of developing a toxic reaction and recommend vitamin supplements for at-risk patients.

The drug has subsequently been approved in both Europe and the United States and is saving lives. Its high level of effectiveness has led it to being studied for other common cancers, including breast and colorectal cancer.[29] It is quite possible that in the future we will come to view small pill bottles containing identical milligrams of medicine as a quaint—or even barbaric—practice. Looking ahead, it is likely that we will receive personalized prescriptions that take into account a large variety of personal markers associated with each drug's effectiveness.

3. The Wonderful World of Consumers

In the immediate future, the area in which it seems likely that we will encounter Optimization most frequently is the world of consumer products. With some estimates of consumer spending comprising as much as 70 percent of the U.S. economy,[30] the rush has already begun to enhance the consumer's experience through the introduction of "smart products."

To get a glimpse of tomorrow, take a ride in Toyota's new Prius V. Not only does its software make recommendations: it executes them. If you slip the car into "parallel-parking mode," it uses a patented optimization system to combine camera and sonar inputs to smoothly steer your car into a parking spot.[31]

A car capable of parking itself? It's hardly child's play, and neither are some of the other features of the Prius V. The car's cameras also track the lane lines on roads. If the car's computer senses that you are starting to drift, it sounds its Lane Departure Warning. Using its Lane Keep Assist, it also helps you stay in your lane by adding additional torque to the steering wheel. If the car senses that you are approaching an object too quickly, its Collision Mitigation Breaking System sounds an alarm and advises you to slow down. If the car concludes that a crash is imminent, it tightens the seatbelts and primes the brakes for you.

In the world of tomorrow, your encounters with Optimization are likely to begin long before you head for work in your automobile. The era of the smart appliance is already upon us. Take refrigerators. There are now brands on the market that are capable of tracking what's inside—and perhaps more importantly, when it was put inside—the refrigerator. Several refrigerator models now come with Wi-Fi capability so they can be accessed from the Internet. Have you ever been in the supermarket but unable to remember whether or not you needed to buy more milk? Not to worry. Just extract your smartphone, launch the browser, and check with your refrigerator how much milk is inside and when it was purchased.

At the moment, there are a number of limitations to new smart refrigerators. One is cost—plan on investing a whopping $2,000 to $3,000 for a unit. The second is data entry. Right now, most entry must be done by hand. Each time you put away the groceries, you must "tell" the refrigerator what you are putting into it. However, some of the newest smart refrigerators have radio-frequency identification (RFID) chip readers. If the food placed in the refrigerator has an RFID chip, the refrigerator automatically reads and remembers it. Unfortunately, only a limited number of foods currently have such chips.

The future seems clear, however. You are likely to be surrounded by an array of Web-enabled smart appliances that possess the "self-knowledge" to tell you what maintenance they require and when they need to be restocked. The day is certainly quickly approaching when you will be able to query your refrigerator from your smartphone for a dinner recommendation. Scanning its leftovers, the refrigerator will let you know that if you just stop and pick up a container of heavy cream you will be able to make a delicious chicken curry.

Once appliances become "Internet enabled," they will be able to "talk" to one another. You might wonder why your refrigerator would want to talk with your air conditioner, clothes dryer, or dishwasher. One reason could be to coordinate their use of energy. Such discussions among machines could reduce expensive peak-power generation and even help ward off the types of power-grid failures that plunged the Midwest into darkness in 1996 and the Northeast into darkness in 2003.

Researchers from the Northwest National Laboratory in Richland, Washington, are looking at ways that smart appliances and homeowners with better information about power usage can reduce power consumption during peak periods, when the power grid is most susceptible to breakdowns.[32] The work includes designing appliances with computer chips that can sense when the transmission system is stressed. This would enable them to turn themselves off or delay initiating a task—after checking with other appliances, of course, to see what they are doing.[33]

Testing the devices with customers, the researchers found that consumers experienced minimal impact from minor interruptions to their appliances' operations. Thus a refrigerator sensing a distressed grid might keep its 20-watt lightbulb on but briefly interrupt the operation of its compressor. Or an electric dryer might briefly allow its heating element to cool down, with minimum disruption to the drying cycle. Rob Pratt, the laboratory's program manager for the project, argues that if such appliances were adopted across the country, over a period of 20 years they could save $70 billion in power-plant-construction and power-distribution costs.

Of course, all these means of saving power have not escaped the notice of such optimizers as McDonald's. McDonald's USA has developed an optimization program dubbed Fire-Up Tool. Based on restaurant-specific equipment and operating hours, the program identifies the optimum times to turn kitchen equipment on or off. Through consistent use of the Fire-Up schedule and associated tools to monitor electricity usage, the average McDonald's restaurant can save up to $1,500 a year on its electric bill.[34] And at the fast-food end of the restaurant business, where margins are paper thin, every dollar counts!

Apart from avoiding darkness, using smart appliances has many other benefits for consumers. Once appliances are connected to the Internet, it becomes possible for them to receive updates on the price of electricity throughout the day and evening. It would be a short step for the appliances to begin regulating themselves in ways that save energy and reduce the electric bill. Energy Star II—or whatever the name it will be given—will likely involve machines that are not only energy efficient, but also smart enough to regulate their own behavior, as well as the behavior of surrounding appliances, to help conserve resources.

If your business is somehow related to consumer appliances, you might consider a recent report by the research and consulting firm Zpryme, which estimates that the global smart-household-appliance market will grow from $3.06 billion to $15.12 billion over the next five years. By 2015, the global market for smart washers and refrigerators alone is projected to be $3.54 billion and $2.69 billion, respectively.[35]

A smart washing machine would be nice, but how about an executive assistant: someone who can set up appointments, make reservations, look up information, and get to know your personal likes and dislikes? Sounds like another page from "The Jetsons," but it's in the works. Several years ago, the Defense Advanced Research Projects Agency (DARPA) approached SRI International, a nonprofit research group, to ask about the possibility of developing a humanlike system that could learn. One of the outcomes of this effort was a spin-off company named Siri, which has set out to bring Cognitive Assistant that Learns and Organizes (CALO) technology to consumers via their smartphones.[36]

Let me introduce you to the company's automated assistant, Siri. She can understand your oral requests, complete tasks, and even learn your preferences. Siri is one smart lady. She not only knows how to access your personal information on your phone, but she can tap into the Internet, both to draw on additional computing power and search for useful information.

Ask Siri for a restaurant nearby, and she will identify your location and make a recommendation. Initially, you may have to tell Siri about the types of food you prefer, but over time, like a real executive assistant, Siri will learn your preferences and act on them. Ask about a concert, and she can not only provide the starting time but also order tickets and make a reservation at a nearby club for you to visit afterward. With the ability to access your calendar and contacts, she can alert you to conflicts in your schedule and perhaps, based on recent dates that you've gone on or gifts that you have sent, recommend a friend who you can ask to accompany you. True, there are things Siri cannot do, such as purchase an airplane ticket. However, given her ability to learn, count on her to master those tasks as well in the near future.

In spite of tough economic times and a flat-to-declining growth in cell-phone revenue, smartphone sales increased rapidly in 2009. The Gartner Group estimates that, worldwide, 172 million smartphones were sold in 2009: a 24 percent increase over 2008.[37] It seems certain that that figure will continue to grow at a double-digit rate. Gartner's latest figures show that, on a quarter-to-quarter basis, smartphone sales surged in the first quarter of 2010 by 48.7 percent—as 54.3 million units flew off the shelves.[38] It is difficult to overstate how quickly optimization capabilities, along with optimization software, are finding their way into the hands and pockets of consumers. And let us not forget: today's smartphone will be tomorrow's "dumb" phone, and tomorrow's smartphone might be unimaginable to most of us. It might not even be recognizable to us as a phone!

As a growing number of organizations and individuals experience Optimization, it is certain to change how organizations view and implement optimization projects. In the next section, we will examine what some of these changes are likely to be.

Optimization in Tomorrow's Organization

The way in which decisions are made goes a long way toward defining an organization and how it operates. As computers increasingly assume decision-making responsibility, at both the individual and organizational levels, it is likely that we will see many changes in organizational structure, as well as in the implementation of optimization projects. Here are a few of the changes that I anticipate seeing in the near future.

Revolutionizing Decision Making

The ascendancy of Optimization should dramatically bring decision making to the forefront of organizations' consciousness. Today, a vast number of decisions continue to be made by people sitting around a conference table, chatting on the phone, or exchanging e-mails. Companies that examine key decision points of their most important business processes and replace jawboning and hand-wringing with Optimization will improve speed, reliability, scalability, and efficiency. Ultimately, these are the companies that will gain a competitive advantage and make it to the top of everyone's "most admired" list.

The Ascendancy of "and" Thinking

Once an individual becomes heavily involved in Optimization, it changes how he or she thinks about problems. One of the most important changes is a shift from "or" to "and" thinking. Faced with the desire to reduce decision making to simple terms, we learn from an early age to think in terms of one option *or* another: "I can either do 'A' *or* 'B.'" "Do you want me to do it quickly *or* well?" "We can deliver it in five days at a standard rate *or* tomorrow at a premium." Such binary thinking is often deemed a necessary trade-off, but it can be a fatal trap that limits the number of alternatives in a decision. Optimizers don't think this way. They think not in terms of "or" but of "and." "How can we make our product or service more customized for each customer *and* less expensive?" "How can we deliver it faster *and* reduce shipping costs?" Exceptional leaders are often characterized as "and" thinkers.

The spirit of "and" thinking is nicely illustrated by the following story of one McDonald's franchisee. Eggs and meat cook at different temperatures. One consequence is that you can order breakfast at McDonald's at 10:20 A.M., but not at 10:40 A.M.—once the grills have been heated to cook lunchtime burgers. One of the most challenging problems for a manager is determining how many eggs to cook: too few and the 10:20 breakfasters don't get any; too many and some have to be thrown out. In San Francisco, an ingenious "and"-thinking store owner has begun selling the Mc10:35—eggs, ham, and a burger piled into one massive sandwich. Customers love it, product waste is eliminated, and everyone wins—but don't try to order a Mc10:35 at any other time of the day![39]

Imagine an organization in which a growing number of employees begin to think like this franchisee! This may be the greatest gift that Optimization offers an organization.

An Increased Focus on the Balance Sheet

As we face climate change, global competition, aspirations of developing countries, imploding banking systems, and exploding oil wells, there seems little doubt that we need to put a new emphasis on resource management. Smart Computers and Optimization will allow both companies and individuals to track, minute-by-minute, how resources are being consumed and then to advise on ways to deploy them more efficiently. The increased balance-sheet focus should lead, in turn, to new organizational structures and leadership positions. Already, new positions and titles are being created: director of decision engineering; director, decision-support modeling; senior director of total yield systems; managing director, enterprise optimization; and VP of solutions on demand.

Organizational structural changes are evolving more slowly. A standing joke at meetings of INFORMS' OR/MS Leader Roundtable is, "Whom are you reporting to today?" The answers vary from finance to operations to research and even to marketing. Currently, operations research (OR) and optimization positions are somewhat transient. Down the road, however, optimization groups seem certain to grow, increasing the likelihood of more permanent structures. The level of investment in Optimization could become so great that both CEOs and boards want an overseer, much as they have come to rely on CIOs and CTOs. A high-level chief of optimization would likely have a range of responsibilities, from helping evaluate new purchases or mergers to playing a key role in formulating business strategy, especially thinking through the next generation of customer demand and the next round of competitive advantage. What could be the level of savings from optimizing organizational structures, processes, and networks or from optimizing suboptimal decisions? In answering the question, the chief optimization officer can play a key role, alongside his counterparts in human resources and finance. One advantage of establishing a permanent, senior-level optimization position is the ability to provide a career path for the best and the brightest optimizers, who today often get redirected to—and buried in—functions such as marketing or IT.

Shortened Learning Time

Today, when our firm begins an optimization project, our consultants often encounter high levels of skepticism as to what kind of decisions a computer can make. Our going-in assumption is that, even when the company has previously implemented an optimization project, we need to be extremely adroit—almost paranoid—in selling, explaining, educating, and looking for data. As Optimization comes to play an increasingly central role in both business and personal lives, people's familiarity with—and acceptance of—decision-making software will increase. This will be especially true for the next generation of corporate leaders, who will have grown up trusting their laptop and smartphone apps.

This increased knowledge and acceptance will mean that less time will be required to educate employees about Optimization. Just as IT teams no longer need to explain the meaning of, "We'll put it in the data warehouse," people will be familiar with common optimization concepts such as "business rules," "constraints," "soft costs," "simulation," and "objective functions."

Specialized Optimization Apps

Today, Optimization is either embedded in large suites of expensive software or in general optimization solvers that need to be programmed from scratch before they can be applied to any business problem. These general solvers are similar to an Excel spreadsheet program. You open a blank spreadsheet to develop your optimization model. There are currently relatively few off-the-shelf optimization-software packages designed to solve a specific class of business problems, but this is already beginning to change. There are already a few specialized software packages that use Optimization to solve specific *industry* problems, such as when and how much a retailer should discount prices.[40] Going forward, there is likely to be a surge in such programs because assets and liabilities—more than general processes such as invoicing—tend to be industry specific. A financial services firm, for example, will focus on optimizing the value of its financial portfolio. In contrast, a transportation firm or utility will focus on optimizing physical assets. Execution of optimization projects should be greatly facilitated by these industry-specific, less-costly packages.

As we think about the world of apps being unleashed by Apple and other smartphone makers, an image arises of a possible new way of building optimization programs. Rather than a large-scale, "boil the ocean" approach, in the future business teams may be able to quickly prototype and solve problems using inexpensive optimization apps that they can connect together. Most optimization projects today require that far too much time be spent on understanding the basic business problem and putting it into a solvable framework. In Chapter 6, we discussed the importance of "early wins" to boost confidence in an optimization project. The ability to jump-start a project from a robust selection of off-the-shelf apps that "know" about specific business problems would surely be a confidence builder.

The Rise of the Hybrid Employee

As Optimization takes center stage, there will be an increasing demand for hybrid employees: those who combine an engineering or mathematical perspective with a deep understanding of the business. Add in a heavy dose of communication skills and some creativity, and you have the perfect job candidate of the future. Companies that are heavy users of Optimization are already searching for and promoting such individuals. Craig Barrett, who went on to become Intel's CEO, was initially recruited from a Stanford engineering department. He, in turn, hired Karl Kempf, another scientist, to launch Intel's Decision Technology Group. Other hybrid individuals are now rising to national prominence. Paul O'Neill, who was trained in OR, became

U.S. Secretary of the Treasury; in Japan, an operations researcher, Yukio Hatoyama, served recently as the country's Premier.

Much has been said about the United States' need to strengthen math and engineering courses in its schools to compete on a global basis. It's a good start, but it is not sufficient. To lead the next wave of innovation, we need not only math majors and engineers, but also individuals with outstanding communication skills and creativity. At Princeton Consultants, we tell our employees that their most valuable asset is their ability to quickly get to state-of-the-art on a new topic. Given the expected pace of change, it will be an essential capability for every successful employee.

Mining the New Gold

Land and the availability of large pools of physical labor once defined the wealth of nations and companies. Today, wealth is more closely linked to access to capital and special contract rights for distribution, natural resources, or intellectual property. Think about AT&T and its exclusive contract with Apple for the latter's iPhone. Tomorrow, it is likely that wealth will increasingly depend on access to data, data networks, and the intellectual capital required to effectively exploit them. Think of Google as a model for tomorrow. Companies will increasingly face questions such as, "How will we gain access to the digitized data that we need?" "Will it be more economical to lease, buy, or manufacture those data?" "What percent of our budget must we dedicate to protecting our data and data networks?" "How can we make better use of existing data to drive greater and greater value from our current assets, to improve our products and services, and to think more incisively about future options?" One very positive note: digital data represent an unlimited resource that is likely to become increasingly inexpensive to produce and manage.

Rocket-Propelled Innovation

One aspect of the coming decade seems clear: the pace of innovation will rapidly accelerate. One reason is that the process of conducting and evaluating experiments has become faster, cheaper, and easier to implement. Google, for example, often runs as many as 200 experiments simultaneously. The Web has made it extremely easy and inexpensive to test new ideas and assess how the public responds. But it is not just Web-based companies that are jumping on the innovation express. Tracking systems that monitor everything from cash register purchases to the movement of products through the supply chain are allowing even brick-and-mortar establishments to collect terabytes of data on customer interactions. Walmart, for example, continually runs in-store experiments to compare the effectiveness of alternative displays, shelf layouts, and signage. Checkout and traffic statistics allow it to see results quickly and cheaply. Not only is it inexpensive to test new ideas, but those ideas that pass the test are becoming increasingly easy to scale up. A change to a Web page can be displayed to millions of viewers in minutes. Since core processes have been digitized, brick-and-mortar establishments can also make almost instantaneous changes. When McDonald's finds a better way to screen new employees, it can implement it and other changes instantly at thousands of stores via its human resource software. Laurie Gilbert, who heads up Innovation Operations at McDonald's, comments on the pace of innovation:

> We have been able to not only grow our value through increased innovative services [and experimentation], but we have also reduced our overall cycle time so dramatically that last year we completed 50,000 experiments . . . we rapidly prototype the design and development of solutions applying a mind-set of "Fail Fast, Fail Forward" . . . it used to take six months to a year to validate a test in a market, but now with the addition of operations research and the use of video analytics, it takes less than three months.[41]

One outcome of all this innovation is a new emphasis on hiring employees with an "experimentation mind-set."[42] Such employees possess both an inquisitive nature and the quantitative skills needed to turn results into tangible rules for optimization software.

Postscript on the Optimized Organization

The Industrial Revolution liberated blue-collar laborers from a great deal of drudgery and backbreaking work. Jobs were lost, but new occupations were created to replace them. Decision-making software seems likely to create a similar revolution for white-collar workers. Increasingly, traditional white-collar drudgery—tasks such as designing schedules, setting prices, managing inventory, preplanning medical procedures, and reviewing supplier contracts—is being assumed by computers.

Computers may even shortly take over the newsroom. In 2009, a group of computer science and journalism students at Northwestern University designed a program called Stats Monkey, which was capable of writing an accurate and compelling description of a baseball game.[43] The program uses the box office score and summary of the play-by-play to analyze the game and write about it. Its stories communicate whether the game was a come-from-behind victory, a pitchers' duel, or a seesaw nail-biter. With a player roster, the program can name names and easily identify key players in the victory. It can also generate a story from the perspective of either team. The technology underlying Stats Monkey should be applicable in many domains with data-driven, recurring story themes. Beyond sports, this would include many business "stories," such as quarterly or annual earnings reports.

While white-collar workers will be needed for many years to monitor the decisions that computers will be making, the more exciting work is likely to involve designing and conducting experiments or formulating hypotheses about how to improve the decision-making capabilities of computers. Whatever decisions remain with humans in the future, keeping ahead of machines will demand a high degree of education and creativity. This is certain to involve a great deal of change. Optimization is the science of "best," and best often entails challenging the status quo and cultural standpattism to make and execute the optimal decision.

Pot Holes and Speed Bumps on the Optimization Highway

While the future of Optimization is likely to be bright, the journey, like any trek forward, will inevitably include potholes, speed bumps, and setbacks. The three biggest challenges to the rapid use of Optimization are likely to be (1) people's inherent reluctance to change, especially when it comes to giving up decision-making control; (2) lack of trust in machine-made decisions; and (3) data management.

1. Losing Control

It is a well-documented fact that, in general, people just don't like to change. This is especially true when you ask them to embrace decision-making software, which involves not only changing, but also giving up decision-making control. While I don't think that we will see many street riots over the use of optimization software, there may well be strikes, sabotage, and attempts to manipulate software to justify preconceived decisions. Such resistance will be fueled by people's excessive confidence in their own decision-making capabilities, along with fear of job loss. Change management will continue to be an important element of successful Optimization for years to come.

Counterpunching Consumers

Employees will not be the only ones who resist Optimization. Consumers have a love-hate relationship with automated decisions. They love the convenience of smart energy-saving appliances, computer-generated driving directions, and even those automated ads on the side of Web pages—provided that they are relevant to what they are looking for. Even with computers becoming increasingly humanlike in their decisions and interaction style, there undoubtedly will be many instances in which the machines just don't seem smart enough, leaving a customer desperate to interact with a real person.

One of the more interesting recent trends involves consumers beginning to use Optimization to fight Optimization. For example, the website bing.com/travel (formerly Fare-Caster.com) uses Optimization to recommend when a traveler should buy an airplane ticket, based on a database of 175 billion previous ticket purchases. The site claims a 70 to 75 percent accuracy rate in predicting whether a ticket price will go up or down a week into the future. If this type of consumer counterattack becomes common, it could mitigate the effectiveness of optimization pricing efforts, possibly slowing its spread.

Consumers will likely find additional ways to use the Internet and social networking to undermine optimization efforts, according to

Yuri Levin, a distinguished faculty fellow in operations management at Queen's School of Business in Kingston, Ontario.[44] He notes that there have always been shoppers willing to play the waiting game to get the lowest price, even before the advent of optimization engines like bing.com/travel. The Web now provides such people ways of becoming more active and aggressive in their search for the best price.

My Web browser, for example, has a plug-in program that whenever I view a product for purchase, searches the Web and automatically recommends sources with lower prices. Online services such as eBay and Craigslist are widely used for the exchange of both old and new merchandise. You can also buy tickets to concerts and athletic events, which often allows late purchasers to obtain entry to the event at the same reduced price that producers offer to advance-ticket buyers. Levin likens such consumer behavior to "tunneling under" the fences that suppliers create to segment their pricing markets. If this were not enough to undermine optimization efforts, the Internet also opens up the possibility of quickly formed, temporary buyers' cooperatives for bulk purchases of a hot new consumer product.

It seems unlikely that resistance to Optimization by either employees or consumer groups will halt its march forward. The long-term benefits to individuals, companies, governments, and society are simply too great. Although we can expect to see skirmishes and an occasional pitched battle, Optimization is on the move and its rapid advance is unlikely to be halted.

2. The Trust Factor

Ultimately, the speed of acceptance of Optimization will depend to a large degree on the levels of trust that people develop in the decisions made by computers. This is one reason that when beginning an optimization project we typically start slowly and invest significant time up front helping users inspect and validate the logic behind each of the computer's recommendations, until they feel comfortable. Several factors, however, may impede trust-building between humans and machines.

First, machines—just like people—can make really bad decisions. After all, computer programs and algorithms are based on human assumptions, making computer infallibility highly improbable. Adding to the bad-decision problem is the fact that computers can operate so quickly that small missteps can be compounded into large problems in an eyeblink.

Consider what *USA Today* labeled the "wildest day in Wall Street history."[45] At 2:30 P.M. on Thursday, May 6, 2010, the Dow Jones Industrial Average stood at 10,591. Sixteen minutes later, at 2:46 P.M., it had dropped 7 percent—to 9,870. By 3:08 P.M. it was back up to 10,569—only 22 points below where it had started at 2:46 P.M. *USA Today*'s headline screamed, "The Machines Took Over."

Such gut-wrenching gyrations are unlikely to instill in investors trust that machines have the situation under control. Inevitably, there will be more surprises in store for us as an increasing number of decisions are machine made. One possible solution to the machines-gone-wild problem is to impose human oversight. Unfortunately, this creates a whole new set of problems. First, in many cases humans are simply too slow to provide effective oversight. A large part of the power of Optimization is the speed with which computers can sort through a vast set of options and make choices. Slowing the process by imposing human oversight is far from an optimal solution.

Even more challenging is the growing body of research showing that having humans review and adjust an optimized recommendation generally decreases the accuracy of the decision. As Ian Ayres extensively documents in *Super Crunchers*,[46] when human experts are given the tools to carry out statistical analyses, their decisions generally improve. However, across a series of decisions the automated decision model still tends to outperform the aided expert. And when an expert is given the opportunity to review and adjust a computer's decision, accuracy typically declines. The expert too frequently dismisses the computer's predictions and sticks to his own misguided, overconfident judgment. All of us, experts included, too often ignore obvious data that does not fit into our preconceived frameworks, as is so aptly described by Christopher Chabris and Daniel Simons in *The Invisible Gorilla*.[47]

Where humans seem able to make their greatest contribution is in generating hypotheses about which important new variables to include in an analysis or in recognizing when the parameters of a situation have changed so radically that the computer model no longer applies. The most accurate model for teamwork between human experts and computers appears to be one that allows the computer to use the expert's recommendation as one data point in its statistical database. If a disagreement occurs between the computer's recommendation and human judgment, exercise great caution before dismissing the computer's analysis as simply "bad data" or a "program bug." Another factor likely to contribute to distrust of computer decisions is the growth of "prepackaged," industry-specific software packages, described earlier in this chapter. When our firm implements an optimization project, we work closely with the client to develop and test the algorithms that will be used in the computer program. We come to know the client's business; they come to know and trust our algorithms. If a user has a question or concern, he knows whom to go to for an answer or explanation.

Prepackaged software is likely to change such relationships. Questions such as the following will be much more difficult to answer: "Who designed the software?" "Under what conditions has it been tested?" "What assumptions are built into it?" "What situations can it handle and not handle well?" While packaged optimization software will lower costs, it is likely to raise levels of uncertainty and mistrust.

One more challenge to humans' trust in machines will be the increased adoption of Optimization and computers by criminals. Estimates of profits from cybercrime vary anywhere from a conservative $1 billion a year to as much as $400 billion a year.[48] One thing is certain: cybercrime is increasing exponentially. The Federal Bureau of Investigation (FBI), in collaboration with the Internet Crime Complaint Center, has tracked computer crime complaints since 2000. The number of complaints has grown 20-fold since the first report and by more than 60 percent in the last two years.[49]

3. Do You Know Where Your Data Are?

In spite of an array of security risks, the public is proving to be extremely trusting in sharing personal data. One-third of all smartphone users have downloaded Google maps on their phone, allowing Google to track their location. Many of us also trust Google with our address books, calendars, and e-mail. More surprisingly, over a million people share their personal financial records with Mint.com. The site has proven so successful that in 2009 it was purchased for $179 million by Intuit, a leading financial-software company. On social-networking sites such as Facebook and Twitter, people share all types of personal information, including pictures of themselves and their children.

There appear to be multiple reasons for widespread data sharing. In some cases, it seems that people are simply unaware of how much data they are sharing. A recent study by ZapShares Inc., for example, found that large numbers of people are inadvertently sharing personal tax returns, banking, credit card, and other financial information without realizing it.[50] More commonly, however, people simply find it convenient or profitable to share their data. By knowing your location, Google can recommend nearby sites and restaurants; Mint.com provides free financial analyses, alerting you when budget categories have been exceeded or where savings can be realized.

Furthermore, new services can be created when data is aggregated. In a number of cities, anonymous location-data from cell phones are being used to provide up-to-the-minute reports on traffic conditions. By analyzing health-related Web searches from different geographical areas, Google was able to estimate, well before the government could do so, the level of flu-like illnesses in regions of the United States. Google was also able to provide map overlays that showed the hot flu spots so people could choose to avoid them. If people begin to share their medical information in real time, you might someday receive an e-mail alerting you to the fact that you have come into contact with someone with a highly contagious disease. There are—and will continue to be—many benefits from sharing personal data.

The increasingly high level of data sharing, however, has created many unresolved issues related to data ownership, access, use, and security. Until recently, anyone could have accessed information from 19,000 stolen credit cards[51] by executing a simple Google search; a criminal group had placed the credit cards on its server without any security, opening it up to Google's powerful optimization search engines. Criminal activity aside, suits have recently been filed in California, Massachusetts, Oregon, and Washington, D.C., by people accusing Google of violating their privacy by collecting data from open Wi-Fi networks. The Canadian government has launched a probe of Google for possibly collecting private data while taking photographs for the company's Street View product.[52]

Tom Mitchell is former president of the Association for the Advancement of Artificial Intelligence (AAAI) and University Professor, the highest faculty distinction at Carnegie Mellon University. He is currently serving on an AAAI panel charged with exploring the societal impact of advances in artificial intelligence. Recently, he published a "Perspectives" column in the prestigious journal *Science*, concluding that:

> Society will be unable to take full advantage of real-time data analysis technologies that might improve health, reduce traffic congestion and give scientists new insights into human behavior until it resolves questions about how much of a person's life can be observed . . . the risks to privacy from aggregating these data are on a scale that humans have never before faced . . . more important than technical approaches will be a public discussion about how to rewrite the rules of data collection, ownership, and privacy . . . . Until these issues are resolved, they are likely to be the limiting factor in realizing the potential of these new data to advance our scientific understanding of society and human behavior, and to improve our daily lives.[53]

There is another data issue, apart from privacy, that may well slow the advancement of Optimization. If data and data networks become the bases of corporate wealth, efforts to "corner the market" for certain types of data seem certain to emerge. We have already seen investment banks corner and hide data about the default rates of subprime mortgages.[54]

If one of the large search engines were to merge with another search company in the near future, it is not hard to imagine the government stepping in to quash the deal. The motivation for such a challenge may not simply be to prevent services from being monopolized, but rather to thwart the megacompany's monopolistic control of the records of people's searches. The Clayton Antitrust Act of 1914 and the Robinson-Patman Act of 1936 were passed to further define antitrust activities not originally covered by the 1890 Sherman Antitrust Act. The act may need to be updated again for a world in which a company's ability to compete is driven by the amount of data that it controls.

This section of our chapter has focused on some of the challenges that Optimization will face as it grows and expands. Again, while such challenges may temporarily slow Optimization's expansion, they seem unlikely to derail it. As a McKinsey report recently concluded:

> . . . the [recent economic] crisis exposed the limitations of certain tools. In particular, the world saw the folly of the reliance by banks, insurance companies, and others on financial models that assumed economic rationality, linearity, equilibrium, and bell-curve distributions . . . It would be wrong to conclude that managers should go back to making decisions only on the basis of gut instinct. The real lessons are that the tools need to incorporate more-realistic visions of human behavior . . . and that business executives need to get better at using them. Companies will, rightly, continue to seek ways to exploit the increasing amounts of data and computing power. As they do so, decision makers in every industry must take responsibility for looking inside the black boxes that advanced quantitative tools often represent and understanding their functioning, assumptions, and limitations.[55]

Way, Way Over the Horizon

Thus far, I have based my thinking about the future on developments already visible in the research pipeline. In the final section of this chapter, I will attempt to extend my vision even further—relying in some cases on that of technology futurists.

From Dust to Light

It seems certain that you will be able to count on computers continuing to expand in power while shrinking in size. One breakthrough already on the horizon is the use of light, rather than electricity, to drive integrated circuits. When electricity flows through a circuit board, it moves relatively slowly—well below the speed of light. Even more problematic, electricity will require prohibitively high amounts of energy to move data over the wider bandwidth of tomorrow's computers. MIT researchers have recently demonstrated lasers that can operate at room temperature, using germanium, an element that can be incorporated easily[56] into existing silicon-chip-manufacturing processes. The introduction of light-based computers could allow the continued doubling of computer power every two years, in accordance with Moore's law.[57]

Computers will also continue to shrink and reshape themselves. Just ask Kris Pister, who has been fiddling with "smart dust" for years. His original idea, germinated 14 years ago, was to deploy dust-sized sensors randomly around the world so that we could monitor Earth in real time. In a few years, HP will begin working with Royal Dutch Shell to install one million smart-dust sensors around the world to measure rock vibrations to provide a smarter way to look for oil.[58] The same system can be used in the future to monitor changes in global temperature and other environmental factors.

Just how powerful are tomorrow's computers likely to become? Ray Kurzweil is a futurist once labeled by *Fortune* magazine as "the smartest futurist on Earth."[59] Bill Gates considers Kurzweil to be a visionary thinker and has invited him to dinner to pick his brain. Among his accomplishments, Kurzweil invented the flatbed scanner and the first large-vocabulary speech-recognition software. He has launched 10 companies, sold 5 of them, and written 5 books on the future of technology. He has a degree in computer science from MIT, 13 honorary doctorate degrees, and a National Medal of Technology that was presented to him by President Clinton. Perhaps most relevant, he has made a number of successful predictions in the past, including predicting, in the 1980s, that in 1998 a computer would beat the world chess champion. It happened in 1997.

Kurzweil preaches what he has labeled as the "law of accelerating returns." Basically, this is the idea that technological change is happening much faster than most of us realize. The reason, Kurzweil argues, is that people tend to think linearly, not exponentially, as implied by Moore's law.

As linear thinkers, most of us are overly preoccupied with small beginnings rather than with how things add up. Just ask the King of Kerala Province in south India. Legend has it that the sage Krishna once challenged the King of Kerala to a game of chess. The prize that Krishna requested, should he win, was rice: the amount of which would be determined by placing one grain of rice on the first square of the chessboard, two grains on the second, four grains on the third, and so on—doubling the grains on each successive square until the board was covered. The prize seemed so inconsequential to the king that he begged Krishna to consider taking some additional jewels and gold, should he somehow win the match. But Krishna was resolute.

Once Lord Krishna won the match and the payout began, the king quickly realized the shortcomings of his linear thinking. By only the twentieth square, the number of rice grains needed had reached a million. The amount of rice required to fill all 64 squares on the board came to an astounding 18×10^{18} grains, or approximately *18 billion billion grains of rice*, weighing approximately *460 million billion tons*. It was enough rice to cover the surface of India to a depth of two meters![60]

Kurzweil believes that we are still in the first few squares of the chessboard as far as computer power and technology discovery are concerned. Few people realize, he contends, what exponential acceleration really means. As a more modern example of the Indian fable, he cites the Human Genome Project. Initially, it was scheduled as a 15-year project. After 7 years, only 1 percent of the project was completed. Linear-thinking critics around the world began to clamor that the project was a waste of money and that it would never be complete. However, if you double 1 percent every year for seven years, you arrive at 100 percent. The Genome Project was finished right on schedule!

Just how powerful will computers become if Moore is correct, and their power continues to double every two years? Before 2020, Kurzweil predicts, a $1,000 personal computer will have as much raw computing power as the human brain; the combined computing power of all the computers in the world will far exceed the total brainpower of the human race. As for size, Kurzweil believes during the 2020s we will see a computer smaller than 100 nanometers. That is 1,000 times smaller than a micrometer or one billionth of a meter: so small that it cannot be seen by a light microscope. Kurzweil believes that by 2029, a decade later, the $1,000 personal computer will be 1,000 times more powerful than the human brain.[61]

Why Can't a Computer Be More like a Human?

Computational power alone does not a thinker make. Clearly, significant advances will be needed in software and optimization algorithms to take advantage of so much computing power. Software research projects are in the works to bring this about.

IBM recently unveiled details of a project to build a computing system that can understand complex questions and answer them with enough speed and precision to compete on the quiz show "Jeopardy!"[62] For those of you who have never seen it, "Jeopardy!" is a contest demanding broad knowledge and quick recall of a wide range of topics, including history, literature, politics, film, pop culture, and science. Clues given to contestants require analyzing hidden meaning, irony, riddles, and other subtleties that human decision-makers excel at compared to their more-literal computer counterparts.

Code-named "Watson," the program will attempt to determine precise answers to natural-language questions, and since "Jeopardy!" players are penalized for giving a wrong answer, it will also evaluate the computer's confidence in its answers. Typically, winning "Jeopardy!" contestants are able to respond in less than a second when they think they can answer a question. To try to keep up, Watson will incorporate massively parallel processing similar to its human competition. And to put it more on par with its human competition, Watson will not have access to the Internet.

If a computer that understands natural language and can match highly knowledgeable humans in answering a broad range of topics sounds improbable, remember that it was an IBM computer—Deep Blue—that defeated World Chess Champion Garry Kasparov in 1997. Watson's "Jeopardy!" run is being targeted for late 2010. After that, call-center employees beware! Watson may be coming after your job. Not only would Watson possess a wealth of product, technical, and organizational knowledge, but "he" would know immediately how confident he was in his answer. He could decide in an instant whether or not to pass a customer on to a supervisor.

Computers excel at pattern recognition and correlation analysis, particularly when large data sets are available. Both Google's language translator and its spell-checker, for example, work from pattern matches to millions of cases. So does the facial-recognition software currently being used by national security organizations around the world.

But human intelligence is composed of much more than an ability to match patterns. Humans possess strong inductive-reasoning capabilities. We are able to consider relatively few examples and make impressive inductive leaps to build powerful theories of causation, such as Darwin's theory of evolution or Einstein's theory of relativity. Josh Tenenbaum, an associate professor in MIT's Department of Brain and Cognitive Sciences, is working to teach computers the same skill. He and his students are training computers to understand the structure of multiple theories of causation and then programming them to use Bayesian probability to decide which theory best fits the situation. The results are a more human brand of intelligence that requires smaller sets of data to reach a conclusion.[63]

Pattern recognition and inductive logic are two aspects of human intelligence. A third is emotional intelligence: the ability to read and appropriately react to the emotions of others. Here again, strides are being made in software development. Researchers at the University of Massachusetts and at Arizona State University are working to build intelligent tutoring systems that can read children's emotions and respond empathetically.[64]

For example, if a student is working on a math problem and suddenly expresses frustration, the computer may respond encouragingly with something like, "This is a tough problem. Let's read it one more time to see if we are sure what it is asking." The system picks up on the student's emotional state through sensors embedded in the student's chair, the student's body, and in the computer itself. A bracelet around the student's wrist, for example, monitors pulse and skin-moisture levels; sensors in the seat of the student's chair can identify nine different postures from which emotional states can be inferred; pressure on the mouse sends signals to the computer about how firmly the student is squeezing the mouse. In combination, the sensors allow the computer to correctly interpret the child's emotions more than half the time, which is better than some inattentive teachers I've had in the past!

Inductive reasoning and emotional intelligence should greatly increase computers' ability to optimize decisions. Some of Kurzweil's predictions about what we will see by the year 2020 include:[65]

- Most business transactions will be conducted by a simulated person—very likely driven by powerful optimization software.
- The majority of learning will be accomplished through intelligent, adaptive courseware presented via computer-simulated teachers that optimize the presentation of learning materials. Human adults will be relegated to the roles of counselor and mentor rather than academic instructor.
- Computers will be driving most of our vehicles. Humans, in fact, will be prohibited from driving on highways unassisted by a computer. The Prius V is just the beginning!
- Creative computer composers will be producing their own art and music. Computers will also become increasingly adept at

monitoring their own performance and writing their own optimization computer programs for self-improvement.

- Accurate simulations of all aspects of the human brain will exist.
- Most human workers will spend the majority of their time acquiring new skills and knowledge.

Kurzweil predicts that by the end of the following decade, in 2030, by scanning the enormous content of the Internet, computers will "know" literally every single piece of public information. As a result, they will become capable of learning and creating new knowledge entirely on their own.

ROSIE ARRIVES AT LAST

I may have been only slightly ahead of my time when I imagined Rosie showing up to clean my house. Kurzweil predicts that automatic house-cleaning robots will be commonplace in 2014. Tokyo University has already produced a Home Assistant Robot—HAR—that can carry out simple cleaning chores such as wiping floors, washing dishes, and even moving furniture. The robot has five cameras, laser sensors, and six hands with three joints each.[66] In Figure 7.4, Rosie is on the left and an HAR on the right.

FIGURE 7.4   Rosie and HAR

 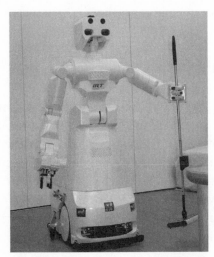

Mind Melds

Researchers at Intel's Pittsburgh lab feel certain that people will become bored using keyboards, mice, and even verbal commands to communicate with computers. Consequently, they are working hard to find ways for people to control computers with brain waves.[67] This is not as far-fetched as it sounds. In 2008, scientists in the United States and Japan used the brain waves of a rhesus monkey to control a robot. Sensors were implanted in the monkey's brain. The Intel team in Pittsburgh hopes to do the same with the human brain. It is currently using functional magnetic resonance imaging machines to determine blood-flow changes in specific areas of the brain, based on the word or image that a person is thinking about. These changes can then be used to send messages to a computer.

Meanwhile, at Caltech, a team is working on a robot probe designed to slowly insert electrodes into a person's brain to connect with specific neurons for advanced controls of prosthetic limbs.[68] If the idea of brain implants makes you feel queasy, you might be surprised to learn that over 10 percent of Americans—33 million—are already cyborgs, possessing some mechanical or electrical body parts.[69] Kurzweil predicts that computer-driven medical technology will reach a tipping point in 2022, after which each new year of research in medical technology will produce at least one more year of life expectancy. Unlikely? Perhaps, but from 1955 to 2010—a period of just 50 years—average life expectancy, worldwide, increased by 21 years: from 47 to 68 years.[70] If you believe in Kurzweil's law of accelerating returns, the one-to-one ratio appears well within reach.

Final Note

If the exponential increase in computers' computational power and software's "intelligence" unfolds as envisioned by Kurzweil and others, there will come a point in time when *artificial* intelligence could surpass *human* intelligence as the smartest, most capable intelligence on the planet. At that point, it would be logical for machines to take over the development of technology, since they could do so at many times the speed of humans. Futurists have labeled the point at which the handoff will occur as the "Singularity." Kurzweil predicts that it will happen in the year 2045. While some have expressed fear that at this point computers will decide to eradicate humankind, Kurzweil feels that this is unlikely, since the large number of cybernetically enhanced humans that will exist will blur the lines between people and machines.

On a further positive note, Kurzweil and other futurists are optimistic about what the future will bring as computers take over more and more decisions. Kurzweil anticipates that poverty, disease, and war will disappear as early as 2029, thanks to technology's ability to alleviate want. Dr. James Canton, CEO and chairman of the San Francisco think tank Institute for Global Futures, also predicts that the superiority of convergent technologies will prevent wars in the 21st century, as robots develop the ability to sense, analyze, authenticate, and anticipate threats. Somehow, I think we'll be reading this in the year 2029 and laughing at their naïveté, just as we now laugh at the threat from "HAL the homicidal AI program" that screenwriter Arthur C. Clarke predicted in *2001: A Space Odyssey*. I am also still waiting for my personal Jetson-style flying saucer.

The introduction to this chapter cited St. Augustine's view that the future evolves from present expectations. It also comes about by having clear, specific goals and by feeling compelled to achieve them. Great athletes often report seeing themselves coming in first across a finish line, hitting a home run, or having a puck glide into the net. Golf great Jack Nicklaus once wrote:

> I never hit a shot even in practice without having a sharp in-focus picture of it in my head. . . . First, I "see" the ball where I want it to finish . . . . Then the scene quickly changes, and I "see" the ball going there: its path, trajectory, and shape, even its behavior on landing. Then . . . the next scene shows me making the kind of swing that will turn the previous images into reality.[71]

In writing this book, I have tried to create a clear, compelling picture of the power and potential of Optimization, so that a great number of people across industries and disciplines will be motivated to step up and take a "swing" at turning the images presented here into reality, now and well into the future.

NOTES

Chapter 1

1. Andrew Martin, "At McDonald's, the Happiest Meal Is Hot Profits,"
   New York Times, January 11, 2009, BU1.
2. Howard Johnson's history was drawn from the following sources: "A
   Chronicle of the Howard Johnson Company—A Hospitality Trail-
   blazer," *Hospitality Accounting Textbooks*, http://raymondcote.com/
   about17.html, accessed July 4, 2010; "References for Business: Howard
   Johnson International, Inc.," *Encyclopedia of Business*, 2nd ed., http://
   www.referenceforbusiness.com/history/He-Ja/Howard-Johnson
   -International-Inc.html, accessed July 4, 2010; and Glenn Wells, "A
   Vanishing Roadside: Icon Howard Johnson's," http://www.roadsidefans
   .com/hojo.html, accessed July 4, 2010.
3. The history of the Hot Shoppes and the Marriott company was taken
   from the following sources: "J. Willard Marriot," *Marriott.com*, http://
   www.marriott.com/corporateinfo/culture/heritageJWillardMarriott
   .mi, accessed July 10, 2010, "J.W. Marriott, Jr.," *Marriott.com*, http://
   www.marriott.com/corporateinfo/culture/heritageJWMarriottJR.mi,
   accessed July 10, 2010; and "The Marriott Timeline," *Marriott.com*,
   http://www.marriott.com/corporateinfo/culture/heritageTimeline.mi,
   accessed July 10, 2010.

4. Jesse Alpert and Nissan Hjaj, "We Knew the Web Was Big . . .," *The Official Google Blog*, http://googleblog.blogspot.com/2008/07/we-knew -web-was-big.html, July 25, 2008.

5. Om Malik, "Google at 10: Larry, Sergey & Me," *GIGAOM*, http:// gigaom.com/2008/09/06/google-at-10-larry-sergey-me, September 6, 2008.

6. Elain Jarvik, "UPS Says Turning Right Saves Time, Money." *bNet*, http://findarticles.com/p/articles/mi_qn4188/is_20060716/ai _n16540534/, July 16, 2006.

7. Jeffery A. Trachtenberg, "Borders Bets a New Chief as It Battles for Survival," *WSJ.com*, http://online.wsj.com/article/ SB123116358050653669.html, January 5, 2009.

8. Andrea James, "Amazon Holiday 'Best Ever' with Peak 73 Orders per Second," *Seattle PI Blogs*, http://blog.seattlepi.nwsource.com/amazon/ archives/157950.asp, December 26, 2008.

9. "Daniel Kahneman on Behavioral Economics," *McKinsey Quarterly Video*, https://www.mckinseyquarterly.com/ghost.aspx?ID=/Video/ Daniel_Kahneman_on_behavioral_economics_2214, May 2008.

10. Taken from author interview of Karl Kempf, March 2, 2010.

Chapter 2

1. John Kellermeier, "How Menstruation Created Mathematics." *Tacoma Community College*, http://www.tacomacc.edu/home/jkellermeier/ Papers/Menses/Menses.htm, accessed October 25, 2009.

2. Picture taken from Wikipedia contributors, "Archimedes." *Wikipedia, The Free Encyclopedia*, http://en.wikipedia.org/wiki/Archimedes, accessed October 23, 2009.

3. Charles R. Shrader, *History of Operations Research in the United States Army* (Washington, D.C: Office of the Deputy Under Secretary of the Army for Operations Research, U.S. Army, For sale by the Supt. of Docs., U.S. G.P.O., 2006), 3.

4. Peter L. Bernstein, *Against the Gods: The Remarkable Story of Risk* (New York: Wiley, 1998), 1–2.

5. Bernstein, 37–72. A majority of the material discussing Pascal's devel- opment of probability comes from this source.

6. Bernstein, 71.

7. "Pascalina Mechanical Calculator," Computer History, http://www .computernostalgia.net/articles/pascalina.htm, accessed July 5, 2010.

Material on Pascal's development of the calculator comes from this source unless otherwise cited.

8. "Gottfried Leibniz (1646–1716 c.e.)," Rational Vedanta, http://www .rationalvedanta.net/bios/rationalists/leibniz, accessed July 6, 2010. Material on Leibniz comes from this source unless otherwise cited.

9. "The Babbage Engine," Computer History Museum, http://www .computerhistory.org/babbage/history, accessed July 6, 2010.

10. Adapted from "Charles Babbage," Wikipedia, The Free Encyclopedia, http://en.wikipedia.org/w/index.php?title=Charles _Babbage&oldid=321596339, accessed October 23, 2009.

11. "Herman Hollerith," U.S. Census Bureau: History, http://www .census.gov/history/www/census_then_now/notable_alumni/herman _hollerith.html, accessed July 6, 2010.

12. Bernstein, 100–143. The majority of the material on the Bernoulli family is taken from this source unless otherwise cited.

13. Eliezer S. Yudkowsky, *An Intuitive Explanation of Bayes' Theorem* (manuscript placed online), http://yudkowsky.net/rational/bayes, accessed October 13, 2009.

14. Daniel and his father were purported to have a stormy relationship, particularly after they tied for first prize in a scientific contest at the University of Paris. See D. A. Quinney, "Daniel Bernoulli and the Making of the Fluid Equation," *+Plus Magazine*, http://pass.maths.org .uk/issue1/bern/index.html, Issue 1, January 1997.

15. Bernstein, 88–96. Unless otherwise cited, the discussion of the history of actuary science is taken from this source.

16. George Dantzig, *Linear Programming and Extensions* (Princeton, NJ: Princeton University Press, 1963), 12–13.

17. "Who Was Frederick W. Lanchester?" INFORMS Online, http:// www.informs.org/Recognize-Excellence/INFORMS-Prizes-Awards/ Frederick-W.-Lanchester-Prize/Who-Was-Frederick-W.-Lanchester, accessed October 23, 2009.

18. S. I. Gass & A. A. Assad, *An Annotated Timeline of Operations Research: An Informal History.* (New York: Kluwer Academic Publishers, 2005), 24–38.

19. Shrader, 9–33. Descriptions of the early operations research efforts in Britain and the United States comes from this source unless otherwise cited.

20. Shrader, 10.

21. Operations Research is called "operational research" in the United Kingdom.
22. Shrader, 10.
23. Shrader, 12.
24. "Britain, Battle of." *New World Encyclopedia* online, http://www .newworldencyclopedia.org/entry/Battle_of_Britain, accessed July 6, 2010.
25. Shrader, 12.
26. Shrader, 6.
27. Shrader, 31–32.
28. Dantzig, 14.
29. The term *programming* was taken from the military's use of the expression to refer to planning or scheduling, not to a set of computer instructions.
30. A number of linear programming concepts were discussed by the Russion L. V. Kantorovich in his 1939 monograph *Mathematical Methods of Organization and Planning Production*. Kantorovich suggested that a linear programming structure could be used to analyze problems in oil refining, scrap minimization, construction planning, and the optimum distribution of arable land to different agricultural products. However, without computers or an algorithm for solving the equations, Kantorovich's proposed techniques were never applied and remained unknown not only abroad but within the U.S.S.R.
31. The example is based on an example presented in "Linear programming," Wikipedia, The Free Encyclopedia, http://en.wikipedia.org/w/index.php?title=Linear_programming&oldid=324379675, October 2009.
32. Gass & Assad, 80.
33. Robert Freund, "Professor George Dantzig: Linear Programming Founder Turns 80," *SOL: Siam News*, http://www.stanford.edu/group/SOL/dantzig.html, November 1994.
34. Jacob Bronowski, *The Ascent of Man* (Boston: Little Brown & Co., 1974), 217.
35. "Alan Mathison Turing," *Encyclopaedia Britannica* online, http://www .britannica.com/EBchecked/topic/609739/Alan-M-Turing, accessed July 6, 2010.
36. The following description of the history of computing was drawn from "Eniac-Definition," wordiq.com, http://www.wordiq.com/definition/Eniac, accessed July 6, 2010; Stephen White, "A Brief History of Com-

puting," http://trillian.randomstuff.org.uk/~stephen/history, accessed July 6, 2010; "UNIVAC I," Wikipedia: The Free Encyclopedia, http://en.wikipedia.org/wiki/UNIVAC_I, accessed September 27, 2009; and IBM:Archives, http://www-03.ibm.com/ibm/history/exhibits/vintage/vintage_4506VV2214.html, accessed July 6, 2010.

37. The American-built Atanasoff-Berry Computer (ABC) introduced in 1941 was in fact the first all-electronic computing device. It was not, however, a general purpose machine, as it was not programmable, being limited to solving systems of linear equations.

38. Freund, http://www.stanford.edu/group/SOL/dantzig.html.

39. Gass & Assad, 144. Unless otherwise cited, the description and capabilities of MYCIN were taken from this source.

40. Victor L. Yu, Lawrence M. Fagan, Sharon Wraith Bennett, William J. Clancy, A. Carlisle Scott, John F. Hannigan, Robert L. Blum, Bruce G. Buchanan, and Stanley N. Cohen, "An Evaluation of MYCIN's Advice," edited version of an article from the *Journal of the American Medical Association*, 242: 1279–1282 (1979), accessed at http://www.u.arizona.edu/~shortlif/Buchanan-Shortliffe-1984/Chapter-31.pdf.

41. The primary ethical concern revolved around the question of who is held responsible for a misdiagnosis by a machine; as for practicalities, an interactive session with MYCIN took up to 30 minutes, more time than a clinician was willing to spend.

42. Gass & Assad, 79–178. Unless otherwise cited, the examples are drawn from this source.

43 A. E. Paul, "Linear programing: A key to optimum newsprint production," *Pulp and Paper Magazine of Canada*, Vol. 57(1), 1956, 85–90.

44. P. Homer, "Eyes on the Prize," *OR/MS Today*, Vol. 18(4), 1991, 34–38.

45. Herbert A. Simon, *Models of Man: Social and Rational; Mathematical Essays on Rational Human Behavior in Society Setting* (New York: Wiley, 1957).

46. Daniel Kahneman and Amos Tversky, "Prospect Theory: An Analysis of Decision Under Risk," *Econometrica*, Vol. 47, 1979, 263–291.

47. Daniel Kahneman, Paul Slovic, and Amos Tversky, *Judgment Uunder Uncertainty: Heuristics and Biases* (Cambridge, U.K.: Cambridge University Press, 1982).

48. Gass & Assad, 176.

49. Gass & Assad, 184.

50. Bo K. Wong and John A. Monaco, "Expert System Applications in Business: A Review and Analysis of the Literature (1977–1993)," *Information & Management*, Vol. 29(3), 1995, 141–152.

51. A. Holohan and A. Garg, "Collaboration Online: The Example of Distributed Computing," *Journal of Computer-Mediated Communication*, Vol. 10(4), art. 16, 2005, accessed at http://jcmc.indiana.edu/vol10/issue4/holohan.html, November 10, 2009.

52. Institute of Transportation Studies, "Mobile Century: Collecting Traffic Data from GPS-Equipped Cell Phones," *California Center for Innovative Transportation*, http://www.calccit.org/?page=projects&id=33, November 10, 2009.

53. J.B. Braklow, W. Graham, K. Peck, S. Hassler, and W.B. Powell, "Interactive Optimization Improves Service and Performance for Yellow Freight System," *Interfaces*, Vol. 22(1), 1992, 147–172.

54. Gass & Assad, 189.

55. "Franz Edelman Award—Past Winners," INFORMS Online, http://www.informs.org/Recognize-Excellence/Franz-Edelman-Award/Franz-Edelman-Award-Past-Winners, November 2009. Unless otherwise cited, the bulleted examples are drawn from this source.

56. "Enterprise-Class Web Analytics Made Smarter, Friendlier and Free," *Google Analytics*, http://www.google.com/analytics/#utm _source=google&utm_campaign=ga-us-googleblog&utm _medium=embedded-text%20, accessed November 11, 2000.

57. "The Marketing Optimization Blog: Turning more visitors into Customers," *Wider Funnel: Marketing Optimization*, http://www.widerfunnel.com/case-study/obama-used-conversion-rate -optimization-to-win, accessed July 7, 2010.

58. Dan Frommer, "Apple Buys Siri, a Mobile Assistant App, as War with Google Heats Up," *Business Insider: SAI*, http://www.businessinsider .com/apple-buys-siri-a-mobile-assistant-app-as-war-with-google-heats -up-2010-4, accessed April 28, 2010.

59. Ian Ayres, *Super Crunchers* (New York: Bantam Dell, 2007), 2–6.

60. *Google Analytics*, http://www.google.com/analytics.

Chapter 3

1. "The Global Competitiveness Report 2009–2010." World Economic Forum, http://www.weforum.org/en/initiatives/gcp/Global%20 Competitiveness%20Report/index.htm, accessed November 25, 2009.

2. Jared Diamond, *Collapse: How Societies Choose to Fail or Succeed* (New York: Viking, 2005), 495.

3. Vanessa O'Connell, "Retailers Reprogram Workers in Efficiency Push," *Wall Street Journal*, September 10, 2008, A1.

4. Weather Eyes, "Dreaming of a White Christmas?" The Weather Doctor, http://www.islandnet.com/~see/weather/eyes/whitexmas.htm, accessed November 25, 2009.

5. Amir D. Aczel, *Chance: A Guide to Gambling, Love, the Stock Market & Just About Everything Else* (New York: Thunder's Mouth Press, 2004), 70–75.

6. "List of cognitive biases," Wikipedia, The Free Encyclopedia, http://en.wikipedia.org/w/index.php?title=List_of_cognitive_biases&oldid=330090177, accessed November 25, 2009.

7. Malcom Gladwell, *Blink: The Power of Thinking Without Thinking* (New York: Little, Brown & Company, 2005), 2–7.

8. Spectrum Massachusetts Institute of Technology, "Emotional Intelligence: Teaching Machines to Care," Massachusetts Institute of Technology, http://spectrum.mit.edu/issue/2006-spring/emotional-intelligence, accessed November 26, 2009.

9. José Vicente Caixeta-Filho, Jan Maarten van Swaay-Neto, & Antonio de Pádua Wagemaker, "Optimization of the Production Planning and Trade of Lily Flowers at Jan de Wit Company," *Interfaces* Vol. 2(1), January–February 2002. Unless otherwise cited, information about the Jan de Wit Company's use of Optimization has been drawn from this source.

10. Caixeta-Filho et al., 42.

11. INFORMS, *The Franz Edelman Award: Achievement in Operations Research* CD, Disc 29.02 http://www3.informs.org/site/edelman_dvd/index.php?c=4&kat=RECENT+DVDs+('03-'09), accessed January 20, 2010.

12. Taken from author interview of Sharon Hormby, February 10, 2010.

13. "Our History: Celebrating Quad/Graphics Milestones," Quad/Graphics, http://www.qg.com/aboutus/qg_story/recognition.asp, December 3, 2009.

14. Rob Walker, "The Song Decoders," *The New York Times Magazine*, October 14, 2009, http://www.nytimes.com/2009/10/18/magazine/18Pandora-t.html?sq=music talents couts&st=cse&scp=5&pagewanted=all, December 1, 2009.

15. Anita Elberse, Jehoshua Eliashberg, and Julian Villaneuva, "Polyphonic HMI: Mixing Music and Math," Harvard Business School Case Study 9-606-009, September 5, 2006, http://cb.hbsp.harvard.edu/cb/product/506009-PDF-ENG, accessed December 4, 2009. Unless otherwise cited, information about Polygenic and Hit Song Science was drawn from this source.
16. Elberse et al., 4.
17. Elberse et al., 12.
18. Benny Evangelist, "Software Predicts Which Songs Will Be Hits," *San Francisco Chronicle*, September 8, 2009, DC-1.

Chapter 4

1. John Toczek, "To Queue or Not to Queue," *OR/MS Today*, Vol. 36(3), December 2009, http://lionhrtpub.com/orms/orms-6-09/frpuzzlor.html, accessed December 19, 2009.
2. Paul O'Neill, "Why the U.S. Healthcare System Is So Sick . . . and What OR Can Do to Cure It," *OR/MS Today*, Vol. 34(6), December 2007, http://lionhrtpub.com/orms/orms-12-07/frhealthcare.html, accessed December 12, 2009.
3. O'Neill, http://lionhrtpub.com/orms/orms-12-07/frhealthcare.html.
4. Steffie Woolhandler, Terry Campbell & David U. Himmelstein, "Costs of Healthcare Administration in the United States and Canada." *New England Journal of Medicine*, Vol. 349, August 2003, 768-775.
5. Tanya G. K. Bentley, Rachel M. Effros, Kartika Palar, and Emmett B. Keeler, "Waste in the U.S. Health Care System: A Conceptual Framework," *Milbank Quarterly*, Vol. 86(4), December 2008.
6. "U.S. Health Care Today," Rand Compare, http://www.randcompare.org/us-health-care-today/waste#measuring-waste, accessed December, 28, 2009.
7. "Waste," *Rand Compare*, http://www.randcompare.org/us-health-care-today/waste#measuring-waste, accessed December 12, 2009.
8. "Life Expectancy—We Are Not Getting Our Money's Worth," April 10, 2009, ChartingTheEconomy.com, http://chartingtheeconomy.com/?cat=18, accessed October 28, 2009.
9. O'Neill, http://lionhrtpub.com/orms/orms-12-07/frhealthcare.html.
10. Marvin Mandelbaum and Myron Hlynka, "Examples of Applications of Queueing Theory in Canada," *INFOR* Vol. 46(4), November 2008, 256–257.

11. Patrik Eveborn, Mikael Ronnqvist, Helga Einarsdottir, Mats Eklund, Karin Liden and Marie Almroth, "Operations Research Improves Quality and Efficiency in Home Care," *Interfaces*, Vol. 39(1), January–February 2009, 18–34.

12. O'Neill, http://lionhrtpub.com/orms/orms-12-07/frhealthcare.html.

13. Chris Born, Monica Carbajal, Pat Smith, Mark Wallace, Kirk Abbott, Surain Adyanthaya, E. Andrew Boyd, Curtis Keller, Jin Liu, Wayne New, Tom Rieger, Bert Winemiller, and Ron Woestemeyer, "Contact Optimization at Texas Children's Hospital," *Interfaces* Vol. 34(1) January–February 2004, via INFORMS at http://pubsonline.informs .org/interfaces/abstract493/year2004/month01/searchkeyTexas/ valueYTo2OntzOjExOiJzZWFyY2hfdGV4dCI7czo1OiJUZXhhcyI7 czoxMDoiY29tYm9fb3B0biI7czozOiJhbGwiO3M6MTToieCI7czoy OiIxNyI7czoxOiJ5IjtzOjE6IjMiO3M6NjNjoic3RhdHVzIjtzOjE6IjIi O3M6Nzoiam91cm5hbCI7czowOiIiO30=/t2, accessed December 14, 2009.

14. O'Neill, http://lionhrtpub.com/orms/orms-12-07/frhealthcare.html

15. Saul I. Gass and Arjang A. Assad, *An Annotated Timeline of Operations Research: An Informal History* (New York: Springer Science, 2005), 48–49.

16. Ian Ayres, *Super Crunchers: Why Thinking-by-Numbers Is the New Way to Be Smart* (New York: Bantam Dell, 2007), 30.

17. Srinivas Bollapragada, Hong Cheng, Mary Phillips, Marc Garbiras, Michael Scholes, Tim Gibbs, and Mark Humphreville, "NBC's Optimization Systems Increase Revenues and Productivity," *Interface* Vol. 32(1), January–February 2002, 47–60, http://www.scienceofbetter.org/ can_do/success_stories/Interfaces/1526-551X-2002-32-01-0047R.pdf, accessed December 29, 2009.

18. "What It Can Do for You: Success Stories," *Operations Research: The Science of Better*, http://www.scienceofbetter.org/can_do/success_alpha .php, accessed January 6, 2010.

19. Stephen Baker, *The Numerati* (Boston: Houghton Mifflin Company, 2008), 34.

20. Ayres, 28.

21. "McDonald's: I'm Lovin' It," slide 35, Slideshare.net, http://www .slideshare.net/dredmonds/mcdonalds-3754675, July 26, 2010.

22. Taken from author interview of Mike Cramer, September 20, 2010.

23. Michael Lewis, *Moneyball: The Art of Winning an Unfair Game* (New York: W.W. Norton, 2004).

24. Steve Reed, "Panther Notebook," *The Star of Cleveland County*, October 9, 2002, http://www.shelbystar.com/sports/panthers-4502-fox-week .html, accessed April 1, 2010.

25. Jeff Winters and Doug Mohr, "O.R. at United Parcel Service." *OR/MS Today*, Vol. 36(6), December 2009, http://www.lionhrtpub.com/orms/ orms-12-09/frroundtable.html, accessed April 1, 2010.

26. Taken from author interview of Jack Levis, February 2, 2010.

27. Taken from author interview of Jack Levis, February 2, 2010.

28. Taken from author interview of Jack Levis, February 2, 2010.

29. Ayres, 144–149.

30. Pierre Haren, *Apply Science to the Art of Business*, keynote address, INFORMS Annual Conference, Plenary Speaker #1, April 26–28, 2009.

31. Taken from author interview of Karl Kempf, March 2, 2010.

32. Christopher Peterson, Steven F. Mailer, and Martin E. P. Seligman, *A Theory for the Age of Personal Control* (Oxford: Oxford University Press, 1993).

33. Taken from author interview of Karl Kempf, March 2, 2010.

34. Nasir Naqvi, Baba Shif, and Antoine Bechara, "The Role of Emotion in Decision Making: A Cognitive Neuroscience Perspective," *Current Directions in Psychological Science*, Vol. 15(5), October 2006, 260–264.

35. Taken from author interview of Jack Levis, February 2, 2010.

36. Berns, Gregory, "In Hard Times, Fear Can Impair Decision-Making," *New York Times*, December 7, 2008. Online edition, http://www.ny times.com/2008/12/07/jobs/07pre.html, accessed July 23, 2010.

37. Thomas Cook, "Bullish on OR," *OR/MS Today*, Vol. 30(1), February 2003, http://www.lionhrtpub.com/orms/orms-2-03/frpres.html, accessed April 1, 2010.

38. "HP Transforms Product Portfolio Management with Operations Research, " *INFORMS Interfaces*, Vol. 4(1), January–February 2010, 17–32.

Chapter 5

1. Kenneth C. Laudon and Jane P. Laudon, "A New Supply Chain Project Has Nike Running for Its Life," Pearson's Companion Website for *Essentials of Management Information Systems*, 6th ed., http://wps.pren hall.com/bp_laudon_essmis_6/21/5561/1423785.cw/content/index.html;

unless otherwise cited, the description of the Nike-i2 case was drawn from this citation.

2. Laudon & Laudon, 1.

3. Taken from author interview of Jack Levis, February 2, 2010.

4. Taken from author interview of Karl Kempf, January 28, 2010.

5. "McDonald's: Our Company," http://www.aboutmcdonalds.com/mcd/our_company.html, accessed September 8, 2010.

6. Taken from author interview of Sharon Hormby, February 10, 2010.

7. Pandora, "Why Was This Song Selected?" http://www.pandora.com/#/playlist/why, accessed February 16, 2010.

8. Paul O'Neill, "Healthcare Code Red: Why the U.S. Healthcare System Is So Sick . . . and What OR Can Do to Cure It," *OR/MS Today*, December 2007, http://lionhrtpub.com/orms/orms-12-07/frhealthcare.html.

9. Taken from author interview of Sharon Hormby, February 10, 2010.

10. Taken from author interview of Sharon Hormby, February 10, 2010.

11. Taken from author interview of Karl Kempf, January 28, 2010.

12. Taken from author interview of Sharon Hormby, February 10, 2010.

13. John P. Kotter, "What Leaders Really Do," originally published in *Harvard Business Review*, December 1, 2001. Reprinted in *Leadership Insights: 15 Unique Perspectives on Effective Leadership*, Article Collection, Harvard Business School Publishing, 26.

14. Taken from author interview of Karl Kempf, January 28, 2010.

15. Taken from author interview of Karl Kempf, January 28, 2010.

16. Randy Henn, "Online Experiments for Optimizing the Customer Experience," presentation to IMTC, April 3, 2008, http://exp-platform.com/Documents/old%20format%202008-04%20Irish%20Microsoft%20Technology%20Conference.ppt.

17. Taken from author interview of Jack Levis, February 2, 2010.

18. Taken from author interview of Jack Levis, February 2, 2010.

19. Taken from author interview of Karl Kempf, January 28, 2010.

Chapter 6

1. Lauriston Sharp, "Steel Axes for Stone Age Australians," in *Man in Adaption: The Cultural Present*, 2nd ed., edited by Yehudi A. Cohen (New York: Aldine de Gruyter, 1974), 116–125.

2. Sharp, 125.

3. Thomas Hobbes, *Leviathan* (Oxford: Oxford University Press, 1998).

4. Ian Johnston, "Men, You Have 30 Seconds to Impress Women," *News. Scotsman.com*, July 2, 2007, http://web.archive.org/web/20070702025413/http://news.scotsman.com/scitech.cfm?id=567952006.

5. Malcolm Gladwell, *Blink: The Power of Thinking Without Thinking* (New York: Little, Brown, 2005), 61–66.

6. Taken from author interview of William Boga, March 26, 2010.

7. Taken from author interview of William Boga, March 26, 2010.

8. Taken from author interview of Karl Kempf, January 28, 2010.

9. Taken from author interview of Karl Kempf, January 28, 2010.

10. Taken from author interview of Jack Levis, February 2, 2010.

11. Taken from author interview of William Boga, March 26, 2010.

12. Taken from author interview of Karl Kempf, January 28, 2010.

13. George E. P. Box and Norman R. Draper, *Empirical Model-Building and Response Surfaces* (New York: Wiley & Sons, 1987), 424.

14. Taken from author interview of William Boga, March 26, 2010.

15. Taken from author interview of Karl Kempf, January 28, 2010.

16. Taken from author interview of Sharon Hormby, February 10, 2010.

17. Taken from author interview of Jack Levis, February 2, 2010.

18. Taken from author interview of Karl Kempf, January 28, 2010.

19. Taken from author interview of Karl Kempf, January 28, 2010.

20. Maurice Schlumberger, "Time to Payback," *Analytics*, January–February 2010, http://analyticsmagazine.com, 22.

21. Taken from author interview of Sharon Hormby, February 10, 2010.

22. Taken from author interview of Scott Abell, March 25, 2010.

23. Taken from author interview of Scott Abell, March 25, 2010.

Chapter 7

1. "9 Life-Changing Inventions the Experts Said Would Never Work," August 22, 2008, http://www.ecosalon.com/9_Life_Changing _Inventions_the_Experts_Said_Would_Never_Work.

2. "Famously Wrong Predictions," *Wilk4: Miscellaneous Humor*, October 15, 2007, http://wilk4.com/humor/humore10.htm.

3. Roger Roberts and Johnson Sikes, "IT in the New Normal: McKinsey Global Survey Results," *McKinsey Quarterly*, December 8, 2009, https://www.mckinseyquarterly.com/Business_Technology/BT_Strategy/IT_in_the_new_normal_McKinsey_Global_Survey _results_2473.

4. Larry Dignan, "Gartner: Cloud Computing, Analytics Top 2010 Strategic Tech List," *Between the Lines*, October 20, 2009, http://www.zdnet.com/blog/btl/gartner-cloud-computing-analytics-top-2010-strategic-tech-list/26191.

5. Andrew H. Bartels, Ellen Daley, Andrew Parker, Boris Evelson, and Chetina Muteba, "Smart Computing Drives the New Era of IT Growth: A New Tech Investment Cycle Holds Seismic Promise—and Challenges," *Forrester Report*, December 4, 2009, http://www-935.ibm.com/services/us/cio/pdf/forrester-smart-computing-drives-new-era-of-it.pdf.

6. Bartels et al., 3.

7. Bartels et al., 3.

8. "Eight Levels of Analytics," *Sascom Magazine*, http://www.sas.com/news/sascom/2008q4/column_8levels.html, accessed May 5, 2010.

9. Neil Craig, "Kurzweil's Predictions—2010 On," a place to stand, January 19, 2010, http://a-place-to-stand.blogspot.com/2010/01/kurzweils-predictions-2010-on.html.

10. Aaron Saenz, "Create an AI on Your Computer," *Singularity Hub*, http://singularityhub.com/2009/05/28/create-an-ai-on-your-computer/, accessed September 7, 2010.

11. Cameron Chapman, "The Future of User Interfaces," *Six Revisions: Useful Information for Web Developers & Designers*, February 11, 2010, http://sixrevisions.com/user-interface/the-future-of-user-interfaces.

12. "Pattie Maes and Pranav Mistry Demo SixthSense," *TED: Ideas Worth Spreading*, March 2009, http://www.ted.com/talks/pattie_maes_demos_the_sixth_sense.html.

13. Dennis McCafferty, "IT Management Slideshow: IT Dream Team on Data Management," *CIO Insight*, May 5, 2010, http://www.cioinsight.com/c/a/IT-Management/IT-Dream-Team-on-Data-Management-500479/?kc=CIOQUICKNL05132010FEA1.

14. McCafferty, http://www.cioinsight.com/c/a/IT-Management/IT-Dream-Team-on-Data-Management-500479/?kc=CIOQUICKNL05132010FEA1.

15. "Statistics," *Facebook Press Room*, http://www.facebook.com/press/info.php?statistics, accessed May 11, 2010.

16. *Twitter Blog*, "Measuring Tweets," February 22, 2010, http://blog.twitter.com/2010/02/measuring-tweets.html.

17. Steve Lohr, "SAS Seeks to Improve Data Mining of Social Media," *The New York Times: Bits,* April 12, 2010, http://bits.blogs.nytimes .com/2010/04/12/sas-seeks-to-improve-data-mining-of-social-media

18. "Google's Head of Research Still Searching for Answers," *Irishtimes.com,* December 19, 2009, http://www.irishtimes.com/newspaper/finance/ 2009/1218/1224260888550.html.

19. Bartels et al., 19.

20. Emily Fredrix, "Wal-Mart Plans $2B Push on Hunger Relief," *Taiwan News,* May 13, 2010, http://www.etaiwannews.com/etn/news_content .php?id=1254760&lang=eng_news&cate_img=logo_world&cate_rss =WORLD_eng

21. "Pioneering Cyber-Security Center to Transform Crime Prevention," *EPSRC: Pioneering Research and Skills,* Press release, September 23, 2009, http://www.epsrc.ac.uk/newsevents/news/2009/Pages/csit.aspx.

22. *EPSRC,* http://www.epsrc.ac.uk/newsevents/news/2009/Pages/csit.aspx.

23. "Warranty Fraud Detection," *Warranty Week,* February 25, 2010, http://www.warrantyweek.com/archive/ww20100225.html.

24. Slide provided by John C. Brocklebank, SAS Advanced Analytics Lab, 2010.

25. Philip Klevin, "MediFraud for Everyone," *The American Spectator,* October 23, 2009, http://spectator.org/archives/2009/10/23/medi-fraud -for-everyone.

26. Eva K. Lee and Marco Zaider, "Operations Research Advances Cancer Therapeutics," *Interfaces* Vol. 38(1), January–February 2008, 5–25.

27. Fran Kelly, "Effectiveness of Prescription Drugs Under Dispute," *The World Today,* ABC Online, December 9, 2003, http://www.abc.net.au/ worldtoday/content/2003/s1006644.htm.

28. Jessica Frazer, "Statistics Prove Prescription Drugs Are 16,400% More Deadly Than Terrorists," *Natural News,* July 5, 2005, http://www .naturalnews.com/009278.html.

29. "Identifying and Neutralizing the Cause of Deadly Side Effects of Eli Lilly & Co. Anticancer Drug ALIMTA," *Operations Research: The Science of Better,* http://www.scienceofbetter.org/can_do/success _stories/iantcodseoelcada.htm, accessed May 26, 2010.

30. "Consumer spending accounts for 70 percent of U.S. economic activ- ity," *Journal of Commerce* Online, August 30, 2010, http://www.joc .com/logistics-economy/consumer-spending-jumped-04-percent-july.

31. "2010 Toyota Prius: Intelligent Parking Assist," YouTube, http://www
    .youtube.com/watch?v=2eng94_flJw, accessed May 26, 2010.

32. Bryn Nelson, "Smart Appliances Learning to Save Power Grid: Wash-
    ers, Dryers, Refrigerators Grow Savvier, Adjust to Demand," *MSNBC
    Business on Main*, November 26, 2007, http://www.msnbc.msn.com/
    id/21760974.

33. Using two-way digital technology to save energy, reduce cost, and
    increase reliability of the electrical grid is often referred to as a Smart
    Grid. It seems certain to be a big area of emphasis over the coming
    decade.

34. "Fired Up About Energy Savings," *bestpractices.mcdonalds.com*, http://
    bestpractices.mcdonalds.com/sections/1/case_studies/63?q=, accessed
    May 26, 2010.

35. R. P. Siegel, "Study Shows Bright Green Future for Smart Appliances,"
    triplepundit, March 10, 2010, http://www.triplepundit.com/2010/03/
    smart-appliances-could-be-the-next-big-thing.

36. John Markoff, "A Software Secretary That Takes Charge," *New York
    Times*, Business Section, December 13, 2008, http://www.nytimes
    .com/2008/12/14/business/14stream.html?_r=1

37. Erick Schonfeld, "Smartphone Sales up 24 Percent, iPhone's Share
    Nearly Doubled Last Year," *TechCrunch*, February 23, 2010, http://
    techcrunch.com/2010/02/23/smartphone-iphone-sales-2009-gartner.

38. Lance Whitney, "Cell Phone, Smartphone Sales Surge," *CNET.News*,
    May 19, 2010, http://news.cnet.com/8301-1035_3-20005359-94.html,
    accessed July 22, 2010.

39. Scott Beaulier, "McOnomics," *The Economic Way of Thinking: Clear
    Conjectures About a Complex World*, March 8, 2010, http://ewot.typepad
    .com/the_economic_way_of_think/2010/03/mconomics.html.

40. See, for example, "Price Optimization Software Overview: Revion-
    ics Delivers a Best-of-Breed Lifecycle Price and Inventory Optimi-
    zation Suite for Retail," *Revionics*, http://www.revionics.com/price
    -optimization-software-overview.aspx, accessed July 16, 2010.

41. Mike Cramer, "The Emerging Role of Operations Research at
    McDonald's," *OR/MS Today*, August 2009, http://www.lionhrtpub
    .com/orms/orms-8-09/roundtable.html.

42. Eric Brynjolfsson and Michael Schrage, "The New, Faster Face of
    Innovation," *The Wall Street Journal Digital Network*, August 17, 2009,

http://online.wsj.com/article/SB100014240529702048303045741308201
84260340.html.

43. Peter Kirwan, "The Rise of Machine-Written Journalism,"
    Wired.Co.Uk, December 16, 2009, http://www.wired.co.uk/news/
    archive/2009-12/16/the-rise-of-machine-written-journalism?page=all.

44. Yuri Levin and Jeff McGill, "Revenue Management in the Era of
    Social Networking," *Analytics*, March–April 2010, http://analytics
    -magazine.com/?p=22.

45. "The Machines Took Over," *USA Today*, May 7–9, 2010, 1A.

46. Ian Ayres, *Super Crunchers* (New York: Bantam Dell, 2007), 116–124.

47. Daniel Simons and Christopher F. Chabris, *The Invisible Gorilla I* (New
    York: Crown, 2010).

48. John Leyden, "'Cybercrime Exceeds Drug Trade' Myth Exploded,"
    The Register, March 27, 2009, http://www.theregister.co.uk/2009/03/27/
    cybercrime_mythbusters.

49. "FBI 2009 Cybercrime Statistics," *ScamFraudAlertBlog*, March 13,
    2010, http://scamfraudalert.wordpress.com/2010/03/13/fbi-2009-cyber
    crime-statistics.

50. "New Study Shows Most People Unaware of Security Risks Posed
    by P2P File-Sharing Software," 24-7 Pressrelease, June 20, 2009,
    http://www.24-7pressrelease.com/press-release/new-study-shows
    -most-people-unaware-of-security-risks-posed-by-p2p-filesharing
    -software-104852.php.

51. Mathew Humphries, "19,000 Stolen Credit Cards Accessible with a
    Google Search," *Geek.com*, March 31, 2009, http://www.geek.com/
    articles/news/19000-stolen-credit-cards-accessible-with-a-google
    -search-20090331.

52. Jim Finkle, "Canada Probes Google on Wi-Fi Data Collection,"
    MSNBC.com, June 1, 2010, http://www.msnbc.msn.com/id/37455927/
    ns/technology_and_science-security.

53. "Carnegie Mellon Researcher Says Privacy Concerns Could Limit
    Benefits from Real-Time Data Analysis," Carnegie Mellon, December
    17, 2009, http://www.cmu.edu/news/archive/2009/December/dec17
    _privacydataanalysis.shtml.

54. Michael Lewis, *The Big Short* (New York: W. W. Norton & Company,
    2010), 126–131.

55. Eric Beinhocker, Ian Davis, and Lenny Mendonca, "The 10 Trends
    You Have to Watch," *Harvard Business Review*, Guest Edition, July 1,

2009, http://hbr.org/web/extras/insight-center/health-care/10-trends
-you-have-to-watch.

56. "Computers That Use Light Instead of Electricity? First Germanium
Laser Created," *ScienceDaily*, Science News Section, February 5, 2010,
http://www.sciencedaily.com/releases/2010/02/100204144555.htm.

57. Moore's law is technically about how many transistors can fit on a
single integrated chip. It has become, however, a proxy for the advance
of computer density and power.

58. Boonsri Dickinson, "With 'Smart Dust,' a Trillion Sensors Scattered
Around the Globe," *Smartplanet*, May 7, 2010, http://www.smartplanet
.com/technology/blog/science-scope/building-a-real-world-web-with
-smart-dust/1673/.

59. Brian O'Keefe, "The Smartest (or the Nuttiest) Futurist on Earth,"
Fortune, May 2, 2007, http://money.cnn.com/2007/05/01/magazines/
fortune/kurzweil.fortune/index.htm.

60. "Ambalappuzha," Wikipedia, The Free Encyclopedia, http://
en.wikipedia.org/wiki/Ambalappuzha, accessed May 26, 2010.

61. Craig, http://a-place-to-stand.blogspot.com/2010/01/kurzweils
-predictions-2010-on.html.

62. "What is Watson?" IBM, http://www.research.ibm.com/deepqa, June
3, 2010.

63. "Davos 2010—IdeasLab with MIT—Josh Tenenbaum," YouTube, June
3, 2010, http://www.youtube.com/watch?v=k9MnT5fOLA0&feature=
channel

64. Debra Viadero, "'Intelligent' Systems Respond to Students' Cues,"
Education Week, June 6, 2010, reprinted in *Behavioral Health Central*, June 6, 2008, http://behavioralhealthcentral.com/index.
php/20091222160291/Latest-News/scholars-test-emotion-sensitive
-tutoring-software-education-week-bethesda-md.html.

65. Craig, http://a-place-to-stand.blogspot.com/2010/01/kurzweils
-predictions-2010-on.html.

66. Julian, "8 Insane Japanese Robots That Will Take Your Job (and Possibly Your Life)," *Business Pundit*, November 16, 2009, http://www
.businesspundit.com/8-insane-japanese-robots-that-will-take-your-job
-and-possibly-your-life.

67. Sharon Gaudin, "Intel: Chips in Brains Will Control Computers by
2020," *Computerworld*, November 19, 2009, http://www.computerworld
.com/s/article/9141180/Intel_Chips_in_brains_will_control_computers
_by_2020?taxonomyId=11&pageNumber=1.

68. "Scientists Working on Matrix-esque Brain-Computer Inter-face," Gizmodo, http://gizmodo.com/393604/scientists-working-on-matrix+esque-brain+computer-interface, accessed June 24, 2010.

69. Gary Robbins, "Futurist Tells O.C. What Lies Ahead," *The Orange County Register*, December 4, 2009, http://sciencedude.freedom blogging.com/2009/12/04/futurist-tells-oc-what-lies-ahead/69991.

70. "'Sharp Increase' in Life Expectancy," *The Belfast Telegraph*, April 10, 2010, http://www.belfasttelegraph.co.uk/breaking-news/world/sharp -increase-in-life-expectancy-14762466.html?r=RSS.

71. "Mental Imagery," *BrainMAC*, http://www.brianmac.co.uk/mental .htm, accessed June 26, 2010.

INDEX

ABOUT THE AUTHOR

Steve Sashihara is the president and CEO of Princeton Consultants Incorporated (http://www.princeton.com), which specializes in a unique blend of information technology and management consulting. While many firms today provide both services, they invariably do so with separate staffs: typically, "computer scientists" for IT and M.B.A.s for management consulting. Princeton Consultants blends the two together, and the same staff members are responsible for both software design and process design, which the firm believes are inextricably mixed. Over one third of the firm's professional staff hold Ph.D.s.

The firm's specialty is "optimization": the application of advanced mathematical programming to ordinary business problems, where the software gives concrete recommendations for action. In its 30-year history, Princeton Consultants has helped its clients achieve transformational and industry-changing improvements to their core operations.

Steve is an active member of the academic society INFORMS (http://www.informs.org) and the INFORMS Roundtable, which includes many of the leading businesses in operations research.

Steve is a director of the Association of Management Consulting Firms (http://www.amcf.org) and has served in a variety of leadership roles, including cochairman, the association's highest elected office. As a thought leader, Steve has spoken at and moderated dozens of events with top executives of other consulting firms.

Steve is a 1980 graduate of Princeton University, where he received an B.A. in philosophy. His undergraduate thesis was titled "The Legal Protection of Computer Software Property" and was an early study in intellectual-property aspects of software algorithms. While at Princeton, Steve worked at Princeton's Computer Center "Clinic," a software help desk for professors and scholars to help them harness the university's large mainframe computers for their research.

Steve and his family reside in New Hope, Pennsylvania.